# Taxpayers, Taxes, and Government Spending

## Perspectives on the Taxpayer Revolt

### Robert J. Dworak

PRAEGER

PRAEGER SPECIAL STUDIES • PRAEGER SCIENTIFIC

**Library of Congress Cataloging in Publication Data**

Dworak, Robert J
   Taxpayers, taxes, and government spending.

   Includes index.
   1. Local taxation--United States. 2. Local
finance--United States. 3. Local government--United
States. 4. Taxation--United States. I. Title.
HJ9152.D94    336.2'00973    80-135

ISBN 0-03-056111-6
ISBN 0-03-056109-4 pbk.

Published in 1980 by Praeger Publishers
CBS Educational and Professional Publishing
A Division of CBS, Inc.
521 Fifth Avenue, New York, New York 10017 U.S.A.

© 1980 by Praeger Publishers

0123456789  145  987654321

Printed in the United States of America

*To Marcia*

# PREFACE

The late 1970s marked the first wide-spread tax revolt in the United States since the Revolutionary War. From California to Massachusetts, taxpayers expressed their discontent over government spending and taxation. Inflation and the energy crisis added to the economic pressures of taxation. The economic problems were so severe that they seemed to cause a crisis in confidence between the people and their leaders. At the national level, the major concerns were energy supplies and inflation. The intense interest in these problems overshadowed concerns about escalating social security taxes and the inflationary effect of the income tax. However, at the state and local level, taxes and government spending were the predominant issues. In many areas of the country, voters made constitutional and legislative changes aimed at reducing their tax payments. Local governments were particularly vulnerable to the taxpayer revolt because of their proximity to the people.

The increased level of interest and activity in regard to local government created a need for an informed citizenry that had not existed before. While the citizens' desire for lower taxes was clear, their understanding of the consequences of tax reduction was less clear. What the citizens lacked was a basic understanding of local government and its financial operations. This lack of knowledge about local government put citizens at a great disadvantage when they had to deal with elected officials and local government administrators. As a result, local government suffered some severe problems and citizens found it difficult to get the tax relief that they wanted.

Taxpayers have to be knowledgeable in three different areas if they are to be effective in their efforts to reduce government spending and taxation. First, they must have a general understanding of the tax burden imposed upon them by all three levels of government: federal, state, and local. By being familiar with the growth patterns of tax revenues, taxpayers can devote their efforts to reducing the taxes that have the greatest impact upon them now and in the coming years.

Second, taxpayers must have a clear understanding of the successes and failures of the tax revolt movements in the various states. They must learn that winning an election is no guarantee that taxes will be lowered or that government spending will be reduced.

Third, taxpayers must know enough about local government operations to understand the potential effects of the various types of tax reductions and expenditure limitations. They must also understand the importance of preserving the autonomy and accessibility of local government against the encroachments of state and federal government. Finally, taxpayers must know enough about the interests and goals of elected officials to be able to work effectively with them.

If taxpayers operate in ignorance of these issues they have no chance of achieving the reductions in taxes that they seek. Ignorance leads to a poorer level of government services at a higher cost. It would be a sad irony indeed if the taxpayer revolt increases the problems that it intends to solve. This book is written with the hope that the revolt will be successful, both for the taxpayers and for local government. In the final analysis, their interests are one and the same.

# TABLE OF CONTENTS

PREFACE                                                    iv
LIST OF TABLES                                             xi
LIST OF FIGURES                                            xi

## Part I: Taxes and Government

1. INTRODUCTION TO TAXES AND GOVERMENT                     3
   Why Taxes Increase                                      5
   Getting Elected                                         6
   Being in Office                                         8
      Cutting Programs                                     8
      Maintaining Programs                                11
      Expanding Programs                                  12
   Getting Reelected                                      14
2. FEDERAL TAXATION                                       16
   Personal Income Tax                                    16
   Employment Tax                                         20
   Corporate Income Tax                                   23
   Excise Tax                                             25
   Estate and Gift Taxes                                  27
   Summary                                                29
3. STATE TAXATION                                         31
   Property Tax                                           33
   Sales and Excise Taxes                                 34
   Income Taxes: Personal and Corporate                   38
   License Fees                                           42
   Summary                                                43

4.  LOCAL GOVERNMENT TAXATION 47
     Property Tax 49
     Sales Tax 55
     Income Tax 60
     Other Taxes 63
     Summary 64

## Part II: The Taxpayer Revolt of 1978

5.  PROPOSITION 13: CALIFORNIA LEADS THE WAY 69
     The Election 70
     Major Provisions of Proposition 13 74
     Implementation of Proposition 13 77
     California After Proposition 13 82
6.  THE PROPERTY TAX LIMITATION MEASURES OF 1978 87
     Idaho 87
     Nevada 90
     Oregon 91
     Michigan 93
     Property Tax Limitation Measures in Other States 94
       Alabama 95
       Massachusetts 95
       Missouri 96
     The Property Tax in Prospective 96
7.  NEW LIMITS ON STATE AND LOCAL EXPENDITURES 100
     Principles of Expenditure 101
     Types of Limitations 103
     Arizona 108
     New Jersey 111
     Hawaii 115
     Colorado 116
     Texas 118
     Tennessee 119
     Illinois 120
     California Revisited: the "Spirit of 13" Initiative 121
     Concluding Comments 122
8.  OTHER RESULTS OF THE TAXPAYER REVOLT 125
     Reforming the Federal Tax Structure 125
       The Constitutional Convention 127
       The Constitutional Amendment Proposed by Congress 128
       The Legislative Approach to National Tax Reform 131
     What Taxpayers Can Do 133

Part III: The How and Why of Local Government Spending
and Taxation

9. THE FUNCTIONS AND SERVICES OF LOCAL
   GOVERNMENT     141
   Types of Local Government     143
   How Local Government Works     149
     Identification and Pricing of Productive Outputs     150
     Raising of Revenue     152
     Allocation of Financial Resources     155
     Management of Fiscal and Human Resources     156
     Audit and Review of Expenditures     157
     Interaction with the Private Economy     158
   Services of Local Government     159
   Conclusion     161
10. THE FUNDAMENTALS OF THE BUDGETARY
   PROCESS     163
   Efficiency     164
   Effectiveness     164
   Economy     165
   Legal and Ethical Requirements     166
   Types of Budgets     167
   Methods of Budgeting     169
     Line Item Budgeting     170
     Performance Budgeting     170
     Program Budgeting     171
     Zero Base Budgeting     172
   How Budgets Actually Work     173
     Setting Policy     173
     Estimating Expenditures     174
     Reviewing Expenditure Estimates     175
     Estimating Revenues     175
     Making Budgetary Forecasts     176
     Preparing the Budget Document     176
     Reviewing and Adopting the Budget     176
     Executing the Budget     177
   Conclusion     177
11. GETTING TO KNOW YOUR LOCAL GOVERNMENT:
   QUESTIONS TO ASK     179
   Criteria for Responsible Local Government     181
   How to Evaluate the Financial Policies of Local
   Government     187

How to Evaluate the Revenues and Expenditures of
  Local Government 195
    Summarizing Revenues 196
    Summarizing Expenditures 201
    Getting the Information 203
  Conclusion 216

## Part IV: Alternatives to Higher Taxes

12. BETTER MANAGEMENT OF LOCAL GOVERNMENT 219
  How to Increase the Efficiency and Effectiveness
    of Local Government 220
    Use Cost/Benefit Analysis 221
    Contract for Services 223
    Evaluate Programs and Services 224
    Train the Workforce 225
    Take Advantage of "Free" Services 226
  Payment-for-Services Programs 227
  How to Reduce and Eliminate Government Services 230
    Consider What Services Can Legally Be Reduced
      or Eliminated 231
    Consider the Different Types of Reduction Decisions 232
    Link Reductions in Services to Reductions in Taxes 232
    Involve Citizens in Reduction and Elimination
      Decisions 233
    Look for Special Constraints on Service Reductions 234
    Concluding Comments About Reductions 234
  Conclusion 235
13. A NEW ALTERNATIVE TO PAYING TAXES:
  VOLUNTEER PERSONAL SERVICE 236
  How Volunteer Personal Service Can Work 236
  How Volunteer Personal Service Benefits the Taxpayer 239
  How Volunteer Personal Service Benefits the Government 241
  How to Fight for the Volunteer Personal Service Program,
    or What to Say When They Tell You It Can't Be Done 243
14. WHAT SHOULD TAXPAYERS EXPECT FROM LOCAL
  GOVERNMENT? 246
  Responsiveness 246
  Communication 247
  Accessibility 248
  Honesty 250
  Satisfaction 252

Organizational Considerations 253
Conclusion 255
INDEX 257
ABOUT THE AUTHOR 260

# List of Tables

1.1 Tax Burden Per Capita, 1950-75   4
2.1 Income Tax Receipts, 1950-75   18
2.2 Income Tax Per Capita, 1950-75   19
2.3 Employment Tax Receipts and Outlays, 1965-77: Old Age, Survivors, and Disability Insurance   21
2.4 Employment Tax Receipts and Outlays, 1965-77: Unemployment Insurance   22
2.5 Corporate Income Tax Receipts, 1960-77   25
2.6 Excise Tax Receipts, 1960-77   27
2.7 Estate and Gift Tax Receipts, 1960-77   28
2.8 Federal Budget Receipts, 1960-77   30
3.1 State Revenue As a Percent of All Government Revenue, 1950-75   31
3.2 State Revenue by Category, 1960-75   32
3.3 Property Tax As a Source of State Revenue, 1960-75   34
3.4 Sales Tax As a Source of State Revenue, 1960-75   35
3.5 Excise Tax As a Source of State Revenue, 1960-75   36
3.6 Excise Tax Revenues by Tax Base, 1960-75   37
3.7 Individual Income Tax Revenues, 1960-75   39
3.8 Corporate Income Tax Revenues, 1960-75   41
3.9 License Fee Revenue, 1960-75   43
3.10 Taxes As a Percent of Total State Revenue, 1960-75   44
4.1 Local Government Revenue As a Percent of All Government Revenue, 1950-75   48
4.2 Local Government Revenue by Source, 1975   49
4.3 Property Tax As a Source of Local Government Revenue, 1950-75   50
4.4 Sales Tax As a Source of Local Government Revenue, 1950-75   56
4.5 Income Tax As a Source of Local Government Revenue, 1950-75   60
4.6 Other Taxes As a Source of Local Government Revenue, 1950-75   63
4.7 Local Government Tax Revenue by Source, 1950-75   64

# List of Figures

9.1 Process Model for Local Government   151
11.1 Summary of Local Government Revenues   198
11.2 Summary of Local Government Expenditures   204

# PART I    Taxes and Government

# 1      INTRODUCTION TO TAXES AND GOVERNMENT

Most citizens feel their taxes have risen sharply in recent years. But because many taxes are hidden from direct scrutiny, it may be difficult for people to realize just how much their tax burden has actually increased. Table 1.1 presents a summary of the per capita tax burden for U.S. taxpayers for the years 1950 to 1975. The dollar figures represent the amount of tax revenue that each level of government collected for each person in the United States for the year indicated. As an example, in a typical family of four in which only one of the members is employed, the total taxes paid should approximate four times the amount shown on the table in any given year. For instance, an average family of four in 1975 probably paid well over $6,000 in taxes to the various levels of government. If this figure seems high, it is because many of the taxes attributed to the family may be paid indirectly; that is, they are included in the cost of goods the family buys. As another example of an indirect tax, a family of four that rents a house rather than owning one does not directly pay any property taxes. Yet the rent the family pays is in part determined by the amount of property taxes the landlord must pay. The result is that the burden of these taxes is passed from the landlord to the tenants. Additionally, the renting family does not receive a tax deduction against its personal income tax as does a family that owns its own home and pays the property tax directly. Therefore, the renting family pays a hidden tax in two ways, as part of the rent it pays each month and as increased income tax due to not having a property tax deduction.

A review of Table 1.1 reveals there have been massive increases in the per capita tax burdens of U.S. citizens during the last three decades.

In the period 1950 to 1975, the per capita overall tax burden for all levels of government has increased over 360 percent from $337 in 1950 to $1,556 in 1975. This is an average increase of more than 14.5 percent per year for 25 years. The breakdown among federal, state, and local governments reveals the increase of the federal tax burden has been somewhat less: almost 285 percent for the 25-year period, an average yearly increase of 11.4 percent. In contrast, the percentage increase in the state and local tax burden for the same period has been a staggering 532.4 percent, a yearly average increase of 21.3 percent per year. A closer look at the table shows only one year in which there was a decrease. In 1971 the per capita federal tax burden fell from $719 to $666. However, this decrease was counterbalanced by an increase in the state and local per capita tax burden of $33 (from $427 to $460 per capita).

TABLE 1.1
Tax Burden Per Capita, 1950-75
(dollars)

|  | Total | Percent Increase | Federal | Percent Increase | State @ Local | Percent Increase |
|---|---|---|---|---|---|---|
| 1950 | 337 | – | 232 | – | 105 | – |
| 1955 | 490 | (45.4) | 348 | (50.0) | 142 | (35.2) |
| 1960 | 629 | (28.4) | 428 | (22.9) | 201 | (41.5) |
| 1965 | 747 | (18.8) | 483 | (12.9) | 264 | (31.3) |
| 1970 | 1146 | (53.4) | 719 | (48.9) | 427 | (61.7) |
| 1971 | 1126 | (-1.7) | 666 | (-7.4) | 460 | (7.7) |
| 1972 | 1260 | (11.9) | 738 | (10.8) | 522 | (13.5) |
| 1973 | 1366 | (8.4) | 789 | (6.9) | 577 | (10.5) |
| 1974 | 1492 | (9.2) | 874 | (10.8) | 618 | (7.1) |
| 1975 | 1556 | (4.3) | 892 | (2.0) | 664 | (7.4) |
| 25 year increase: | 361.7 percent | | 284.5 percent | | 532.4 percent | |
| Average increase: | 14.5 percent | | 11.4 percent | | 21.3 percent | |

*Source:* U.S. Bureau of the Census, *Statistical Abstract of the United States: 1977* (Washington, D.C., 1977), p. 281, #460.

The data clearly show that individual perceptions of an ever growing tax burden are accurate, perhaps to an extent that goes beyond the imagination of even the most disgruntled taxpayer. While statistics of this sort are interesting, it is more important to understand why these increases have taken place.

While there can be no argument about the massive increase in the tax burden, there is considerable disagreement about the reasons for these increases. Most explanations for the increases in government spending and taxation are based upon economic grounds. They suggest that, for one reason or another, people have demanded their government provide a greater quantity and variety of services that were not provided by private industry. Additionally, international politics has played some part in these increases. The problem with these explanations is that they provide no understanding of how spending and taxing decisions are made in government. They do not examine the dynamic interaction between the various actors in the political system. They do not reflect the political complexity of the democratic form of government. But worst of all from the point of view of the taxpayer, they do not suggest any strategies or means for halting this seemingly inexorable growth in government and taxation. It would be inconsistent with the purpose of this book not to offer an explanation for the growth of government spending and taxation that includes ways to reverse the trend.

## WHY TAXES INCREASE

The key to understanding why taxes increase lies in the complex interactions taking place between the groups of people who are the primary actors in the democratic political process. These actors are the elected government officials, top level government managers, public employee groups, and the public. The composition of this last group requires further elaboration. In a general sense, the public is composed of all citizens living within a particular governmental unit. These citizens, either when acting as individuals or when organized into groups, have a variety of different relationships with government. There are four major types of relationships that citizens have: citizens are voters; citizens are political activists; citizens are consumers of government services; and, of course, citizens are taxpayers. People in these roles have different parts to play in the process of making government expenditure and taxation decisions.

Most traditional theories of government decision making concentrate on the legislative process with emphasis on the interaction between the members of the various branches of government. The Promise Model of the decision process offered here has a much broader scope in terms of time and participants. The decision process can be conveniently divided into three parts: (1) getting elected, (2) holding office, (3) getting reelected. From these titles, the focus of the model should be obvious. The primary concern is with the electoral process and its effect on government expenditure and taxation decisions. Discussion of the model will show how each of these three parts contributes to the relentless rise in the cost of government.

## GETTING ELECTED

An election is a communication process that focuses on making promises to the electorate. In all election campaigns there are three types of promises. These promises differ in the scope of the audience to which they are addressed and the level of specific information that they contain.

The first type of promise is designed to appeal to a majority of the citizens. Since a candidate is never certain who will vote in any particular election these promises are broad, general, and draw upon those issues and values that the candidate feels will appeal to almost every citizen. Also, they are structured so that they do not offend any significant group of citizens.

Examples of this type of promise might include the following:

"I promise to serve the needs of the people."
"I promise to work for the public good."
"I promise to put leadership back into government."
"I promise to make government more efficient and/or effective."

The reader will undoubtedly recognize these bland generalities as being a part of virtually every political campaign. They should be regarded as harmless trademarks of the American political system having no significant impact on any future actions that the successful candidate might take. These promises do not make a significant contribution to the steady increase in government spending and taxation.

The second type of promise made during a campaign is neither bland nor harmless. Almost all candidates running for office have a list of things they feel the government should do:

1. Improve service(s) that the government currently offers.
2. Identify a group of citizens that have unmet demands for government services and promise to see what can be done to meet their needs.
3. Identify some area where they feel government should be providing a service, but is currently not doing so.

In any of these situations, the candidate promises to see what can be done to meet the needs that have been uncovered. The candidate is hopeful that these actions will strike a positive and responsive cord with a large number of citizens. Second, the candidate is hopeful that a specific group of citizens (presumably those who stand to benefit directly from the promised service) will be pleased and excited enough to become actively involved in the campaign—volunteering their time, money, and political resources. Third, in making this type of promise the candidate hopes to avoid making any group of citizens angry enough to take an active role in opposing the candidate or in supporting the candidate's opponent. Finally, it may be possible to gain a strategic advantage by making the opponent adopt a "me too" approach to the issue or by forcing the opponent to come out against the promised improvement thereby alienating the activist group created by the candidate. This kind of promise is a prime contributor to increased government spending for the simple reason that when elected the candidate must try to make good on the promise. This can only mean expanding the services and costs of government. This expansion leads inevitably to a rise in taxes.

The third type of promise is similar to the second because it is aimed at a group of citizens who have established themselves as activists in regard to a political issue or government program. In this instance, the candidate sees the activist group is organized and has some ability to influence the outcome of the election. Therefore, the candidate feels it is in the best interest of the campaign to make promises that are likely to attract the group to support the candidate. This type of promise is directly related to increased spending and taxes because it represents a public commitment for which the candidate can be held accountable.

Thus far, the promises described have been aimed at providing new or increased government services. It would be erroneous to leave the impression that candidates promise only to spend and never to save. Particularly in the last few years, it has been commonplace for candidates to make general statements about holding the line on taxes or government spending. The problem is that these types of promises are almost always addressed to the general citizenry, not to a specific group of activist citizens. Unfortunately, the general citizenry does not have the capacity to force delivery on its promises with the same authority that the groups of activist citizens do.

In fairness, it must be said that there is no agreement among experts about what factors are crucial in winning elections. No matter what the reason for success and no matter which candidate is the winner, in terms of promises the result is always the same. The winning candidate has a list of promises that were made to specific groups of citizen activists. The candidate also has a collection of general promises including those of fiscal restraint that were made to the general citizenry. It is quite likely that some of these promises may be in conflict with one another. The manner in which the candidate resolves these conflicts and the determination of which promises to keep is the key factor in increasing government spending and taxation.

## BEING IN OFFICE

It is an unfortunate fact of American political life that upon achieving an elective office, the candidate must start to think about retaining that office or moving on to a higher one. This preoccupation colors all the candidate's actions and is the predominate factor in determining which promises will be kept and which will be forgotten.

When a successful candidate assumes a hard-won office, there is an immediate and strong desire to begin doing things, to begin establishing a record of accomplishment. Unfortunately for the taxpayer, records of accomplishment are best made by the creation of new programs and services as well as by the expansion of existing activities. Why is this so? The reasoning is quite simple. The elected official when faced with budgetary decisions has essentially three choices:

1. To attempt to cut services and programs.
2. To maintain the existing level of services necessitating an actual increase in budgeted funds due to inflation.
3. To propose new programs and services with corresponding increases in funding.

The ramifications of pursuing these three courses of action must be examined in turn.

### Cutting Programs

Attempting to cut budgets and programs is a certain road to trouble for the newly elected public official. Going back to the campaign and the promises that came so easily, it is likely that very little was said about eliminating existing programs and services. To have advocated elimination would probably have alienated one or more groups of activist citizens. This action would give the opponent an opportunity to come to the aid of the activist group thereby strengthening the opponent's position in the election. Therefore, the public official is probably on record as supporting new and expanded programs rather than for reducing and eliminating programs. Even if a public official comes to believe that a program has outlived its usefulness and, therefore, should be reduced or eliminated, the official's record of election promises may be an insurmountable barrier to acting on that belief. But what happens if the official decides to try to go ahead and cut programs without regard to the pre-election promises? In attempting to cut programs, the official will immediately be confronted by one or more groups allied in strong opposition to the proposed reduction. These groups will include other elected officials in the legislative body, the appointed managers who are responsible for the affected programs, and the public employee association that has organized the workers in the program.

Opposition from other members of the legislative body may come for the simple reason that these officials are not willing to make the same political sacrifices as the reduction-minded official. Opposition will be even stronger from those officials who count as political allies:

1. The management of the affected program.
2. The employee association that represents workers in the affected program.
3. Those members of the public who are the direct recipients of the threatened service. Unless there is strong public support for reduction or elimination of a given program, the budget-minded official can expect little or no support in the legislative chamber.

An official proposing reductions in established programs can expect loud and strong opposition from the administrative officials responsible for the program under attack. A proposed reduction is a bodily assault on top management. It says that their program is inefficient, ineffective, and not needed by the public. Managers have no choice but to resist with all the resources they have available. Many managers regard reductions as a personal attack on their competence and integrity. (After all, if the program is so unworthy that it should be eliminated, the managers should have come forward with this information before. They are closest to what is going on and they should be able to judge whether or not the public is getting full value for its tax dollar.) The problem lies in the managers' ability to make judgments in an objective manner. Managers tend to see their own success or failure in terms of what happens to their programs. Additionally, they are accustomed to defending their programs in the yearly budget process. Therefore, they develop a sense of protectiveness for their programs. To support an attempt to cut a program that they have worked long and hard for goes against the managers' nature. It is a rare day indeed when managers will admit to a newly elected public official that their programs can be reduced or eliminated to the benefit of the taxpayer.

The circle of resistance to program reduction is completed by the public employee association and its position in the matter. Any union or other type of employee association can be expected to defend vigorously the livelihood of its membership. In the government sector, this means defending already existing programs from reduction or elimination. Programs mean jobs. Reducing jobs means reducing the power and influence of the employee association. Because of the strength of this opposition, officials often propose that program reductions be carried out in a way that insures no public employees will lose their jobs. Reducing personnel without layoffs can be achieved through natural attrition, early retirement and hiring freezes. Even these mild and indirect measures will not meet with the approval of the employee association leadership. The management of employee associations can be expected to behave in the same manner as any other management. That is, they can be expected to identify with the mission and goals of their organization. They tend to see their own success and failure in terms of the success and failure of the organization they lead.

For employee associations, one of the major criteria for success is membership and the increasing of that membership. Obviously, reductions in programs are not conducive to enlarging membership. Therefore, employee association management has a clear and logical reason to oppose any effort to reduce government programs. These managers have an additional reason to oppose any attempt at program reduction.

Employee-management relations in the government sector as elsewhere are based upon conflict. Employee association managers are judged by how well they fare in the conflict with management. An image of strength is not projected by going along with proposals to reduce programs and jobs. Just the opposite. Opposing a reduction proposal provides a good opportunity for the employee association leader to demonstrate strength. Chances for success are good because the employee association manager can count on legislators and the government managers themselves as allies. A last point that must be considered about the opposition of employee association groups is that they often wield a good deal of political clout, especially in local elections. Therefore, an official who angers them with proposals for program reductions can expect retribution at the next election. This not only discourages reduction proposals, but makes it very difficult to gather support for such proposals from other legislative officials.

By this time, it should be abundantly clear that the newly elected official seeking to reduce government spending will face strong opposition with little or no prospects for support. The official that continues to pursue this course of action is likely to be a one-term office holder. The message is clear for the taxpayer who wonders why government always grows and never decreases in size or budget. It is inconsistent with political survival for elected officials to advocate and actively fight for significant reductions in government programs or spending. Unless the political chemistry of program reductions changes, the taxpayer can expect to see little or no reduction in government spending.

## Maintaining Programs

The second of the three budgetary choices available to the elected official is to maintain the existing levels of programs and services. Because government is no more immune from inflation than the individual, maintaining the status quo in terms of programs means increasing the size of the budget. In making this choice, the public official avoids the violent opposition associated with program reduction. This course of action is considered "business as usual" because many legislative officials find this a reasonable position to take. Also, government managers find this position a reasonable base from which to work. It allows them to maintain the status quo while they wait for an opening to expand an existing program or perhaps even create a new one. Employee association officials, like the managers, find this choice to be a comfortable starting place both for salary negotiations and for the establishment of political relationships with newly elected officials. Their main concern is the dimension of the salary increase compared to inflation. Disagreements with public management can be reduced to a matter of trading a few percentage points in salary increase back and forth. (In this congenial arrangement, there is only one loser—the taxpayer.) The result is all programs will be continued regardless of their worth or effectiveness. There will be upward adjustments for inflation and perhaps even some programmatic increases. The taxpayer can count on an increase in the tax burden sufficient to cover this budgetary expansion.

Referring to Table 1.1, the reasons for the long term pattern of annual increases in the tax burden should become clear. There is one other conclusion to be drawn from this state of affairs and that concerns the longevity of government programs: once a program has been initiated, the chances are excellent that it will enjoy a long trend of gradual increases in its funding. In other words, once a program has been approved it almost certainly will become a permanent fixture of government. This fact of public life highlights the importance of that initial funding decision.

Something should be said about the political consequences for a newly elected official pursuing this second course of action. It does not really have a political payoff. The official cannot return to the electorate and merely say that business has been conducted as usual. There have been no programs eliminated. There have been no programs created. Government services will continue to operate as usual. The only difference is that the cost will be a little higher. This kind of political report card is not consistent with any of the campaign promises that have been discussed previously in this chapter. Nor is it consistent with a successful reelection campaign. Since cutting government programs is politically destructive, there is only one alternative available to the public official who wishes to remain in office. The official must do something. The official must try to make good on some of the specific campaign promises that were made, thereby creating a record of achievement. All of these dictates of political reality may be translated into one course of action: seeking new government programs or the expansion of existing ones, thus, continuing to increase the tax burden.

### Expanding Programs

The third and most expedient choice for the newly elected public official is to propose some modest increases in existing programs or to propose the creation of a new program or service. Because other legislative officials can be expected to pursue this same course of action and because the amount of funds available for new and expanded programs is limited, a great deal of debate and controversy will take place regarding these proposals. It is at this point that the question of expertise becomes important. In most instances legislative officials do not have sufficient expertise to formulate realistic, workable proposals for expanding or creating programs.

Developing such expertise requires a long-term involvement with the operation of a particular type of program. Additionally, it is necessary to have a good understanding of how the overall government bureaucracy works. Because most legislative officials are sadly lacking in both of these areas, they must rely on others for this expertise. In most instances, particularly in local government, the staff provided for the legislative officials is not capable of providing the necessary information. They are usually too few in number and often have not been on the job long enough to acquire a clear view of how things get done in government. Therefore, legislative officials find themselves seeking information from the managers involved in the programmatic area they are interested in expanding. In government as in any organization, information is power. When legislative officials are forced to rely on managers for the information needed to formulate their program proposals, they are giving away to these officials a great deal of power and influence. By being selective about what information is given to the legislative official, managers can strongly influence the nature of the program expansions. In most instances, the legislator has no choice but to accept the information given by the managers with little serious question. Based upon the information received, the legislative official is able to develop a set of program proposals that can be presented publicly as serious, well thought out attempts to fulfill campaign promises.

It is extremely important to understand the implications of this situation. What is supposed to happen is that the elected official responds to the will of the people with positive actions. Presumably, the official was elected because of the specific promises made to the groups of activist citizens who supported the official's candidacy. But, in fact, the official is forced to propose what is deemed favorable by the government managers.

Proposals for program expansion have no difficulty in finding supporters. Managers in different program areas tend to reach agreements of mutual support designed to encourage the expansion of their programs. Their rationale is that by providing more and better services, they are able to do a more effective job of caring for the public's interest. Also, expansion has the happy coincidence of enhancing the prestige and professional reputations of the managers.

From the point of view of the employee association, expansion of programs is usually a very desirable state of affairs. For the association management, expansion means more members, more dues coming in—with the result being more power and prestige. These things are as important to the managers of employee associations as they are to the administrative managers of government.

As a result of this cooperation, the newly elected official finds that proposals for program increases can make life quite pleasant in most instances. There is little reason to think about trying to undertake the difficult task of reducing the overall scope of government activity. Even if a particular official is inclined in this direction, it will soon become apparent that this is a swift route out of office, or to isolation in the legislative body at the very least. There is clearly a strong bias in our governmental processes toward spending and against conserving tax dollars.


## GETTING REELECTED

In the absence of exceptional circumstances, the chances for reelection most often depend on what an official has done while in office. Those officials who can show a record of achievement, who can show that government is doing more or performing a function better because of their efforts, stand the best chance for reelection. They are the ones who government managers mention in press conferences as being knowledgeable and dedicated representatives of the people. They are the ones that the employee associations regard as honorable and reasonable opponents in the bargaining process and, therefore, worthy of reelection. They are the ones who are complimented by their colleagues for being responsible and productive members of the legislative body.

In addition to all this support within the government, these officials can now go to the special interest groups who are the recipients of the expanded programs and seek their support. In all likelihood, they will get it. Except for something as extraordinary as a taxpayers' revolt, the reelection of these officials should be relatively easy and straightforward.

But what about the first-term official who has not worked to maintain the status quo program and has not advocated a few increases here and there? What are this official's chances for reelection? There is no need to look for support from the government structure. The official's colleagues will not reward what they consider to be irresponsible behavior with supportive and complimentary statements. Instead this official will be termed "difficult to work with" and be mentioned as a generally ineffective member of the legislative body. The government managers will not have anything positive to say about this official. The terms likely to be used are "not knowledgeable," "meat-axe" approach to government, and "unconcerned about the needs of people." The management of the employee associations will feel they are dealing with someone who does not understand the rules of the game, or, if the rules are understood, who does not abide by them. The reduction-minded official is quite likely to be at the head of the "hit" list of the employee association. The "hit" list is, of course, the list of those candidates that the association will oppose most strenuously during the next election. The result is that the official has drawn a blank as far as support from the government structure is concerned.

What about support from the people? No need to go out in search of citizen special interest groups who have benefited from the official's actions during the first term of office. There will not be any. The reduction-minded official cannot even appeal to the general public on the grounds of trying to reduce taxes and eliminate unnecessary government spending. Such an appeal would be worthless because it is highly unlikely that the official was really able to make much of a reduction in overall government spending. One or two officials cannot turn the tide against spending.

What conclusions can be drawn about reelection campaigns? The primary one is that favoring reduced government spending is not conducive to reelection. The plain fact is that advocating less government is not good politics. Principally because there has not been a general public sentiment that says "we have too much government activity at too high a price and we want less of it." Additionally, the general public has not been in a position to judge which government programs are effective and should be continued and which are ineffective or no longer needed. The entire political system, particularly at the local level, is geared toward more and bigger government. New programs and increased spending are the characteristics of the successful politician. Programs are almost always maintained at existing levels with appropriate adjustments for inflation. The result is that local government just keeps on getting bigger.

The evidence of this trend toward more government spending and taxation is presented in the three chapters that follow. The federal, state, and local government tax structures are examined with particular emphasis on the rationale, structure, yields, and operating characteristics of each of the major taxes.

The federal government with its massive expenditures and seemingly limitless supply of tax revenues is the focal point of all government activity. Although state and local governments spend more money and collect more tax dollars than the federal government, there can be no doubt that the federal government exercises a predominant influence on the financial affairs of the states and their local government subdivisions. This predominance can be directly attributed to the vast revenue resources that the federal government enjoys. Federal revenues come from two major sources, taxation and borrowing. The deficit spending habit of the federal government is a topic that deserves complete and separate coverage at another time. Federal taxation, however, is directly related to understanding the taxpayer revolt and its effect on local government. In this chapter, the major taxes of the federal government will be reviewed with emphasis on how they affect the financial situation of state and local government. The effect of these taxes on taxpayer attitudes will also be examined. While it is not possible to provide an exhaustive review of federal taxation in a single chapter, enough information will be presented to provide an adequate background for the chapters that follow.

## PERSONAL INCOME TAX

Virtually every taxpayer in the United States pays personal income tax. This tax is the mainstay of federal revenues and the primary concern of every taxpayer at least for a few weeks each year. The influence of this tax on the financial affairs of government at all levels makes it necessary for the well-informed taxpayer to know more about the tax than merely how to fill out a return.

The basic principle of the income tax is that each person should be taxed in accordance with the amount earned. The more a person earns, the higher the rate at which those earning are taxed. This is in theory. In practice, the tax liability of any individual is based upon a percentage of that individual's *taxable* income. Taxable income is the income that remains after deductions and exemptions are taken. Deductions and exemptions are reductions in the amount of income that is subject to tax. These reductions are granted for a variety of purposes that range from subsidizing local and state governments to stimulating homeowner investment in energy-conserving improvements. Generally, the more income a person has, the easier it is to take advantage of these income reductions. The result is that those individuals who earn the highest incomes, do not pay the highest percentage of taxes. By far the greatest part of the income tax burden is borne by the middle income taxpayer.

For most taxpayers, this burden is relatively painless because tax payments are deducted regularly from a person's paycheck. The "pain" occurs for a few weeks in the spring of each year, when taxpayers must submit their returns to the Internal Revenue Service. Even then, the amount of money withheld during the tax year is usually sufficient to cover the amount of tax owed. Ideally, a taxpayer should neither receive any money back from the government nor have to pay any money when the return is filed. The amount withheld should equal the amount of tax owed. For many people, filing an income tax return means they will receive a much-welcomed check back from the government. This goes against the long-run interest of the taxpayer for two reasons. First, the money returned represents an overpayment of tax. The taxpayer was thus deprived of the use of these funds for a lengthy period of time. Even worse, receiving a tax refund tends to prevent people from realizing how much of their earnings they actually pay in income taxes each year.

If people don't really know how much they pay, there is no way for them to evaluate whether or not the services they receive from government are worth what they are paying for them in taxes. This inability to calculate the benefit received against taxes paid is one of the biggest problems with the federal tax system, and the income tax is the greatest offender.

Table 2.1 summarizes income tax receipts for the 25 year period 1950 to 1975. During that time revenue from the income tax increased from 18.4 billion dollars to 124.8 billion dollars. This represents a 578.3 percent increase over the 25 year period or a yearly average

*Federal Taxation*

increase of 23.1 percent. During the same period the number of taxpayers increased from 84.6 million to 126.3 million. This represents only a 49.3 percent increase as compared to the 578.3 percent increase in taxes. These figures portray a massive increase in the burden imposed by the income tax. Perhaps the most significant statistic in terms of the future is the yearly average increase of over 23 percent. There is absolutely no reason to think that this rate of increase will lessen in coming years. Even if this figure is adjusted for inflation, the result is still a whopping increase in the income tax burden. For instance, the annualized inflation rate for the first half of 1978 is 13.2 percent. If the 23 percent tax increase figure prevails in 1978, this will represent a significant decrease in purchasing power for the average taxpayer. The essential question is: Will the value of government services to the taxpayer increase by a similar amount? If it does not, then the overall quality of the taxpayer's economic position has decreased.

TABLE 2.1
Income Tax Receipts, 1950-75

|  | Total Income Tax (billions of dollars) | Percentage Increase | Number of Returns (millions) | Number of Tax Payees (millions) |
|---|---|---|---|---|
| 1950 | 18.4 | – | 52.6 | 84.6 |
| 1955 | 29.6 | 60.9 | 57.8 | 93.9 |
| 1960 | 39.5 | 33.4 | 60.6 | 98.7 |
| 1965 | 49.5 | 25.3 | 67.2 | 107.6 |
| 1970 | 83.9 | 69.5 | 73.9 | 117.0 |
| 1972 | 93.6 | 11.6 | 77.6 | 120.9 |
| 1973 | 108.1 | 15.5 | 80.7 | 124.3 |
| 1974 | 123.6 | 14.4 | 83.3 | 127.6 |
| 1975* | 124.8 | 1.0 | 82.1 | 126.3 |

Income tax 25-year increase: 578.3 percent

Income tax 25-year average
increase: 23.1 percent

*Preliminary estimate
*Source:* U.S. Bureau of the Census, *Statistical Abstract of the United States: 1977* (Washington, D.C., 1977), p. 259, #424.

Table 2.2 presents the burden of the income tax spread over the entire population of the United States. During the period 1950 to 1975 the income tax per capita has increased from $121 to $586. This an increase of 384.3 percent for 25 years, an annual average increase of almost $19 or 15.4 percent. If this trend continues, the average family of four can expect to pay an additional $76 to the federal government in income tax every year. Summarizing the data from Tables 2.1 and 2.2, one point is very clear: the income tax has a 25-year history of significant increases. There is absolutely no reason to believe that this trend will abate in the future.

### TABLE 2.2
### Income Tax Per Capita, 1950-75

| | Income Tax Per Capita (dollars) | Percentage Increase |
|---|---|---|
| 1950 | 121.00 | – |
| 1955 | 179.00 | 47.9 |
| 1960 | 219.00 | 22.3 |
| 1965 | 256.00 | 16.9 |
| 1970 | 413.00 | 61.3 |
| 1972 | 450.00 | 8.9 |
| 1973 | 515.00 | 14.4 |
| 1974 | 585.00 | 13.6 |
| 1975* | 586.00 | .2 |
| Per capita 25-year increase: | 384.3 percent | |
| Per capita 25-year average increase: | 15.4 percent | |

*Preliminary estimate
Source: U.S. Bureau of the Census, *Statistical Abstract of the United States: 1977* (Washington, D.C., 1977), p. 259, #424.

What is the effect of the federal income tax on taxpayer attitudes? Consider these facts. The income tax combined with inflation places an additional hidden tax on every wage earner who receives a raise. As a typical example, assume that in a given year the annual rate of inflation is 10 percent. During that year a wage earner receives a raise of 8 percent that is supposed to compensate for the effect of inflation. It is obvious that the worker is short 2 percent. But if this 8 percent raise pushes the worker into a higher tax bracket, the marginal tax rate will increase. Therefore, the worker will have to pay a greater share of earnings to the federal government. The result is that, in addition to the 2 percent loss of purchasing power caused by inflation, a further loss of purchasing power is inflicted by the additional tax. The inevitable result is a lowering of the worker's standard of living.

Traditionally, America has been a place where most people looked forward to the future with optimism. This sense of economic optimism is one of the reasons why Americans have not been overly concerned about the dimensions of the tax burden they carry. As this sense of optimism decreases, people tend to be more concerned about what they get for their tax dollars. The taxpayer revolt of the late 1970s represents the start of a serious questioning of the value citizens receive for their tax dollars. This questioning focuses on those taxes that are the most highly visible to the taxpayer. As has been shown, the income tax is not highly visible and, for most people, not particularly painful to pay. In fact, a great many people may look forward to tax time with anticipation because in return for the time spent on a tax return, they may receive money back from the government. This kind of thinking prevents a serious examination of the efficiency and effectiveness of the federal government. Unfortunately, this kind of serious examination seems to be reserved for units of government whose taxes are neither hidden nor painless.

## EMPLOYMENT TAX

"Employment Tax" is a term used to describe a group of taxes whose revenues are paid into a trust fund that provides money for certain types of social purposes. There are three general types of assistance funded by federal employment taxes: retirement in the form of Social Security benefits, income protection during periods of forced unemployment, and income protection during periods of physical disability. Employment taxes are collected from both employers and employees. They are calculated on the basis of a percentage of employee earnings and employer payrolls. These funds are earmarked; that is, they can only be used for the payment of benefits under one of the three categories of general assistance. The theory of the trust fund system is that the contributions of the employer and employee should be sufficient to provide the funds necessary for the payment of benefits. For instance in the case of the retirement benefit, the funds paid in by an employer and a given employee should be sufficient to provide the benefits received by that employee upon retirement.

There has been a good deal of questioning in regard to the practice of this principle. One cause for questioning has been the increased longevity of retirees. The level of payments made by current retirees and their employers during the working years was determined by calculations dependent upon projected lifespans that were a good deal shorter than the actual life spans of the retirees. The result is a shortfall in the funds necessary to pay retirement benefits. This slack is made up out of the tax payments of people currently in the work force, thus raising a question about the adequacy of their contribution toward their own retirement. Despite these actuarial shortcomings, employment taxes are the federal government's best example of linking benefits received directly to taxes paid. This linkage provides a reasonable means for the taxpayer to determine the efficiency and effectiveness of government programs.

Table 2.3 summarizes the receipts and outlays for the Old Age, Survivors, and Disability Insurance trust fund (OASDI) for the years 1965 to 1977. Between the years 1965 and 1977 employment taxes earmarked for the OASDI trust fund increased 360.2 percent from 17.6 billion to 81 billion dollars. In the same years, outlays from the trust fund increased 384 percent from 17.5 billion dollars in 1965 to 84.7 billion dollars in 1977. Taxes supporting this fund increased an average of 15.8 percent per year during the same period. In the years 1976 and 1977 the fund ran at a deficit: 3.2 billion dollars in 1976

TABLE 2.3
Employment Tax Receipts and Outlays, 1965-1977:
Old Age, Survivors, and Disability Insurance
(billion dollars)

|  | Receipts | Outlays | Surplus or (Deficit) | % Increase Receipts | % Increase Outlays |
|---|---|---|---|---|---|
| 1965 | 17.6 | 17.5 | .1 | – | – |
| 1970 | 36.1 | 30.3 | 5.8 | 105.1 | 73.1 |
| 1971 | 38.9 | 35.9 | 3.0 | 7.8 | 18.5 |
| 1972 | 43.2 | 40.2 | 3.0 | 11.1 | 12.0 |
| 1973 | 49.6 | 49.1 | .5 | 14.8 | 22.1 |
| 1974 | 57.7 | 55.9 | 1.8 | 16.3 | 13.8 |
| 1975 | 66.7 | 64.7 | 2.0 | 15.6 | 15.7 |
| 1976 | 70.7 | 73.9 | (3.2) | 6.0 | 14.2 |
| 1976 TQ[a] | 18.4 | 19.8 | (1.4) | n.a. | n.a. |
| 1977[b] | 81.0 | 84.7 | (3.7) | 14.6 | 14.6 |

1970-77 estimated cumulative surplus or (deficit):   7.8 billion
12-year (1965 vs. 1977) increase in receipts:   360.2 percent
Average 7-year (1970-77) increase in receipts:   12.3 percent
12-year (1965 vs. 1977) increase in outlays:   384 percent
Average 7-year (1970-77) increase in outlays:   15.8 percent

[a]TQ—Transition Quarter: July to September.
(due to change in federal fiscal year)

[b]Preliminary estimate

*Source:* U.S. Bureau of the Census, *Statistical Abstract of the United States: 1977* (Washington, D.C., 1977), p. 252, #412.

and 3.7 billion dollars in 1977. Overall, the table reflects a reasonable balance between the tax revenue received and the benefits provided. It appears that taxpayers as a group are getting what they paid. However, if the data reported for 1976 and 1977 represent a future trend, there could be some real problems in regard to the financial viability of the OASDI fund.

Table 2.4 summarizes the receipts and outlays of the Unemployment Insurance trust fund for the period 1965 to 1977. As in the case of the OASDI fund, there appears to be a reasonable balance between taxes paid into the fund and the benefits paid out. Between the years 1965 and 1977 taxes earmarked for this fund increased 282.9 percent from 4.1 billion to 15.7 billion dollars paid in annually. Annual outlays increased from 3 billion dollars in 1965 to 15.4 billion dollars in 1977, representing an increase of 413.3 percent. In the period 1970 to 1977 outlays exceeded tax revenues by 6.7 billion dollars. Concern over

TABLE 2.4
Employment Tax Receipts and Outlays, 1965-77:
Unemployment Insurance (billions of dollars)

| | Receipts | Outlays | Surplus or (Deficit) | Increase or (Decrease) % Receipts | Increase or (Decrease) % Outlays |
|---|---|---|---|---|---|
| 1965 | 4.1 | 3.0 | 1.1 | – | – |
| 1970 | 4.1 | 3.6 | .5 | 0 | 20.0 |
| 1971 | 4.3 | 6.1 | (1.8) | 4.9 | 69.4 |
| 1972 | 5.4 | 6.9 | (1.5) | 25.6 | 13.1 |
| 1973 | 6.7 | 5.4 | 1.3 | 24.0 | (21.7) |
| 1974 | 7.5 | 6.2 | 1.3 | 11.9 | 14.8 |
| 1975 | 8.2 | 13.2 | (5.0) | 9.3 | 112.9 |
| 1976 | 16.2 | 17.9 | (1.7) | 97.6 | 35.6 |
| 1976 TQ[a] | 3.4 | 3.5 | (.1) | n.a. | n.a. |
| 1977[b] | 15.7 | 15.4 | .3 | (3.1) | (14.0) |

1970-77 estimated cumulative surplus or (deficit): (6.7 billion)
12-year (1965-77) increase in receipts: 282.9 percent
Average 7-year (1970-77) increase in receipts: 24.3 percent
12-year (1965-77) increase in outlays: 413.3 percent
Average 7-year (1970-77) increase in outlays: 30.0 percent

[a]TQ—Transition Quarter: July to September (due to change in federal fiscal year).

[b]Preliminary estimate

*Source:* U.S. Bureau of the Census, *Statistical Abstract of the United States: 1977* (Washinton, D.C., 1977), p. 252, #412.

this deficit, coupled with the fact that the law governing the Unemployment Insurance trust fund remained essentially unchanged since its enactment in 1935, caused Congress to pass Public Law 94-566 effective January 1, 1978. PL 94-566 restructured both the benefits and the supporting tax system of the Unemployment Insurance trust fund. Presumably the new structure will reduce or eliminate future deficits.

Employment taxes are relatively unique in the federal tax structure because they are used to fund a service that can be directly linked to a specific set of tax revenues. This direct linkage provides the taxpayer with the opportunity to make an evaluation of the service received contrasted with the amount of taxes paid. The problem is that this evaluation must be made in a general way by all citizens. The OASDI trust fund involves two different groups of citizens: those that pay into it and those that receive the benefits. The time delay between payment and benefit makes it difficult for one individual to evaluate whether or not the benefit received is worth the cost incurred.

Employment taxes are relatively painless for the taxpayer because they are deducted from employee paychecks and paid by the employer who passes them on to the consumer. These taxes are hidden because no return has to be filed by the employee and individuals do not usually know how much they have paid. They are not hidden from the employer because strict recordkeeping and payment schedules are required. While the general citizenry does not evidence much concern about employment taxes, employer groups spend a great deal of time and money attempting to influence legislation that governs the collection and use of employment taxes. It would appear that hiding taxes and making them relatively painless to pay is an effective way of keeping people from being too concerned about their tax burden.

## CORPORATE INCOME TAX

Most citizens view the corporate income tax as the business equivalent of the personal income tax. It is quite similar to the personal income tax in that the basis of the tax is the profit of a "legal person," i.e., the corporation. The corporation is allowed deductions for the cost of doing business, while individuals are allowed deductions for expenditures that do not add to their net worth such as medical expenses, taxes, and losses due to theft and other misfortunes. In both cases, the federal government can use deductions as a means to encourage or discourage certain kinds of behavior. This use of deductions is termed a "tax expenditure." A certain amount of tax is foregone in order to encourage some desirable activity such as adding energy-conserving improvements to an existing structure whether it is a place of residence or a place of business.

Perhaps the greatest differences between the two taxes are the rates of taxation and in the ultimate burden of the tax. The personal income tax has a progressive rate structure that ranges from 14 percent to 70 percent. The corporate tax has only two rates: 25 percent for earnings under $100,000, and 48 percent for everything over that amount. The rate structure used for the corporate tax is commonly referred to as a proportional rate structure; that is, the amount of the tax paid increases as earnings increase but the percentage tax rate remains the same. The other major difference between the two taxes is in the way the burden of the tax is distributed. The burden of the personal income tax is borne by the person who files the return. There is little or no opportunity to pass the burden on to someone else. In the case of the corporate taxpayer, there are two options. First, the burden may be borne by the owners of the corporation, the stockholders. This burden is in the form of reduced dividend payments to stockholders. The second option is for the corporation to decide what level of after-tax profits it wants and then to adjust its operating procedures to yield that level of profit. In this case, the consumers of the corporation's goods and services bear the ultimate burden of the tax. On an overall basis, it is difficult to determine just where the ultimate burden of the corporate income tax falls.

Table 2.5 shows corporate income tax receipts for the period 1960 to 1977. The annual revenues from this tax were 163.3 percent higher in 1977 than in 1960, rising from 21.5 billion to 56.6 billion dollars. The average yearly increase for the period 1971 to 1977 was 9.2 percent. When adjusted for inflation, this average yearly increase would be quite a bit smaller. It is interesting to note that the corporate tax as a percent of total federal revenues fell from 23.2 percent in 1960 to 16.0 percent in 1977. The low point for this period was 1976 when the tax constituted only 13.8 percent of all federal revenues.

The corporate income tax has had little significance for the citizens concerned about their tax burden. The only individual taxpayers that really feel any impact from the corporate tax are those who enjoy a substantial amount of income in the form of corporate dividends. The average U.S. taxpayer does not have this worry and, therefore, what happens to the corporate tax sturcture is usually of little consequence. The only exception is in the instance when special purpose surcharges are proposed for specific industries and time periods. President Carter's proposal in 1979 for a windfall profits tax on the oil industry did arouse some general taxpayer concern, but it appeared to be primari-

## TABLE 2.5
### Corporate Income Tax Receipts, 1960-77

| | Corporate Income Tax Receipts (billions of dollars) | Percent Increase or (Decrease) over previous period | Percent of Total Federal Receipts |
|---|---|---|---|
| 1960 | 21.5 | – | 23.2 |
| 1965 | 25.5 | 18.6 | 21.8 |
| 1970 | 32.8 | 28.6 | 16.9 |
| 1971 | 26.8 | (18.3) | 14.2 |
| 1972 | 32.2 | 20.1 | 15.4 |
| 1973 | 36.2 | 12.4 | 15.6 |
| 1974 | 38.6 | 6.6 | 14.6 |
| 1975 | 40.6 | 5.2 | 14.5 |
| 1976 | 41.4 | 2.0 | 13.8 |
| 1976 TQ[a] | 8.5 | n.a. | 10.4 |
| 1977[b] | 56.6 | 36.7 | 16.0 |

17-year (1960-77) increase in receipts: 163.3 percent
7-year (1970-77) average yearly increase in receipts: 9.2 percent

[a]TQ—Transition Quarter: July to September (due to change in the federal fiscal year).

[b]Preliminary estimate

*Source:* U.S. Bureau of the Census, *Statistical Abstract of the United States: 1977* (Washington, D.C., 1977), p. 249, #407.

ly a reaction against oil company profits rather than a question of an increased tax burden.

## EXCISE TAX

The excise tax is a form of sales tax that applies only to specific items at the time of purchase. The tax is generally levied for one of two reasons. The first is as payment for benefits received. The primary example of the benefit-based excise tax is the federal tax on motor fuel. These funds are specifically earmarked for use in interstate highway construction. The idea is that the motorists who buy gasoline are the prime beneficiaries of the interstate highway system. Therefore, they ought to pay the costs for the benefits they receive. The second rationale for excise taxes is to control the consumption of certain goods and services. This control may be imposed for "moral" reasons in the case of the excise tax on alcohol and tobacco products or it may be imposed for reasons of conservation such as the tax on rubber products imposed during World War II.

When excise taxes are levied for purposes of controlling the consumption of goods or services, they are known as sumptuary taxes. The purposes of these sumptuary taxes change over time. Few would argue that the current purpose of the excise taxes on alcohol and tobacco is to limit their use. The magnitude of these taxes is not enough to discourage people from using these products. The reason that these taxes remain in force is simply because they are useful sources of revenue to the federal government and there is no political advantage to be gained by politicians in attempting to remove them. If they were removed, either programs would have to be reduced or new sources of revenue would have to be found to replace what was lost. As we saw in Chapter One, there is no political payoff for politicians who attempt either one of these actions.

Table 2.6 reviews federal excise tax receipts from 1960 to 1977. The table reveals that receipts from the exise tax have increased relatively little over the 17-year period. The yield in 1977 was only 54.3 percent greater than it was 17 years before in 1960. The average yearly increase between 1971 and 1977 was only 1.9 percent. If inflation were taken into account, this would constitute an actual decrease in revenue. As might be expected, the importance of excise taxes as a part of overall federal revenues declined from 12.6 percent in 1960 to 5.1 percent in 1977.

The federal excise tax is a classic example of a tax that has outlived its usefulness both as a revenue source and in terms of the goals that it was originally created to achieve. Its declining importance as a part of federal revenues suggests that the time is right for the federal government to give up this tax and thus encourage its use by state and, especially, local governments. Local governments are particularly in need of broad-based revenue sources in order to reduce their reliance on the property tax. However, if the reasoning described in Chapter One holds true, it is extremely unlikely that federal lawmakers will go through the political inconvenience of eliminating this tax.

As far as the original goals of the excise taxes are concerned, their time has come and gone. The tax on motor fuels has built a large and complex highway system. However, the current emphasis at all levels of government is on transportation rather than merely highways. Also, the benefits derived from the national highway system no longer go only to the motorists that use them. The economic benefits of highway transportation permeate to every sector of the economy and include every individual. The benefit theory of taxation no longer operates with the motor fuels excise tax.

TABLE 2.6
Excise Tax Receipts, 1960-77

|  | Excise Tax Receipts (billions of dollars) | Percent Increase or (Decrease) in Receipts | Excise Tax Receipts As a Percent of Total Receipts |
|---|---|---|---|
| 1960 | 11.6 | – | 12.6 |
| 1965 | 14.6 | 25.9 | 12.5 |
| 1970 | 15.8 | 8.2 | 8.1 |
| 1971 | 16.6 | 5.1 | 8.8 |
| 1972 | 15.5 | (6.6) | 7.4 |
| 1973 | 16.2 | 4.5 | n.a. |
| 1974 | 16.8 | 3.7 | 6.4 |
| 1975 | 16.5 | (1.8) | 5.9 |
| 1976 | 17.0 | 3.0 | 5.7 |
| 1976 TQ[a] | 4.5 | n.a. | 5.5 |
| 1977[b] | 17.9 | 5.3 | 5.1 |

17-year (1960-77) increase in receipts: 54.3 percent
7-year (1970-77) average yearly increase in receipts: 1.9 percent

[a]TQ—Transition Quarter: July to September (due to change in the federal fiscal year).

[b]Preliminary estimate

*Source:* U.S. Bureau of the Census, *Statistical Abstract of the United States: 1977* (Washington, D.C., 1977), p. 249, #407.

As far as the sumptuary taxes are concerned, alcohol and tobacco might be considered unhealthy, but few people would agree that they are immoral. In any event, these taxes are not high enough to discourage even the poorest citizen from smoking or drinking.

The time has come for the federal excise taxes to be eliminated. Elimination would encourage the development of additional revenues at the state and local level and would be a step toward making the federal tax structure more visible and understandable to the average taxpayer.

## ESTATE AND GIFT TAXES

The estate and gift taxes are two federal taxes that most taxpayers do not experience. The estate tax is a tax on the property and material wealth left when an individual dies. The history of the tax is one of controversy between the states and the federal government: the states wishing to retain for themselves a needed source of revenue, and the federal government unwilling to give up any tax dollars no matter how small and insignificant they might be. The tax is generally encountered only by the wealthy citizen because small inheritances are not subject to the tax. (PL 94-455 increased the size of an estate that a person could leave to a spouse tax free to $250,000, or half the estate, whichever is greater.)

The gift tax is applied to property or money that one person gives to another. Gifts on which the gift tax has been paid are not subject to the federal income tax. The gift tax like the estate tax is structured in such a way that only the wealthy taxpayer is likely to encounter it. In addition to its role as a revenue source, the gift tax makes avoidance of the inheritance tax difficult. If it were not for the gift tax, wealthy people could give away the majority of their estates before death and thus avoid the estate tax. Despite its relatively small yield,

TABLE 2.7
Estate and Gift Tax Receipts, 1960-77

|  | Estate and Gift Tax Receipts (billions of dollars) | Percent Increase or (Decrease) in Receipts | Estate and Gift Tax Receipts As A Percent of Total Receipts |
| --- | --- | --- | --- |
| 1960 | 1.6 | – | 1.7 |
| 1965 | 2.7 | 68.8 | 2.4 |
| 1970 | 3.6 | 33.3 | 1.9 |
| 1971 | 3.7 | 2.8 | 2.0 |
| 1972 | 5.4 | 46.0 | 2.6 |
| 1973 | 4.9 | (9.3) | 2.1 |
| 1974 | 5.0 | 2.0 | 1.9 |
| 1975 | 4.6 | (8.0) | 1.6 |
| 1976 | 5.2 | 13.0 | 1.7 |
| 1976 TQ[a] | 1.5 | n.a. | 1.8 |
| 1977[b] | 5.9 | 13.5 | 1.7 |

17-year (1960-77) increase in receipts: 268.8 percent
7-year (1970-77) average yearly increase in receipts: 8.6 percent

[a]TQ—Transition Quarter: July to September (due to change in federal fiscal year).

[b]Preliminary estimate

*Source:* U.S. Bureau of the Census, *Statistical Abstract of the United States: 1977* (Washington, D.C., 1977), p. 249, #407.

the gift tax plays a valuable role as a companion to the estate tax and the personal income tax.

Table 2.7 summarizes receipts from the estate and gift taxes for the period 1960 to 1977. During this 17-year period the annual receipts increased by 268.8 percent from 1.6 billion dollars in 1960 to 5.9 billion dollars in 1977. The average yearly increase in receipts from 1971 to 1977 was 8.6 percent per year. The relationship of estate and gift tax receipts to federal tax receipts overall has remained relatively stable at somewhat less than 2 percent of the total.

While these taxes are not an important source of revenue to the federal government, they do play a significant role in closing potential loop holes in the personal income tax structure. It would be possible to accomplish this by other means, thereby allowing for the elimination of these taxes from the federal revenue structure. However, there is no reason to believe that federal lawmakers will remedy the situation and thereby give state and local government a chance to obtain additional revenue.


## SUMMARY

Table 2.8 shows the total federal budget receipts for the period 1960 to 1977. During this period annual receipts increased from 92.5 billion dollars in 1960 to 354 billion dollars in 1977, an increase of over 282 percent. The average increase in federal receipts for the last seven years was 9.2 percent. Considering adjustments for inflation, this does not appear to be a tremendous increase in taxes. Because of this relative stability, federal taxation has thus far escaped a great deal of attention from irate taxpayers. In addition to being stable, federal taxes are usually well hidden from the attention of the general public, thus creating a pleasant situation for both politicians and bureaucrats.

If citizens do harbor negative feelings about their federal government, it is because of failures to deliver service. As described in Chapter One, this failure provides politicians with the opportunity to make specific promises to specific groups and thereby keep the political process going as usual.

Although the federal government is not a direct target of the taxpayer revolt, it is certainly a causal factor. First, the federal government's failure to control inflation in the late 1970s has contributed to a general deterioration of the financial position of most citizens. Second, most of the federal government's taxes are hidden and relatively painless. In addition, the federal political process is so far removed from the influence of most citizens there is very little that

TABLE 2.8
Federal Budget Receipts, 1960-77

|  | Total Receipts (billions of dollars) | Percent Increase or (Decrease) over Previous Period |
|---|---|---|
| 1960 | 92.5 | – |
| 1965 | 116.8 | 26.3 |
| 1970 | 193.7 | 65.8 |
| 1971 | 188.4 | (2.7) |
| 1972 | 208.6 | 10.7 |
| 1973 | 232.2 | 11.3 |
| 1974 | 264.9 | 14.1 |
| 1975 | 281.0 | 6.1 |
| 1976 | 300.0 | 6.8 |
| 1976 TQ[a] | 81.8 | n.a. |
| 1977[b] | 354.0 | 18.0 |

17-year (1960-77) increase in receipts: 282.7 percent
7-year (1970-77) average yearly increase in receipts: 9.2 percent

[a]TQ—Transition Quarter: July to September (due to change in federal fiscal year).

[b]Preliminary estimate

*Source:* U.S. Bureau of the Census, *Statistical Abstract of the United States: 1977* (Washington, D.C., 1977), p. 249, #407.

they can do about it. So, the taxpayers turn to the state and local governments, which suffer from the disadvantages of:

1.  Having to greatly expand their scope of operations as a result of federal mandates.
2.  Being relatively accessible to the taxpayer.
3.  Being supported by a set of taxes that are somewhat more visible and painful than those of the federal government.

During the 25-year period of 1950 to 1975 states contributed an increasing amount to the overall tax burden. In 1950 state revenue constituted 16.4 percent of all government revenues collected. By 1975 this percentage had risen to 22.6 percent. Table 3.1 shows that

TABLE 3.1
State Revenue As a Percent of All Government
Revenue,1950-75

|      | Revenue, All Governments (billions of dollars) | State Revenue (billions of dollars) | State Revenue As a Percent of Total Revenue | State Revenue Per Capita (dollars) |
|------|------|------|------|------|
| 1950 | 67   | 11   | 16.4 | 73   |
| 1955 | 106  | 17   | 16.0 | 105  |
| 1960 | 153  | 26   | 17.0 | 145  |
| 1965 | 203  | 39   | 19.2 | 201  |
| 1970 | 334  | 69   | 20.7 | 340  |
| 1971 | 345  | 73   | 21.2 | 354  |
| 1972 | 384  | 84   | 21.9 | 405  |
| 1973 | 434  | 97   | 22.4 | 463  |
| 1974 | 485  | 108  | 22.3 | 511  |
| 1975 | 517  | 117  | 22.6 | 548  |

25-year increase in all government revenue: 771.6 percent
25-year increase in state revenue: 1,063.6 percent
25-year increase in state revenue per capita: 750.7 percent

Source: U.S. Bureau of the Census, Statistical Abstract of the United States: 1977 (Washington, D.C., 1977), p. 276, #455.

the per capita burden of state taxes increased from $73 per person in 1950 to $548 per person in 1975. This represents an average yearly increase of just over 30 percent during the entire 25-year period. The message from these statistics is quite clear: state taxation is increasing at a very fast rate and, therefore, is assuming an increasingly important role in the total tax burden. There is no reason to expect that this increase will slow down during the next few years.

Table 3.2 shows the major sources of state revenues for a 15-year period from 1960 to 1975. The table presents three major types of revenues: taxes, intergovernmental revenue, and other sources. The category of intergovernmental revenue represents transfers of funds from either the federal government or local governments to the state level. As might be expected, the vast majority of these funds flow from the federal government to the states. The flow of funds from the local to the state level is primarily accounted for by a sharing of property tax revenues collected by local government for the state. The "other sources" category includes such items as payments into retirement trust funds and revenues from state-run enterprises such as toll roads and liquor stores.

Examination of the data for the 15-year period reveals that there has been a gradual shift in the sources of state revenue. In 1960 taxes accounted for 56.3 percent of all state revenues. In 1975, fifteen years later, taxes accounted for only 51.9 percent of revenues, a decline of 4.4 percent. With revenue from "other sources" remaining about the same, intergovernmental revenues rose from 20.4 percent of the total

TABLE 3.2
State Revenue by Category, 1960-75
(billions of dollars)

|  | Total Revenue | Taxes | Percent of Total Revenue | Inter-govern-mental Revenue | Percent of Total Revenue | Other | Percent of Total Revenue |
|---|---|---|---|---|---|---|---|
| 1960 | 32.8 | 18.0 | 56.3 | 6.7 | 20.4 | 8.1 | 23.3 |
| 1965 | 48.8 | 26.1 | 53.5 | 10.3 | 21.1 | 12.4 | 25.4 |
| 1970 | 88.9 | 48.0 | 54.0 | 20.3 | 22.8 | 20.6 | 23.2 |
| 1972 | 112.3 | 59.9 | 53.3 | 28.0 | 24.9 | 24.4 | 21.8 |
| 1973 | 129.8 | 68.1 | 52.5 | 32.7 | 25.2 | 29.0 | 22.3 |
| 1974 | 140.8 | 74.2 | 52.7 | 33.2 | 23.6 | 33.4 | 23.7 |
| 1975 | 154.6 | 80.2 | 51.9 | 37.8 | 24.5 | 36.6 | 23.6 |

*Source:* U.S. Bureau of the Census, *Statistical Abstract of the United States: 1977* (Washington, D.C., 1977), p. 294, #476.

in 1960 to 24.5 percent of the total in 1975, a gain of 4.1 percent. Most of these increased revenues have come in the form of federal aid to the states. It is likely that this trend will continue well into the 1980s.

The whole question of local and state reliance on federal support will be examined later in this book. At this point, suffice it to say that the net effect of this influx of federal funds to state government is to undermine the autonomy of the states in regard to making their own policy and financial decisions.

The Promise Model presented in Chapter One provides an explanation of why federal funds are so readily accepted by state governments. These funds provide the opportunity for elected officials and other members of the government structure to develop and implement new programs with little or no increase in state taxes. The elected official can go to the citizenry at election time with the welcome news that new services are available, promises of action have been kept, and, best of all, the bulk of the cost is borne by the federal government. One can hardly expect state officials to say no to a situation like this, especially when the alternative is to be accused of depriving the state and its citizens of "free" federal dollars. The fact that these dollars are not "free," that they restrict the ability of states to make their own decisions usually goes unnoticed.

An increased reliance on federal aid makes it very difficult for citizens to evaluate the performance of the state government because it is almost impossible to determine the cost of the services to the state taxpayer. Without direct information on services and costs, citizens cannot determine if they are getting their money's worth out of state government.

This chapter is devoted to examining the dimensions of the state tax burden with a focus on the five major sources of tax revenue. The purpose is to give the reader a basic understanding of how state tax systems work and of how they contribute to the growing trend of taxpayer unrest.

## PROPERTY TAX

The property tax has been the major focus of the taxpayer revolt. It is a major source of revenue for local governments and at one time was also a major source of revenue for state governments. This is no longer the case. Table 3.3 shows the decline of the importance of the property tax as a source of state revenue for the 15-year period 1960 to 1975. Around the turn of the century, the property tax was an important source of revenue. By 1960 it had declined to only 1.8 percent of total state revenues. By 1975 it had declined further to only .9 percent of state revenues. In terms of dollars of tax collected, the annual increase over 15 years was only 139 percent, not even enough of an increase to overcome the effect of inflation.

TABLE 3.3
Property Tax As a Source of State Revenue, 1960-75

|  | State Property Tax Revenues (millions of dollars) | Percent Increase or (Decrease) | As a Percent of Total State Revenues |
|------|------|------|------|
| 1960 | 607 | – | 1.8 |
| 1965 | 766 | 26.2 | 1.6 |
| 1970 | 1,092 | 42.6 | 1.2 |
| 1972 | 1,257 | 15.1 | 1.1 |
| 1973 | 1,312 | 4.4 | 1.0 |
| 1974 | 1,301 | (.8) | .9 |
| 1975 | 1,451 | 11.5 | .9 |

15-year increase: 13.9 percent

*Source:* U.S. Bureau of the Census, *Statistical Abstract of the United States: 1977* (Washington, D.C., 1977), p. 294, #476.

The tax that is currently collected by the states comes primarily from tangible, personal property: business inventories, motor vehicles, and the like. State tax on real property and intangible personal property (stocks, bonds, cash in banks, etc.) was almost non-existent in the late 1970s.

The state property tax as such has had little or no impact on the development of the taxpayer revolt. Of much more interest is the role of the state in supporting the administration of the local property tax. Many states have laws that require the equalization of tax rates throughout the state and provide for the training and licensing of property tax assessors. These will be discussed in the next chapter.

## SALES AND EXCISE TAXES

While sales and excise taxes are both taxes on consumption, there are major differences between the two taxes. The sales tax is a general tax on a wide variety of goods and services, levied at a fixed percentage statewide. As of 1976 all but five of the states had some form of general sales tax. Where the tax is applicable to food and drug purchases, the criticism can be made that it is a regressive tax; that is, its heaviest burden is on those persons who are least able to pay the tax. The criticism rests on the assumption that poor people spend a large percentage of their income on food and other necessities. Therefore, the amount of sales tax they pay constitutes a larger percentage of their income than that paid by people who spend only a small portion of their overall income on these items.

Aside from being a reasonably good source of state revenues, the major advantage of the tax is that it is easy to collect. The tax is usually collected from retailers on a monthly basis. The cost of collection is borne by retailers in the form of elaborate reporting systems.

In some states, the sales tax is used as a means to provide revenues for local governments. In these instances local governments have the option of adding an additional percent of tax on top of the state levy. The state then collects all of the tax from the retailers and returns the add-on portion to the local government. This system works well for local government because it represents a stable and significant source of revenue without placing any additional restraints or "strings" on local government operations.

Table 3.4 reviews state sales tax revenue from 1960 to 1975. During that 15-year period sales tax revenue rose from approximately 4.3 billion dollars a year in 1960 to approximately 24.8 billion dollars in 1975, an increase of 476 percent. As a part of the total tax revenues

TABLE 3.4
Sales Tax As a Source of State Revenue, 1960-75

|  | General Sales Tax Revenues (millions of dollars) | Percent Increase or (Decrease) | Percent of Total State Revenue |
|---|---|---|---|
| 1960 | 4,302 | – | 13.1 |
| 1965 | 6,711 | 56.0 | 13.7 |
| 1970 | 14,177 | 111.3 | 15.9 |
| 1972 | 17,619 | 24.3 | 15.7 |
| 1973 | 19,793 | 12.3 | 15.2 |
| 1974 | 22,612 | 14.2 | 16.1 |
| 1975 | 24,780 | 9.6 | 16.0 |
| 15-year increase: 476 percent | | | |

*Source:* U.S. Bureau of the Census, *Statistical Abstract of the United States: 1977* (Washington, D.C., 1977), p. 294, #476.

available to state government, the take from the sales tax rose from 13.1 percent in 1960 to just over 16 percent in 1975. The importance of the sales tax as a revenue source is likely to continue to increase because of its responsiveness to inflation. Any significant rise in consumer prices is reflected in increased sales tax revenues. Overall, the tax is a good one for the use of state governments especially when it is shared with local governments through the use of the add-on arrangement described earlier. However, on the basis of equity, a good case can be made for eliminating the sales tax on food and drugs.

State-levied excise taxes have the same characteristics as the federal excise taxes described earlier. They are either levied as benefit taxes, such as the motor fuels tax, or as sumptuary taxes, such as those on alcohol and tobacco. Like the sales tax, the excise tax is a tax on consumption, but it is selective because it applies to only a few goods and services. As might be expected in the case of a tax with such a limited base, its importance as a source of state revenue has been declining in recent years.

## TABLE 3.5
### Excise Tax As a Source of State Revenue, 1960-75

|      | Excise Tax Revenues (millions of dollars) | Percent Increase or (Decrease) | Percent of Total Tax Revenue |
|------|-------------------------------------------|--------------------------------|------------------------------|
| 1960 | 6,208                                     | –                              | 18.9                         |
| 1965 | 8,348                                     | 34.8                           | 17.0                         |
| 1970 | 13,076                                    | 56.6                           | 14.7                         |
| 1972 | 15,631                                    | 19.5                           | 13.9                         |
| 1973 | 17,329                                    | 10.9                           | 13.3                         |
| 1974 | 17,944                                    | 3.5                            | 12.7                         |
| 1975 | 18,565                                    | 3.5                            | 12.0                         |
| 15-year increase:  199 percent |                              |                                |                              |

*Source:* U.S. Bureau of the Census, *Statistical Abstract of the United States: 1977* (Washington, D.C., 1977), p. 294, #476.

Table 3.5 summarizes excise tax revenues for the period 1960 to 1975. Although revenues increased from approximately 6.2 billion dollars in 1960 to approximately 18.6 billion in 1975, as percent of total states revenues, the excise tax declined from 18.9 percent in 1960 to only 12 percent in 1975. In fact, the annual increase in excise tax revenues in 1974 and 1975 was only 3.5 percent. This was not even enough to compensate for inflation.

Table 3.6 provides a closer look at the distribution of excise tax revenue. It reveals that the tax on motor fuels, while still the single largest source of revenue, has led the decline in the overall importance of the excise tax as a source of revenue. In 1960 motor fuel tax revenues constituted 53.7 percent of all state excise tax revenues. In 1975 they were only 44.5 percent. During the same period alcohol and tobacco tax revenues increased almost 3 percent from 25.4 percent to 28.3 percent. The largest increase was in the revenues generated by taxes on miscellaneous goods and services. These rose from a 20.9 percent share of overall excise tax revenues in 1960 to a 27.2 percent share in 1975. This increase in the face of declining revenues from other excise taxes can probably be accounted for by the levying of new taxes on hotel occupancy and entertainment.

TABLE 3.6
Excise Tax Revenues by Tax Base, 1960-75

| | Excise Tax Revenues (millions of dollars) | Motor Fuel Tax Revenues (millions of dollars) | Alcohol and Tobacco Tax Revenues (millions of dollars) | Other Excise Tax Revenues (millions of dollars) |
|---|---|---|---|---|
| 1960 | 6,208 | 3,335 (53.7%) | 1,573 (25.4%) | 1,300 (20.9%) |
| 1965 | 8,348 | 4,300 (51.5%) | 2,201 (26.4%) | 1,847 (22.1%) |
| 1970 | 13,076 | 6,283 (48.0%) | 3,728 (28.5%) | 3,065 (23.5%) |
| 1972 | 15,631 | 7,216 (46.2%) | 4,515 (28.9%) | 3,900 (24.9%) |
| 1973 | 17,329 | 8,058 (46.5%) | 4,929 (28.4%) | 4,342 (25.1%) |
| 1974 | 17,944 | 8,207 (45.7%) | 5,159 (28.8%) | 4,578 (25.5%) |
| 1975 | 18,565 | 8,255 (44.5%) | 5,249 (28.3%) | 5,061 (27.2%) |

15-year increase in motor fuel tax revenues: 147.5 percent
15-year increase in alcohol and tobacco tax revenues: 233.7 percent
15-year increase in other excise tax revenues: 289.3 percent

*Source:* U.S. Bureau of the Census, *Statistical Abstract of the United States: 1977* (Washington, D.C., 1977), p. 294, #476.

The future prospects of the state excise tax are clouded. In addition to its declining revenue potential, the motor vehicle fuel tax faces other problems. This tax is normally earmarked for use in developing and maintaining state highway systems either directly through state transportation departments or as a subsidy given to local governments for road work. In the late 1970s the automobile has been beset with problems ranging from fuel shortages to increased traffic congestion to stricter air pollution control standards. These problems have caused groups of citizens in several states to work for the removal of the earmarking requirement for motor fuel tax revenues.

The idea is for these funds to be used to support transportation systems other than the automobile. These growing political problems coupled with dropping revenue yields serve to indicate a troubled future for motor fuel excise taxes.

The future prospects of the alcohol and tobacco taxes are equally troubled. The small growth in revenues prior to 1975 is threatened in the late 1970s by several factors. Anti-smoking campaigns may make further cuts in this national habit, thereby reducing tobacco-generated tax revenues. As far as alcohol is concerned, the future may not look too promising. Due to their original moralistic purpose, excise taxes on alcohol are based upon the alcoholic content of each type of beverage: distilled liquors having the highest tax rate, being followed by wine and beer. One explanation for the slow rise in alcohol tax revenues may be that more Americans seem to be switching to wine and away from distilled liquors. In any event, this tax like other sumptuary taxes has long outlived its morality-based beginnings. As a source of revenue it ranks low because of its limited yield and its high costs for collection and enforcement.

Excise taxes are best used to fund specific activities because they provide a means of directly linking the benefits of a service with the payment for that service. But problems occur when priorities change and the earmarked funds keep coming in. The motor vehicle tax provides the example here. Even though these moneys might well be used for a different purpose (transportation instead of merely highways), few states have been able to make this change. Why not? The model presented in Chapter One provides ample explanation for this failure. If earmarked taxes are to be used, the political system must have the ability to change the services they support when it becomes necessary. Otherwise, earmarked taxes can become a negative component of the overall tax structure instead of the positive contributor they should be.


## INCOME TAXES: PERSONAL AND CORPORATE

Personal and corporate income taxes may well be the mainstay of state finances for years to come. Potentially, they enjoy all of the advantages of their federal equivalents. Perhaps the only major problem they face is the question of distributing the tax liability for persons and corporations who are employed or do business across state lines. Even this problem does not significantly affect the yield of the tax, but rather it affects the equity of the tax burden.

TABLE 3.7
Individual Income Tax Revenues, 1960-75

|  | Income Tax Revenues (millions of dollars) | Percent Increase or (Decrease) | Percent of All State Revenue |
|---|---|---|---|
| 1960 | 2,209 | – | 6.7 |
| 1965 | 3,657 | 65.6 | 7.5 |
| 1970 | 9,183 | 151.1 | 10.3 |
| 1972 | 12,996 | 41.5 | 11.6 |
| 1973 | 15,587 | 19.9 | 12.0 |
| 1974 | 17,078 | 9.6 | 12.1 |
| 1975 | 18,819 | 10.2 | 12.2 |

15-year increase in income tax revenue: 752 percent

*Source:* U.S. Bureau of the Census, *Statistical Abstract of the United States: 1977* (Washington, D.C., 1977), p. 294, #476.

Table 3.7 reveals the income tax has dramatically increased its position as a source of state revenue. From 1960 to 1975 income tax revenues increased from 2.2 billion dollars to 18.8 billion dollars. This represents an increase of over 750 percent. As a percent of overall state revenues, the income tax has almost doubled in importance from 6.7 percent in 1960 to 12.2 percent in 1975. An evaluation of the future revenue potential of the individual income tax indicates very positive prospects. The major reason is the high degree of compatibility between prevailing economic conditions (i.e., inflation) and the nature of the tax itself.

It is quite likely that inflation will be the dominant factor of economic life for the foreseeable future, certainly through the early 1980s. The previous chapter on federal taxation explained how the progressive rate structure of the income tax acted to keep government revenues on a par with, if not ahead of, inflation. While this "inflation tax" may not be good news for the taxpayer who is losing purchasing power to the tax collector, it is good news for those who spend government revenues.

The key to states cashing in on this inflation bonanza is conformity with the federal income tax structure.[1] There are four generally accepted levels of conformity with the federal structure. The highest level is complete conformity. This level requires that the taxpayer compute the state income tax as a percentage of the federal income tax owed. The Tax Reform Act of 1976 provides that the Internal

Revenue Service may collect state income taxes for any state whose tax laws are in complete conformity with federal law without any expense to the state. The next level is substantial conformity. In this instance taxpayers calculate the state tax due by applying the state tax rate to their federal taxable income. The third level indicates only partial acceptance of the federal income tax structure. The last level is made up of those states that are considered to be either low-conforming or non-conforming.

As of 1977 a little more than one-half of the states having an income tax fell into one of the last two categories. On the basis of yield and ease of administration, it would seem to be advantageous for states to place themselves in complete conformity with the federal income tax structure. There is, however, a distinct disadvantage to doing this. Complete conformity means that the state has given up the right to make its own income tax policies. It must not only follow the legal requirements of the federal tax structure, but it is also bound by the administrative interpretations of the U.S. Internal Revenue Service. Therefore, state elected officials are in a position of having to choose between a high yield, easy-to-administer tax and an independent and autonomous tax policy. The answer to this dilemma should depend on whether or not an autonomous state tax policy will result in significant benefits to the state's taxpayers.

For states that choose substantial rather than complete conformity there are still administrative advantages to be gained. One of the most important advantages is the sharing of audit information with the Internal Revenue Service to assist in enforcement. In the long run it is not necessary for states to be in complete or even substantial conformity in order to have high yield individual income tax structures, but in the short run an increasing number of states will probably find it highly desirable to match up with the federal system.

The corporate income tax is another strong source of state revenue. Table 3.8 shows that corporate tax revenues went from approximately 1.2 billion dollars in 1960 to approximately 6.6 billion dollars in 1975, a percentage increase of 462.9 percent over the 15-year period. As a percent of total state revenue corporate income tax revenues increased slightly during the same time period from 3.6 percent to 4.3 percent in 1975.

In regard to administration the corporate income tax poses the same problems as the individual income tax only they are more severe. In the matter of conformity the difference is that in a number of states the tax is in the form of a corporate franchise fee based either on profits or some other measure of corporate activity. In these states conformity with the federal tax structure would be difficult. Because

TABLE 3.8
Corporate Income Tax Revenues, 1960-75

|      | Income Tax Revenues (millions of dollars) | Percent Increase or (Decrease) | Percent of All State Revenue |
|------|------|------|------|
| 1960 | 1,180 | – | 3.6 |
| 1965 | 1,929 | 63.5 | 3.9 |
| 1970 | 3,738 | 93.8 | 4.2 |
| 1972 | 4,416 | 18.1 | 3.9 |
| 1973 | 5,425 | 22.8 | 4.2 |
| 1974 | 6,015 | 10.9 | 4.3 |
| 1975 | 6,642 | 10.4 | 4.3 |

15-year increase in corporate tax revenue: 462.9 percent

*Source:* U.S. Bureau of the Census, *Statistical Abstract of the United States: 1977* (Washington, D.C., 1977), p. 294, #476.

corporations are more likely than individuals to do business in more than one state, the problem of establishing tax liability among one or more states is especially severe. Companies most affected are the small and medium size corporations that may not have the accounting and legal staff to deal with a multitude of state requirements.

One possible solution to this problem is for the federal government to establish a tax sharing plan for its corporate income tax. A portion of these tax revenues could be allocated to the states where corporations conducted business based upon a standard formula. This plan would relieve corporations, small and large, of the high cost of complying with the income tax laws of several states; instead, only the federal tax return would be required.

From the point of view of the taxpayer, whether corporate or individual, the income tax is likely to be the most important aspect of state taxation in the coming years. Its potential for high yield is unmatched by any other tax source. This is particularly true in times of inflation where the progressive rate structure of the income tax will insure high government revenues. What is revenue to the government official is a tax burden to the citizen. Because of the certainty that inflation will drive up the income tax burden, citizens would be well advised to actively work for tax reforms that will keep their tax burden at a level consistent with the level of services they desire.

A suggestion can be made here. Taxpayers should push for an indexing of the progressive tax rate structures, so that as inflation increases the boundaries of the rate bracket also increase. This would eliminate the "inflation tax" discussed in the previous chapter. Drawing a conclusion from the model presented in Chapter One, it is clear that if taxpayers do nothing, the ever-increasing yields of the state income taxes will inevitably result in additional or expanded programs—not because these are the things that citizens want, but because the nature of the political system supports increased spending rather than the conserving of tax resources.

## LICENSE FEES

In a technical sense, a license fee is not a tax. It is a reimbursement to the state for the cost of licensing and regulating some type of activity or property. In actual fact, license fees exist for two reasons: first, to provide a convenient means to control an activity or to keep track of different kinds of property, second, to provide a source of revenue for the state. In most instances, the revenue from fees is earmarked for a specific purpose associated with the licensed activity or property. In terms of revenue produced, the major areas of license activity are motor vehicles and corporations. Other areas that are important in terms of regulation, but not necessarily revenue, are: occupations and professions, driving, hunting, and fishing licenses, boat and aircraft registration.

Table 3.9 shows the pattern of state license revenue for a 15-year period. Between 1960 and 1975 revenues increased from approximately 2.5 billion dollars to approximately 6.3 billion dollars. This was an increase of 152.1 percent. As a percent of total state revenues, license fees declined from 71.6 percent in 1960 to 4.1 percent in 1975. It is obvious that license fees are of declining importance when only their yield is considered. However, there are other considerations.

License fees are important to the control functions of government because they provide the funds necessary for the operation of registration and testing programs for a wide variety of occupations and professions. Additionally, these fees represent a good example of a direct linkage between the cost of a government service and the benefits resulting from that service. This kind of direct linkage helps to insure that government is providing a reasonable level of service in return for the revenue collected. A clear service/cost relationship is necessary in order for government to be held accountable by the taxpayers. The same principle of fee and service operates with the other types of license fees as well. The only cautionary note is that care must be taken to ensure that the programs supported by the earmarked revenues do not become obsolete and lose their usefulness for the citizenry.

TABLE 3.9
License Fee Revenue, 1960-75

| | License Revenue (millions of dollars) | Percent Increase or (Decrease) | Percent of Total State Revenue |
|---|---|---|---|
| 1960 | 2,495 | – | 7.6 |
| 1965 | 3,218 | 29.0 | 6.6 |
| 1970 | 4,615 | 43.4 | 5.2 |
| 1972 | 5,374 | 16.4 | 4.8 |
| 1973 | 5,753 | 7.1 | 4.4 |
| 1974 | 6,055 | 5.2 | 4.3 |
| 1975 | 6,289 | 3.9 | 4.1 |
| 15-year increase in license revenue: 152.1 percent | | | |

*Source:* U.S. Bureau of the Census, *Statistical Abstract of the United States: 1977* (Washington, D.C., 1977), p. 294, #476.

What is needed is a periodic, regular evaluation of these functions. The state of Colorado has made a good start in this direction by implementing a "sunset" law that forces regulatory agencies (mostly concerned with licensing) out of business unless their life is specifically extended by the legislature. This periodic review provides citizens with the opportunity to evaluate and comment on the activities of a specific agency. Hopefully, "sunset" laws will start to appear in other states with a scope that goes beyond regulatory agencies to include all the functions of state government.

## SUMMARY

Table 3.10 reveals the relative contributions of the various taxes to overall state revenues. Three of the taxes increased their standing as contributors to state revenues during the 15-year period from 1960 to 1975. The sales tax share increased from 13.1 percent to 16 percent of total state revenue. The individual income tax and the corporate income tax increased from 6.7 percent to 12.2 percent and from 3.6 percent to 4.3 percent respectively. Three taxes decreased their share of overall state revenues: the property tax from 1.8 percent to .9 percent, the excise taxes from 18.9 percent to 12 percent, and the license fees from 7.6 percent to 4.1 percent. These patterns are especially interesting in that all the taxes with increased revenue yields are quite responsive in terms of inflation and were originally implemented for purposes of revenue. In contrast, all three of the taxes whose position decreased are relatively non-responsive to inflation.

TABLE 3.10
Taxes As a Percent of Total State Revenue, 1960-75

|      | Property Tax | Sales Tax | Excise Tax | Individual Income Tax | Corporate Income Tax | License Fee |
|------|------|------|------|------|------|------|
| 1960 | 1.8 | 13.1 | 18.9 | 6.7 | 3.6 | 7.6 |
| 1965 | 1.6 | 13.7 | 17.0 | 7.5 | 3.9 | 6.6 |
| 1970 | 1.2 | 15.9 | 14.7 | 10.3 | 4.2 | 5.2 |
| 1972 | 1.1 | 15.7 | 13.9 | 11.6 | 3.9 | 4.8 |
| 1973 | 1.0 | 15.2 | 13.3 | 12.0 | 4.2 | 4.4 |
| 1974 | .9 | 16.1 | 12.7 | 12.1 | 4.3 | 4.3 |
| 1975 | .9 | 16.0 | 12.0 | 12.2 | 4.3 | 4.1 |
| Percent increase or (decrease) from 1960 to 1975: | | | | | | |
| | (50.0) | 22.1 | (36.5) | 82.1 | 19.4 | (46.1) |

*Source:* U.S. Bureau of the Census, *Statistical Abstract of the United States: 1977* (Washington, D.C., 1977), p. 294, #476.

Another significant point is that excise taxes and license fees have goals other than the generation of revenue. Therefore, they must be evaluated differently than taxes whose purpose is purely the generation of revenue. This is especially the case with license fees and some excise taxes that were enacted solely to support regulation functions. Part of this evaluation should be a periodic review of each earmarked revenue to determine whether or not the function being supported is still needed and whether or not it still is a productive and appropriate service area for state government to be involved in. In sum, the utility of earmarked funds must be constantly protected through periodic reevaluation.

How do these revenue sources look from the point of view of the taxpayer? The property tax should definitely be slated for elimination on the state level. Aside from the fact that its yield is decreasing rapidly as a part of overall revenues, it is very difficult to administer, taking more than its fair share of time from consolidated state departments of revenue that are responsible for the collection of all state taxes.

Excise taxes do not present as clear a picture. Sumptuary taxes such as those on alcohol and tobacco still contribute a substantial amount to state revenues. In the minds of most citizens, the moral goals of these taxes have fallen by the wayside. The question of their retention resolves itself into one of how much revenue they generate and how difficult they are to administer. It can be expected that elected officials and others in the government structure will resist any proposals to eliminate these taxes for the reasons described earlier; that is, there is no political advantage to be gained because elimination means either reducing existing programs or replacing the lost revenue by other means (increasing other taxes). If taxpayer groups decide to fight to eliminate some of these sumptuary taxes, they can expect an uphill battle.

Excise taxes whose revenues are earmarked for specific purposes can be evaluated a little more easily. The place to start is with the function they are supporting. Is this the kind of service that taxpayers want to continue to receive? Are the original goals still relevant to the current needs of the state? If the service in question fails these tests, then it is time for taxpayer groups to push for either a reallocation of these funds to other purposes (such as highway funds to rapid transit) or to push for elimination of the service and the excise tax that provides the revenue.

License fees can be subjected to the same test as earmarked excise taxes. The same kind of questions apply, and negative answers will suggest the same type of remedies. A defense of license fees or earmarked excise taxes purely on the basis of revenue yield should not be accepted by taxpayer groups.

The general sales tax and the personal income tax are the mainstays of state tax revenues. Any significant reductions in these taxes will have to come about as a result of either cutting existing levels of service or by preventing government officials from spending tax moneys on new and expanded programs. In the late 1970s there have been several instances of states accumulating vast surpluses as a result of the responsiveness of these taxes to high rates of inflation. When this occurs taxpayers should not be satisfied with one-time tax reductions or one-year tax rebates. Instead, they should push for revision of the tax structure to eliminate the excess taxes due to inflation. For the income taxes this means indexing tax brackets to compensate for inflation. Times of high tax yields are also good times to push for the removal of food and drugs from the general sales tax. Coverage of these items creates an inordinate hardship on lower income taxpayers. This hardship ultimately has a negative effect on the economic well being of taxpayers at all levels.

The corporate income tax is too important a part of the state revenue picture to be eliminated without a sharing of the federal corporate income tax to take its place. If this were to happen, it would be a great benefit for small and medium size corporations that now struggle with a multitude of state tax laws. But the initiative for this action must come from the federal level, and, in these years of an increasing federal debt, this is not likely to occur. Even though it is in the ultimate interest of the individual taxpayer to encourage small and medium size business, there probably is little that can be done by individual states to ease the burden of this tax.

## NOTE

1. *State and Local Government Finance and Financial Management: A Compendium of Current Research.* (Washington D.C.: Municipal Finance Officers Association, 1978), pp. 12-13.

# 4    LOCAL GOVERNMENT TAXATION

Local governments are legal subdivisions of the individual state governments. Therefore, as might be expected, there are essentially 50 different systems of local government in the United States. All states have counties (parishes in Louisiana) as the basic local government unit, and from that point on similarity ceases. In 1977 there were a total of 31,659 local governmental units in the United States.[1] Each of these has its own set of revenues and expenditures. The only reasonable way to deal with this diversity is to treat all local governments as one for the purposes of examining their tax revenues and structures.

Table 4.1 examines local government revenues as a component of total government revenues in the United States. In 1950 local government revenues constituted 17.9 percent of all government revenues, some 12 billion out of 67 billion dollars. This works out to $80 for each man, woman, and child. Some 25 years later in 1975 the revenue burden had risen to $459 per person. Local government revenue was 98 billion out of a total of 517 billion dollars, some 19 percent of all government revenues. Between 1950 and 1975 local government revenues increased by 816.6 percent. There is every reason to believe that this trend toward growth will continue into future years.

Table 4.2 examines the sources of local government revenue in 1975. The single largest source of revenue was in the form of intergovernmental transfers from state and federal governments, some 38.8 percent of the total. The remaining 61.2 percent of the revenue was generated by local government itself. The largest source of locally generated revenue was taxation, which accounted for 38.4 percent or 61.3 billion dollars. Fees and charges followed with 14.4 percent

TABLE 4.1
Local Government Revenue As a
Percent of All Government Revenue,
1950-75

|  | Revenue, All Governments (billions of dollars) | Local Government Revenue (billions of dollars) | Local Government Revenue As a Percent of Total Revenue | Local Government Revenue Per Capita (dollars) |
|---|---|---|---|---|
| 1950 | 67 | 12 | 17.9 | 80 |
| 1955 | 106 | 18 | 17.0 | 111 |
| 1960 | 153 | 27 | 17.6 | 151 |
| 1965 | 203 | 38 | 18.7 | 195 |
| 1970 | 334 | 60 | 18.0 | 296 |
| 1971 | 345 | 67 | 19.4 | 324 |
| 1972 | 384 | 74 | 19.3 | 356 |
| 1973 | 434 | 81 | 18.7 | 387 |
| 1974 | 485 | 88 | 18.2 | 416 |
| 1975 | 517 | 98 | 19.0 | 459 |

25-year increase in all government revenue:  771.6 percent
25-year increase in local government revenue:  816.6 percent
25-year increase in local government revenue per capita:
573.8 percent

*Source:* U.S. Bureau of the Census, *Statistical Abstract of the United States: 1977* (Washington, D.C., 1977), p. 276, #455.

or approximately 23 billion dollars. Utility revenues accounted for 10.9 billion dollars or about 6.8 percent of total revenues. Liquor store revenues and insurance trust payments made up the remainder. Intergovernmental transfers and taxation are by far the largest sources of local government revenues. Intergovernmental revenues are the fastest growing source of local government revenue. In 1902 they accounted for only 6.1 percent of total revenues. By 1932 they were 13 percent. Eight years later in 1940 the share had risen to 25 percent of total local government revenue. In 1970 intergovernmental revenues were 33 percent, only 5.8 percent behind the 1975 figure.

What is the significance of this growth in non-locally generated revenue? The answer lies in the concept of control. In almost every instance, money from the state or federal government comes with strings attached. These rules and requirements result in a reduction of local autonomy. This is particularly unfortunate because it is at the local government level where the taxpayer has the best chance of making an impact on the way government is run. As local government re-

TABLE 4.2
Local Government Revenue by Source, 1975

Total Local Government Revenue: 159,731
(millions of dollars)

| | | |
|---|---|---|
| Intergovernmental Revenue: (millions of dollars) | 61,975 (38.8%) | |
| Tax Revenue: (millions of dollars) | 61,310 (38.4%) | |
| Charges and Miscellaneous General Revenue: (millions of dollars) | 23,047 (14.4%) | Revenue from Own Sources (millions of dollars) 97,756 (61.2%) |
| Utility Revenue: (millions of dollars) | 10,867 (6.8%) | |
| Liquor Stores Revenue: (millions of dollars) | 338 (.2%) | |
| Insurance Trust Revenue: (millions of dollars) | 2,194 (1.4%) | |

*Source:* U.S. Bureau of the Census, *Statistical Abstract of the United States: 1977* (Washington, D.C., 1977), p. 283, #463.

liance on state and federal funds increases, taxpayers can expect their local government officials to be less responsive to their needs and desires.

However, there are ways for local government to receive financial assistance from state and federal governments without undue regulation and control. Tax sharing and the general revenue sharing program are two means of accomplishing this that will be discussed later on. For now, the focus will be on the tax revenues that support local government. This chapter examines four major types of taxes: property taxes, income taxes, sales taxes, and other miscellaneous taxes.

## PROPERTY TAX

The property tax has been and remains the single most important source of tax revenue available to local governments. Table 4.3 demonstrates this point for the 25-year period from 1950 to 1975. In 1950 property tax revenues topped 7 billion dollars and generated over 88 percent of all local government tax revenues. Twenty-five years later in 1975 revenues from the property tax were over 50 billion dollars and amounted to over 81 percent of all tax revenue. Growth in property tax revenues between 1950 and 1975 was over 610 percent. As any property taxpayer knows, this trend of growth has continued unabated into the late 1970s and, if it remains unchecked, will continue to grow rapidly in the years ahead. This high rate of growth has been the catalyst for the taxpayer revolt of the late 1970s. Before the impact of the property tax on the taxpayer revolt can be examined, a basic understanding of how the property tax works is necessary.

TABLE 4.3
Property Tax As a Source of Local
Government Revenue, 1950-75

|  | Local Property Tax Revenues (millions of dollars) | Percent Increase or (Decrease) | As a Percent of All Local Tax Revenue |
|---|---|---|---|
| 1950 | 7,042 | – | 88.2 |
| 1955 | 10,323 | 46.6 | 86.9 |
| 1960 | 15,798 | 53.0 | 87.4 |
| 1965 | 21,817 | 38.1 | 86.7 |
| 1970 | 32,963 | 51.1 | 84.9 |
| 1971 | 36,726 | 11.4 | 84.6 |
| 1972 | 40,876 | 11.3 | 83.6 |
| 1973 | 43,970 | 7.6 | 82.9 |
| 1974 | 46,452 | 5.6 | 82.2 |
| 1975 | 50,040 | 7.7 | 81.6 |

25-year increase in local property tax revenues: 610.6 percent

*Source:* U.S. Bureau of the Census, *Statistical Abstract of the United States: 1977* (Washington, D.C., 1977), p. 281, #460.

In the past the property tax was applied to both personal and real property. Although some local government jurisdictions still derive a substantial amount of income from taxing personal property, the bulk of property tax revenues are raised as the result of the taxation of real property, principally real estate and improvements to real estate.

The first step in any taxing process is the establishment of a tax base. For taxes on income or expenditure this is a relatively easy process involving an objective judgment of income levels or the simple counting of expenditures. The property tax as a levy on wealth requires the placement of a value on the object to be taxed. In the case of real property there must be an assessment of the value of each and every piece of property in a manner consistent with state and local law. The assessment of property for tax purposes is one of the most difficult chores in tax administration. Although great strides have been made in recent years toward the professionalizing of the assessment field, a great deal remains to be done in terms of equalizing tax assessments on a statewide basis (i.e., making certain that a $50,000 house is assessed at the same value no matter where in the state it happens to be located). Another problem with the assessment process is the scheduling of reassessments. Ideally, every piece of property should be reassessed every year in order to accurately reflect the value of that property. For most local governments yearly reassessment is impossible. Actual practice may range from once every two years to once a decade.

Property being resold is more likely to be reassessed than other property. The reason is that lists of real estate transfers provide a convenient means for local assessors to reevaluate property. This practice can give rise to the situation where two taxpayers live side-by-side in houses of equal value and the one who has just purchased the house may be paying three times the tax of the long-time resident next door. To the new owner this situation appears to be a gross injustice. The owner does not care that it is perfectly legal and in conformance with "good" assessment practice. It is of these situations that tax revolts are made.

Once each piece of property has been assessed, these individual assessments are combined into the total assessed valuation for the local government unit. Not all pieces of property are subject to local property tax. The list of properties that are exempt from taxation is long and diverse. Exceptions start with government property. No government property, neither local, state, nor federal, is subject to local property tax. Although in some instances, the federal and state governments may pay a yearly fee to the local government to help to compensate for the loss of value from the tax base. Other kinds of exempt property include private schools, churches, hospitals, and other property belonging to non-profit organizations. The exact determination of what property will be exempt is made either by each local jurisdiction or by state law, depending on the practices of each state. As explained later, the loss of these properties from the total assessed valuation will increase the taxes other property owners must pay.

Once the total assessed valuation has been established, a tax rate is decided upon and applied to valuation. The rate multiplied by the valuation yields the amount of tax to be collected. As an example, if a house and property are assessed at $50,000 and the tax rate is $36.00 per thousand dollars of assessed valuation, then the tax owed by the land owner is $1,800 ($36 x 50 = $1,800.)

The decision regarding the tax rate is made in different ways in different states. Some states have a maximum legal rate that cannot be exceeded. In these instances it is common practice for the rate to be kept at the maximum. In other states a town meeting is required to set the tax rate. In these instances the property tax is a "budget balancing" tax. It operates this way. Local officials tentatively approve a list of expenditures for the coming fiscal year. They estimate as closely as possible the anticipated revenues from other sources. Anticipated revenues are subtracted from proposed expenditures. The amount remaining is the revenue yield that must come from the property tax in order to have a balanced budget. (Almost all local governments are required by law to enact a balanced budget. Whether or not a budget is balanced in fact depends on the accuracy of revenue and cost projections as well as the quality of the government's financial management system.) The amount of revenue required is divided into the total assessed valuation, thus yielding the rate of tax that will be used to determine each individual's tax bill. This rate when applied to the total assessed valuation will yield the amount of revenue necessary to create a balanced budget.

For example, assume that $100,000 is required from property tax revenues to balance the budget. Assume that the total assessed valuation is $5,000,000. $5,000,000 divided into $100,000 equals .020. The tax rate needed to balance the budget is 20 mills or $20 per one thousand dollars of assessed valuation. Applying this tax rate to $5,000,000 ($5,000,000 x .02 = $100,000) yields the $100,000 necessary to balance the budget.

In summary, the proposed budget will include the following items: proposed expenditures, anticipated revenues from all sources except the property tax, and the tax rate necessary to balance the budget. If officials feel that the tax rate is too high, they have no alternative but to cut the proposed expenditures. How far they must cut depends on the tax rate officials feel is appropriate for the year. This is a loaded political question that often requires a good deal of time and effort to work out. From the taxpayer's point of view, this is one of the few opportunities available to directly influence the amount of tax that must be paid.

In addition to being the mainstay of local government revenues, the property tax is also the most controversial of the local government taxes because of its high degree of visibility and because the payment is usually required in a large, lump sum. In order for taxpayers to take an intelligent position on the property tax, either pro or con, they must have an understanding of how elected officials and local government managers view the property tax—in a sense, a "professional" view rather than a taxpayer view.

In government management circles, there are some generally accepted advantages and disadvantages associated with the property tax.[2] Leading off the list of advantages is that the property tax is a consistent producer of revenues that keeps up with the rate of inflation. The second advantage often cited is that the property tax is based upon the benefit principle of taxation, and since most local government services are property-related (fire, police, roads, sewage, etc.), those who receive the most benefit from local government services pay the major share of the cost of those services. A third advantage attributed to the property tax is based upon the idea that the value of the property a person owns is a reflection of the relative ability of that person to pay taxes. Therefore, the property tax can be justified not only upon the benefit principle of taxation, but on the ability-to-pay principle as well.

The concerned taxpayer will not see these "advantages" in the same light as the government official. There can be no quarrel with the statement that property taxes keep up with inflation. Most property taxpayers in the late 1970s would probably say that taxes are ahead of inflation, especially those that live in areas where property values have doubled or tripled in the last ten years. The logic of the second advantage is eroded for those taxpayers who feel that the increased social services provided by local governments do not really constitute a service to property owners, but are really for the benefit of those who are too poor to be property holders. These taxpayers find logic in the argument that the state and federal governments with their larger financial resources should bear the costs of these social programs. Their rationale is that the benefits of these social programs accrue to society as a whole, not to just the property owner. The third advantage is based upon the assumption that the value of property is an indication of the owner's ability to pay taxes consistent with the value of that property. For those homeowners living on a fixed income, this assumption does not hold true. For example, a couple living on retirement income may have paid off their home mortgage over 20 or 25 years only to find that their property taxes, rising along with the value of their house, are too much to pay. They may have no alternative other than to sell their home, leave their neighborhood, and move elsewhere. An economic approach to the property tax can find no fault with this solution; taxpayers, however, have other ideas.

So much for the "professional" approach to advantages, what about the disadvantages? First, the tax is regressive; that is, it will take a larger portion of a low income homeowner's salary than of a high income homeowner's salary. Taxpayers will not argue on this point. Second, financial officers (and some elected officials) take the position that the large amounts of property that are exempt from the property tax create an additional hardship on those taxpayers who can least afford to bear it. These exemptions are in fact cash subsidies to the organizations involved. Taxpayers should look long and hard at those non-profit organizations that are on the receiving end of this arrangement. The question to be asked is: Does the organization involved provide a service of such value to the community that it "earns" its tax exemption? (Note: The property of state and federal government is exempted from taxation for legal reasons. However, it is possible this could be changed if sufficient pressure were brought to bear on elected officials.) If the organization does not "earn" its way, there is good reason to remove its exemption and put its property back on the tax rolls. A third criticism that government officials level at the property tax is that it does not respond quickly enough to inflation, leaving the local government facing inflated costs in carrying out its operations without the increased income to pay for them. Whether this happens in any particular situation depends on whether or not property values are part of a general inflationary trend.

The most time-consuming problem created for local officials by the property tax is that of administration, specifically the assessment of property. Taxpayers should be careful on this issue. The tax a person pays depends on the rate as well as the assessment. Poor assessment procedures can be countered by astute use of the rate structure. Also, taxpayers can be victimized or benefited by poor assessment administration. For the community overall, there is no doubt that standardized assessment procedures and a professionally trained assessment staff are a great benefit. But taxpayers should realize that as individuals they can lose as well as gain by improvements in property tax administration.

Another point should be made about the property tax. The typical homeowner is paying more than one property tax. A quick examination of the typical tax bill will reveal that the property is in a number of taxing districts and that each one is levying its own tax rate on the assessed value of the property. This can be either an advantage or disadvantage depending on the knowledge and sophistication of the taxpayer. Being part of a number of local government units instead of just one, gives the aggressive taxpayer just that many more opportunities to have an impact on the taxes that are paid. On the other hand, the less aggressive taxpayer may find it very easy to be confused by this multiplicity of governments. Also, some of these units may have been created only to levy taxes (and provide services) that were beyond the legal ability of existing local government units. Therefore, the astute taxpayers who want fair value for their tax dollar will find that a knowledge of local history is a valuable aid in assessing the quality of service each local government unit provides in return for the tax dollars it receives.

To sum up, the property tax receives attention far out of proportion to the burden it actually imposes on most taxpayers. This is because it is a painful tax with payment usually required in one or two large sums. Also, it is not a hidden tax such as the sales or income tax. Most people receive a bill in the mail, thus making the tax very obvious. For these reasons, it has been the focal point of taxpayer unrest. The concerned taxpayer would do well to devote some time and energy to understanding the impact of the other taxes that support local government. Overall improvements in the service/tax ratio cannot be expected from a single minded assault on the most vulnerable tax.

## SALES TAX

As a source of local government revenue, the sales tax takes two distinct forms: a general sales tax, and a selective sales tax. Table 4.4 examines the growth of revenues from these two sources over a 25-year period. Between 1950 and 1975 local sales tax revenues increased an astounding 1236.4 percent from 484 million dollars to approximately 6.5 billion dollars. As these figures indicate quite clearly, sales tax revenue also increased its contribution to overall local government revenues. In 1950 it accounted for 6.1 percent of the total, and by 1975 its share had risen to 10.5 percent.

The type of sales tax structure available to any particular unit of local government is determined by applicable state law, the state constitution, and the local government charter if one exists. These sources of regulation will either spell out in detail what the local sales tax structure is or they will provide options that may or may not be adopted by local government units within the state. Any sales tax structure will make use of one or both of the forms of the sales tax that are discussed here.

The general sales tax is a broad-based tax on consumption. It is collected at the time of sale by retailers. Retailers are usually required to file monthly tax returns including data on sales and payment of the tax money collected. The administration of the tax is handled in one of two ways: either by the state's department of revenue, or by the local government.

In instances where the state collects the tax, it usually exists as an "add-on" to the state's own sales tax levy. Local governments are

TABLE 4.4
Sales Tax As a Source of Local Government Revenue, 1950-75

|  | Local Sales Tax Revenues (millions of dollars) | Percent Increase or (Decrease) | As a Percent of All Local Government Tax Revenue |
|---|---|---|---|
| 1950 | 484 | – | 6.1 |
| 1955 | 779 | 61.0 | 6.6 |
| 1960 | 1,339 | 71.9 | 7.4 |
| 1965 | 2,059 | 53.8 | 8.2 |
| 1970 | 3,008 | 46.1 | 7.7 |
| 1971 | 3,662 | 21.7 | 8.4 |
| 1972 | 4,238 | 15.7 | 8.7 |
| 1973 | 4,924 | 16.2 | 9.3 |
| 1974 | 5,542 | 12.6 | 9.8 |
| 1975 | 6,468 | 16.7 | 10.5 |

25-year increase in local government sales tax revenues:
1,235.4 percent

*Source:* U.S. Bureau of the Census, *Statistical Abstract of the United States: 1977* (Washington, D.C., 1977), p. 281, #460.

given the option of adding a fixed percentage to the state's tax rate. (For example: A local government may elect to add 1 percent to the state's rate of 5 percent, yielding an overall sales tax of 6 percent.) The state collects the tax, provides auditing and other administrative services, and remits local government's share. Sometimes a charge is made for collection and handling. This arrangement has distinct advantages for local governments, especially the smaller ones. They do not have to maintain their own revenue department for collection and auditing. Even if they are charged a service fee by the state, this is usually less expensive than if they provided the services themselves. It is also better for the businesses collecting the tax because they only have to deal with one set of regulations and one set of auditors rather than two. Another important advantage to this system is that local governments tend to utilize this option when it is available to them. Thus, the local government does not run the risk of discouraging business and sales as it might if it had a locally enacted sales tax and surrounding communities did not. There is a disadvantage to the state collection plan and that is the local government does not have the autonomy to set its own tax rate. It must either accept or reject the rate that the state offers. Also, there is no control over the administrative and auditing procedures affecting local businesses. The advantages and disadvantages are essentially a question of economic efficiency versus local autonomy.

If a local government has the option of enacting its own general sales tax, it can enjoy exercising autonomy, but it can also look forward to a host of problems. The first and foremost can be a negative effect on the local economy. If a local government enacts a sales tax and surrounding governments do not, there may be a tendency for people to shop out of the area to avoid the tax. Businesses may relocate out of the area to lure patrons for "tax-free" shopping. Such a tax may also be detrimental to the establishment of new businesses and shopping centers within the boundaries of the local government. (However, as is the case with most disadvantages, there is another side to the story. If a community wishes to discourage further business development within its borders and is willing to bear the added burden, a heavy local sales tax can be a very effective way to accomplish this goal.) Another problem is the one of administration. A large city or county may be able to set up a department to collect its tax with a reasonable degree of efficiency. However, a small local government unit is likely to find that the costs of collecting and enforcing a tax may be very great when compared to the revenue the tax is yielding.

A point about the coverage of general sales taxes should be made. Many persons regard the sales tax as regressive, particularly when it applies to all retail sales including food and prescription drugs. A sales tax on food and drugs places an excessive burden on poor families who must spend a large portion of their income for these necessities of life. It is very doubtful that the additional revenue gained by this broad coverage offsets the hardship imposed on the poor and the negative economic affects on citizens as a whole. Local governments that have the option of imposing a general sales tax would do well to avoid taxing these necessities of life and thereby imposing an additional hardship on their poorer families. Also, groups of citizens who are interested in tax reform should demand that government officials provide a vigorous economic rationale demonstrating why a sales tax on food and drugs should be continued or implemented. The rationale should go beyond a mere question of revenues. It should include an analysis of the economic impact of the tax on the poor and on taxpayers as a whole.

Gross receipts taxes are considered to be a part of general sales tax revenue as far as local government finance is concerned because they are levied against the sales of businesses and professions. They are not, however, paid by the consumer directly. They are paid by the seller. Since the total amount of the tax may be easily passed on to the consumer by the seller, the question of who ultimately bears the burden of the tax is quite vague. Gross receipt taxes are usually levied at a very low percentage because of possible negative effects on marginal businesses. To a small business on the brink of bankruptcy, losing 4 percent or 5 percent of its gross income to such a tax could prove to be disastrous. Gross receipt taxes are usually levied in the .5 percent to 1 percent range. They are almost always levied by local option. This means careful consideration must be given to the possible negative economic effects of the tax.

Generally speaking, gross receipts taxes are subject to the same advantages and disadvantages as the general sales tax. The exception is that questions of coverage are answered by the determination of what types of businesses and professions are subject to the tax. To exempt food stores from the tax would be analogous to having a sales tax that did not apply to food. In many ways, a gross receipts tax may be a better tax than the general sales tax for local government because it allows more flexibility in determining just which types of consumption are to be taxed. This flexibility is important to a local government that is trying to tailor its overall tax structure to its particular revenue needs and trying to use the tax structure as a means of guiding the future economic development of the community.

Although revenues from general sales taxes and gross receipts taxes have grown over a thousand times in the first 70 years of this century (from 3 million dollars in 1913 to over 3 billion dollars in 1970), they still yield less than half the revenue of the selective sales taxes that are used by local governments.[3] For instance, in 1970 the yield from selective sales taxes on public utilities alone was 6.6 billion dollars. Selective sales taxes are taxes on consumption that apply only to a particular service or particular goods. The most common targets of local government selective sales taxes are public utility bills, tobacco, admissions and amusements, motor fuels, alcoholic beverages, and hotel and motel bills. The purpose of these taxes is primarily revenue. Each of these types of tax has its own particular method of implementation. Utility taxes are either levied on the utility company as a form of gross receipts tax or directly on the user as a form of selective sales tax. In either event, the effect is the same: the utility user is the one who pays the tax, directly or indirectly. This tax is very regressive, particularly in geographic locations where utility bills are a major factor in the family budgets of lower and middle income groups. They are quite popular with local governments because they yield good revenues, are very easy to collect and administer, and are very well hidden from the taxpayer. They are well hidden because not many people make it a habit to look at their utility bills to see how their charges are calculated. The reasons that make the utility tax popular with local government officials are the very reasons that taxpayer groups should take a close look at these taxes when considering ways to reform and improve their local tax systems.

Tobacco, admissions and amusement, and alcoholic beverage taxes are usually levied for purely revenue purposes. Unlike the utility taxes, they are not regressive because they apply only to expenditures that are discretionary in nature. Happily, they enjoy all the advantages of the utility taxes because they are easy to collect and enforce and yield good revenues in relation to their costs of collection.

Selective sales taxes on motor fuels are usually associated with earmarked funds set aside for the purpose of improving and maintaining local streets and roads. Earlier in this century they were levied mostly by local governments on their own authority. But as highway systems grew beyond the bounds of towns and counties, states began building intrastate roadways and adopted statewide motor fuel taxes for financing. In most states, these taxes put an end to locally originated taxes. The states filled the gap by redistributing some of the tax revenue they collected to the local governments. Today, only a relatively small number of local governments levy and administer their own motor fuel sales taxes. No matter how they are derived, earmarked revenues provide a good means for taxpayers to analyze benefits received in return for taxes paid. But once again the caution must be given that this arrangement is beneficial only as long as the programs supported with these funds have not outlived their usefulness and as long as there is a reasonable balance between the funds available and the amount necessary to provide the level of service the taxpayers want. Close taxpayer scrutiny is essential in order for earmarked funds to yield the full benefits of which they are capable.

The taxation of hotel and motel bills by local government is a good way for visitors to a community to pay a share of the cost of public services they enjoy. These taxes are applied to bills on a fixed percentage basis, collected by the hotel, and remitted to the local government on a regular basis. Like the other selective sales taxes, collection and administration are usually problem free and the yield is very good when balanced against the administrative costs. This tax is likely to be popular with the local taxpayers because they are unlikely to be affected by it.

In summary, the sales tax in all of its forms is becoming an increasingly important component of local government revenues. It should be of particular interest to taxpayer groups because of its many forms and variations. It can be used to accomplish a variety of purposes: to raise tax revenues, to reduce other taxes, to shift part of the tax burden to some particular segment of the community, or to encourage or discourage some particular type of economic activity.


## INCOME TAX

Table 4.5 shows the income tax to be a small but growing part of the local government revenue picture. In 1950 total local government income tax revenue was only about 71 million dollars, less than 1 percent of total local government tax revenue. By 1975 revenues were up to approximately 2.6 billion dollars or about 4.3 percent of the local government tax yield. This amounts to over a 36-fold increase in a 25-year period. The income tax does not enjoy wide-spread use by local government. It is most common in the eastern part of the United States, particularly in the states of Ohio and Pennsylvania. There has been a slow but gradual rise in the number of local governments that are utilizing the income tax.

TABLE 4.5
Income Tax As a Source of Local
Government Revenue, 1950-75

|  | Local Income Tax Revenues (millions of dollars) | Percent Increase or (Decrease) | As a Percent of All Local Government Tax Revenue |
|---|---|---|---|
| 1950 | 71 | – | .9 |
| 1955 | 150 | 111.3 | 1.3 |
| 1960 | 254 | 69.3 | 1.4 |
| 1965 | 433 | 70.5 | 1.7 |
| 1970 | 1,630 | 276.4 | 4.2 |
| 1971 | 1,747 | 7.2 | 4.0 |
| 1972 | 2,241 | 28.3 | 4.6 |
| 1973 | 2,406 | 7.4 | 4.6 |
| 1974 | 2,413 | .3 | 4.3 |
| 1975 | 2,635 | 9.2 | 4.3 |

25-year increase in local government income tax revenues:
3,611.3 percent

*Source:* U.S. Bureau of the Census, *Statistical Abstract of the United States: 1977* (Washington, D.C., 1977), p. 281, #460.


Local income taxes are, for the most part, structured quite a bit differently than the federal income tax and most state income taxes. In fact, local income taxes as a group are very diverse in terms of rate structure and coverage. There are five possible areas of coverage for the tax.[4] These are:

1. The salaries and wages of residents no matter where they have been earned.
2. Salaries and wages of non-residents that were earned within the geographic boundaries of the local government unit.
3. The net profits of occupations and unincorporated businesses run by residents regardless of where they were earned.
4. The net profits of occupations and unincorporated businesses inside the geographical boundaries of the local government unit.
5. The net profits of corporations derived from operations carried on within the geographical boundaries of the local government unit.

These areas of coverage represent the range of possible tax bases available to local government. They can be used singularly or in conjunction with one another. The decision of which of these to use should be based on an analysis of the economic, social, and geographical characteristics of the local government and its surrounding area. Diversity in the local income tax is not limited to its coverage. There are a wide variety of rate structures that can be applied. The two most common are progressive structures such as that of the federal income tax and what is called a proportional structure in which a single rate of tax is applied regardless of the level of income involved. (For example: a 1 percent rate in a proportional structure would yield $100 on a $10,000 dollar income and $1,000 on a $100,000 dollar income.) The amount of tax paid increases with income, but not the rate of taxation. Local income tax structures may or may not provide for a system of deductions and exemptions similar to that of the federal income tax.

To most taxpayers (except those few who may have become used to them) the idea of a local income tax is probably very unsettling. Nevertheless, there are advantages to its use. Unfortunately, these advantages are almost always from the point of view of the government official rather than from that of the taxpayer. The principle advantage is the potential for a great deal of revenue, particularly if the coverage of the tax is wide and the rate structure progressive. Such a tax would be very similar to the federal version and thus not only keep pace with inflation, but actually keep ahead of it due to the "inflation tax" phenomenon discussed in the earlier chapter on federal taxation. An additional advantage is that the tax can be made relatively painless and hidden quite well by using a system of withholding payments so that taxpayers never really "see" the money before they pay it out. A third advantage is that such a strong source of local revenue can do a great deal to assure the autonomy of the local government vis-a-vis the state and federal governments. Are these advantages to the tax-payer? Unfortunately, the answer is "not usually."

What is a great deal of revenue to the government official trans-lates into high taxes for the citizen. It can be assumed citizens will only favor a high rate of taxation if they feel they are getting their money's worth in terms of services. The taxpayer revolt of the late 1970s makes a clear statement that citizens are generally very un-happy with their tax burden. It can be safely said that few citizens would view the high yields of progressive local income taxes as an advantage. This is especially the case in times of high inflation when progressive income taxes tend to increase the impact of inflation. In terms of the third advantage, there is a good deal to be said for the autonomy of local government if, and only if, it is responsive to the needs and desires of its citizens. However, once autonomy is lost it is next to impossible to regain. If taxpayers are faced with the choice of supporting or not supporting a local income tax, a good part of the decision will hinge on the level of confidence they have in their elected officials.

There are many severe disadvantages to the use of the income tax at the local level, and, in this instance at least, government officials and taxpayers may well find they have the same perspective. All of the disadvantages are administrative in nature. The primary one arises from the fact that many people live in one jurisdiction and earn all or part of their income in another jurisdiction. The question simply put is: what jurisdiction taxes what portion of the income? Double taxation is a problem, as is capturing all the income legally subject to taxation. For governments to work out these problems re-quires not only a high level of administrative skill, but a good deal of intergovernmental cooperation. Usually only the largest of local gov-ernments have the capacity to overcome these problems. Even if these problems can be resolved, there is still a massive burden of record keeping placed on the businesses that must calculate and collect the tax.

Assuming that these administrative problems can be worked out, there is another potential disadvantage to be considered. The imposi-tion of the local income tax may be so much of a burden that it drives both businesses and workers out of the area. New York City is a case in point. It has a stiff municipal income tax that, combined with an unusually heavy state tax burden, has contributed to a mas-sive exodus from the city. Of all the taxes available to local govern-ments, the income tax has the greatest likelihood of causing adverse economic effects because of its administrative and economic burden on businesses and employees.

To sum up, the wary taxpayer should approach local income taxes with a good deal of care. These taxes usually place a heavy burden on taxpayers that is quite likely to get heavier with time. Inflation seems to be a permanent fixture of American life that serves to amplify and increase the burden of all income taxes. If taxpayers decide they want an income tax they should be sure the government has the administrative expertise required and that the tax does not have negative economic effects on the local business community. Even more important than these considerations, taxpayers must resolve to keep a close watch on the finances of their government. They must assure that government officials do not spend for the sake of spending, that administrators do not build their empires at the expense of the taxpayer, and most of all, that it is possible to adjust revenues and taxes downward as well as upward.

## OTHER TAXES

Two types of local government taxes fall into this category. The first is special purpose taxes. An example of one such tax might be

TABLE 4.6
Other Taxes As a Source of Local Government Revenue, 1950-75

|  | Other Tax Revenues (millions of dollars) | Percent Increase or (Decrease) | As a Percent of All Local Government Tax Revenues |
|---|---|---|---|
| 1950 | 387 | – | 4.8 |
| 1955 | 634 | 63.8 | 5.3 |
| 1960 | 692 | 9.1 | 3.8 |
| 1965 | 807 | 16.6 | 3.2 |
| 1970 | 1,173 | 45.4 | 3.0 |
| 1971 | 1,298 | 10.7 | 3.0 |
| 1972 | 1,575 | 21.3 | 3.2 |
| 1973 | 1,731 | 9.9 | 3.3 |
| 1974 | 2,108 | 21.8 | 3.7 |
| 1975 | 2,166 | 2.8 | 3.5 |

25-year increase in other tax local government revenues:
459.7 percent

*Source:* U.S. Bureau of the Census, *Statistical Abstract of the United States: 1977* (Washington, D.C., 1977), p. 281, #460.

an instance where a local government levies a tax on the receipts of a local race track betting operation or some other form of legal gambling. Special purposes taxes can be enacted to raise revenues or to control or discourage a particular type of activity. The second type of tax to fall into the "other tax" category is fees and charges. They are placed in this category largely for technical reasons. In instances where a fee charged for a service or license is in excess of the cost, the amount over and above the cost is considered to be a tax. Since it is not possible to determine on a general basis where the cost line is, the entire amount is considered to be a tax.

Table 4.6 shows a 25-year history of local government revenues derived from these taxes. In 1950 the total was 387 million dollars, which amounted to 4.8 percent of all local government tax revenues. By 1975 revenues had risen to a little over 2 billion dollars. While this was an increase of over 459 percent for the 25-year period, as a share of overall local government tax revenue "other taxes" had dropped to 3.5 percent. With the sharp rise in revenues generated by local taxes on consumption and income, this figure will in all likelihood continue to drop in the years ahead.

## SUMMARY

Table 4.7 presents the sources of local government tax revenues over a 25-year time period. The pattern revealed is quite clear. The

TABLE 4.7
Local Government Tax Revenue by Source, 1950-75 (percent)

|  | Property Tax | Sales Tax | Income Tax | Other Taxes |
|---|---|---|---|---|
| 1950 | 88.2 | 6.1 | .9 | 4.8 |
| 1955 | 86.9 | 6.6 | 1.3 | 5.3 |
| 1960 | 87.4 | 7.4 | 1.4 | 3.8 |
| 1965 | 86.7 | 8.2 | 1.7 | 3.2 |
| 1970 | 84.9 | 7.7 | 4.2 | 3.0 |
| 1971 | 84.6 | 8.4 | 4.0 | 3.0 |
| 1972 | 83.6 | 8.7 | 4.6 | 3.2 |
| 1973 | 82.9 | 9.3 | 4.6 | 3.3 |
| 1974 | 82.2 | 9.8 | 4.3 | 3.7 |
| 1975 | 81.6 | 10.5 | 4.3 | 3.5 |

Percent increase or (decrease) from 1950 to 1975:

|  | | | | |
|---|---|---|---|---|
|  | (7.5) | 72.1 | 377.8 | (27.1) |

*Source:* U.S. Bureau of the Census, *Statistical Abstract of the United States: 1977* (Washington, D.C., 1977), p. 281, #460.

sales and income taxes are becoming more important as sources of revenue. Both showed substantial increases in their contributions to overall tax revenue. Property taxes declined in importance between 1950 and 1975 by about 7.5 percent. Also, the importance of the "other tax" category dropped sharply. Taxpayers can expect this pattern to continue well into the future. The effects of the on-going taxpayer revolt have not yet been felt in these statistics. When they are, the drop in the importance of the property tax will be accelerated. Whether or not sales and income taxes will show a significant rise depends on how taxpayers and local government officials react to the financial crunch caused by the loss of property taxes. It may well be that the gap will be filled by additional grants from the state and federal governments and by a sharp increase in locally generated revenues from non-tax sources. The chapters that follow provide an in-depth look at these questions.

## NOTES

1. United States Bureau of the Census, *County and City Data Book, 1977*, p. 903.

2. Lennox L. Moak and Albert M. Hillhouse, *Concepts and Practices in Local Government Finance.* (Chicago, Ill.: The Municipal Finance Officers Association, 1975), pp. 130–131.

3. United States Bureau of the Census, *Historical Statistics of the United States, Colonial Times to 1970.* Bicentennial Edition, Part II (Washington, D.C., 1975), p. 1133.

4. Moak and Hillhouse, *Concepts and Practices*, pp. 156–57.

# PART II The Taxpayer Revolt of 1978

# 5

# PROPOSITION 13:
## CALIFORNIA LEADS THE WAY

The passage of Proposition 13 in the 1978 spring primary election was the most significant event of the taxpayer revolt of the late 1970s. California voters by a margin of 65 percent to 35 percent voted themselves a massive reduction in their local property taxes and severely restricted the process by which new or increased taxes could be levied. This action was taken in the face of dire warnings from government officials and public labor organizations that passage of "13" would effectively destroy local government. The popular governor of California, Jerry Brown, warned that while tax relief was needed, "13" was not the answer; it was too drastic and imposed hardships on those citizens dependent upon local government services for their subsistence. While Brown opposed "13," his Republican opponent for the governorship, Evelle J. Younger, gave luke-warm support to the measure. When the dust cleared after the June election, both Brown and Younger had won their respective primaries, but the big winner was Proposition 13.

There are four important points to the Proposition 13 story. The first is the election, itself. Why did the measure pass? What were the major factors that influenced the thinking of California citizens on election day? Was "13's" passage predictable or was it the result of the strange coincidences that sometimes shape American politics? The second point is the effect of Proposition 13 on the state and local tax structures. Did it effect only the property tax? What kind of impact is it likely to make on California State government? What was the immediate reaction of state and local officials to the passage of "13"? The third aspect of the Proposition 13 story is its implementation in the months that followed the election. Could a governor who opposed the measure provide effective leadership in making "13" work as the people intended? If local government was to be saved from financial ruin by the state, was there a price to be paid? The specific requirements of "13" aside, how did public officials react to the "message" of the irate taxpayers? The last part of the story focuses on California one year after "13." Were the unemployment lines full of ex-government workers? Did the garbage lie stinking in the California sun? Did the taxpayers get all that "13's" advocates promised them? What was the real impact of Proposition 13?

If Proposition 13 is to be more than a local victory in the taxpayer revolt, its lessons must be examined and understood. Taxpayers all across the country must decide if they want to do something about their own growing tax burden. If they do, then the California story is an important source of information. It is important because it contains all the ingredients necessary for a successful taxpayer revolt anywhere in the country.


## THE ELECTION

To understand the dynamics of that fateful California election, it is necessary to start with the legalities of the situation. The United States form of government is one of representation; that is, the welfare of the citizenry is in the hands of the elected representatives. These representatives, not the citizens themselves, are charged with the responsibility of governing. Governing is primarily a process of raising revenues and expending funds for programs and services. The citizen is in nominal control of this representative process by virtue of periodic elections. There are limited opportunities for citizens to take matters directly in their own hands. Prior to 1978, the most well known of these opportunities was the New England-style town meeting where citizens could voice their opinion and make the final decisions for their elected representatives. Californians do not enjoy the advantage of having town meetings. In fact, the sheer size of most of the cities and towns makes the notion absurd. What they do have is a device much more suited to a large, modern society—the constitutional initiative.

The initiative process in California allows propositions designed to amend the state constitution to be placed on the ballot of any statewide election. To place a proposition on the ballot, a petition signed by a small percentage of the registered voters in the state is all that is required. If the proposition passes by a simple majority of those voting in the election, it becomes an amendment to the state constitution. Issues resolved by the initiative process are beyond the reach of the state legislature because constitutional provisions take precedence over legislative action. The constitutional initiative provides citizens with the means to "go over the heads" of their elected officials and change the fundamental legal structure of the state. By doing this, citizens can affect not only the state government, but the actions and structure of local government as well.

As might be expected, this kind of process is not overly popular with elected officials or other groups with vital economic interests in the operation of government. It is unpopular because it has the potential to disturb the "business as usual" mentality that prevails at all levels of government. The use of the initiative is a type of action politicians must praise openly because to do otherwise would be to express lack of confidence in the public. But privately, most public officials probably wish that this type of direct governing process did not exist. Citizens use such direct means only rarely and only when there is an issue of great importance being ignored by the representative processes of government.

In the constitutional initiative, the citizens of California had the perfect means to take matters into their own hands. By using the initiative process, they accomplished two things: substantial changes were made in the tax structure, and they sent a strong message to their government officials. Neither of these things could have been accomplished without such a powerful and direct tool. Without the initiative process, there would have been no taxpayer revolt in California and the national tax reduction movement would have been deprived of one of its most powerful assets.

What were the forces that caused Californians to take matters into their own hands? There are as many answers to this question as there are voters in California, but some major causal factors can be identified. What is most surprising about these factors is that they are not unique to California. They are being experienced by most taxpayers around the country.

Without a doubt the number one factor is inflation. The continuing high rate of inflation had three distinct effects on most California taxpayers. The first is related to real estate values. California has experienced a very heavy growth in population in the 1960s and 1970s. This growth and the corresponding demand for housing made California real estate a very good investment. It was not unusual to find the market value of houses doubling in less than ten years. In general, real estate values grew at a much higher rate than the incomes of most homeowners. Of course, as the value of real estate goes up, so do property taxes. An earlier chapter showed the local property tax to be one of the most painful and obvious taxes a citizen has to pay. It becomes more painful and more obvious when it is administered in an efficient and effective manner. California local government is one of the best examples of efficient public management anywhere in the country. This high level of professionalism and expertise is especially noticeable in the ranks of California's county tax assessors. Most California real estate is reassessed every three years. This means the assessed valuation is usually close to the true market value. In addition, California local governments have a tradition of keeping local tax rates at or near the maximum allowed by law. As a result of both inflation and efficiency, California land owners paid more property tax to local government than did taxpayers in any other state. In the years immediately preceding the passage of Proposition 13 local property taxes in California increased at an astonishing rate. Many middle-class taxpayers found that, for the first time, they had to struggle to make their property tax payments.

Inflation effects not only expenses, but also the income a person earns. California government is "blessed" with having a highly progressive state income tax. As inflation drove up the salaries of California taxpayers, it also forced them into higher tax brackets. Many Californians found themselves earning more and having less. State elected officials found themselves in a situation where they had more revenue coming in than they knew how to spend. In early 1978 the State of California had a surplus of about five billion dollars. The legislature and the governor could not decide how to spend it. While Californians struggled to pay their property taxes, their elected representatives in Sacramento were engulfed with excess tax dollars.

The third effect of inflation on the California taxpayer was not unique to California, but was one that made itself felt throughout the country. In the late 1970s the cost of living went up so high and so fast that the income of most people could not keep up with it. In addition, the federal income tax as well as some state income taxes levied an "inflation tax" that widened even further the gap between the increased income and the increased expenses. For the first time, many Americans seemed to lose the sense of future optimism that has been the trademark of the United States. They began to realize that they would probably be poorer rather than richer in the years to come. This sense of economic foreboding caused an acute sensitivity to their current financial situation. Economic pessimism had the predictable effect of causing people to think more about their own economic welfare and less about the welfare of less fortunate citizens who rely on local government for health and welfare benefits. The result was the building of a negative attitude toward local government that needed only a catalyst to set it off. Enter Howard Jarvis and Paul Gann.

Until Proposition 13 neither of these gentlemen could claim much in the way of success in a long record of fighting government taxation. But this time their efforts struck fertile ground. People were ready for an abrasive, direct approach to solving the problems of government spending and taxation. The message of the "13" campaign was clear and simple: Government was needlessly big and wasteful. Therefore, it could get along on fewer tax dollars than it was currently collecting. A massive cut in the property taxes supporting local government would be a move toward eliminating needless programs and all too numerous government employees. In addition, the cut would force the state to use its massive surplus to help local governments maintain essential services. The taxpayers would do directly what their elected representatives had been either unwilling or unable to do. In the end, the "We're mad as hell and we're not going to take it anymore" approach worked well in conjunction with the support of the big land owners to convince voters that "13" held a message that government needed to receive in the strongest way possible.

Opposition to the tax cutting measure was predictable. Public employee organizations waged a massive campaign. They were joined by local government officials, the academic community, and an assortment of special interest groups dedicated to preserving the educational, health, and welfare services provided by local government. If the proponents of "13" went beyond the bounds of reason in their campaign rhetoric, the opponents went just as far in the other direction with their dire forecast of thousands of local government employees on unemployment and their promise of the total collapse of local government. State politicians including Governor Brown tried to offer a middle-of-the-road alternative that would have limited state and local spending without imposing drastic tax cuts. Their efforts were received with a "too little, too late" attitude by many citizens. For many voters who were having difficulty making up their minds the decision was made much easier just a few days before the election. About one-third of the property owners in Los Angeles County received their 1978 tax bills before the normal date of July 1st. These tax bills reflected massive increases in assessed valuations that in some cases doubled property taxes. As might be expected, this news got a good deal of attention in the few days remaining before the election. If "13" needed a final push toward victory, this was it. On election day Proposition 13 was approved by an overwhelming two to one margin. Some 4.2 million California voters had taken matters into their own hands.

## MAJOR PROVISIONS OF PROPOSITION 13

Although "13" primarily focuses on the local property tax, other areas of taxation are affected. The amount of tax any property owner has to pay is determined by the provisions of "13" and the imposition of any new taxes by either state or local government is curtailed. Additionally, new processes for raising existing state taxes were put into effect. The overall result of these provisions was to:

1. Roll back existing property tax levels.
2. Make it extremely difficult to enact any new taxes or to raise existing ones.

The details of Proposition 13 are given below.

1. The maximum property tax allowable is 1 percent of the full cash value of the property. The 1 percent is to be collected by the counties and distributed to the taxing districts within the counties. The limit does not apply to property taxes or special assessments necessary to pay the interest or retire the principal of bond issues approved by the voters prior to July 1, 1978.

2. Full cash value is defined as the cash value of property as stated on the 1975–76 tax bill. In the case of property with new construction and property that was purchased or otherwise changed ownership after the 1975 assessment had been made, the full cash value is defined as the appraised value at the time of construction or the time of change of ownership.

3. The value of the property may not be increased by more than 2 percent per year. If the consumer price index drops in any given year, the value of the property may be adjusted downward.

4. Increases in existing state taxes must be approved by a margin of two-thirds of the elected members of both houses of the legislature. The legislature is prohibited from enacting any new taxes on real property or the transfer of real property.

5. In order to enact new non-property taxes, local governments must secure the approval of two-thirds of all registered

voters living within the boundaries of the local government. Local governments are prohibited from enacting new taxes on property or on the transfer of real property.

6. The provisions of the amendment take effect on July 1, 1978.

The most obvious effect of "13" was to cut 30 percent out of the property tax revenue of local government. It would seem logical to assume that a 30 percent cut in government revenue translates into a 30 percent cut in taxes. Unfortunately, this is not quite true. Property taxes are deductible from state and federal income taxes. Therefore, the gains made with lower property taxes are partially offset by higher income taxes. In a stroke of supreme irony, the success of the California taxpayer revolt added "windfall" profits to the coffers of both the state and federal governments. Perhaps more important than the rollback of taxes was the guarantee that assessments could not be raised by more than 2 percent per year. This was a far cry from the 100 percent increase that some taxpayers were facing in 1978. Since the property tax is tied to the assessment, it cannot increase by more than 2 percent per year.

Proposition 13 also anticipated the natural reaction of local governments to severe losses in property tax revenues. "13's" requirement that two-thirds of the electorate approve new taxes made it a virtual certainity that new taxes would not be enacted. Two-thirds of the electorate is very different from a two-thirds majority of those voting. Most elections do not get a turnout of two-thirds of the voters, much less a vote of this magnitude on any one side of an issue.

What "13" did not do in this case was to close the door on fees and charges. Fees and charges are not considered to be taxes unless the fee exceeds the actual cost of providing the service. Since most local government fees are set at a level much below the actual cost of the service, local governments could safely raise most fees by significant amounts. The details of some of the fee changes that took place will be examined later in this chapter.

Some local governments took the precaution of raising many of their non-property taxes in the weeks immediately preceding the election. These kinds of actions demonstrated the almost incredible disregard that some local government officials had for the desires of the electorate.

In regard to state taxation, Proposition 13 left a good deal to be desired from the point of view of lightening tax burdens. True, no new property taxes can be enacted. Also, any additions to existing taxes require a two-thirds vote of both houses of the legislature.

However, the two taxes responsible for the massive state surplus were left untouched. California's 6 percent sales tax and highly progressive income tax continue to generate huge revenues, and the income tax continues to burden taxpayers with its "inflation tax."

In order to see why these taxes escaped "13," certain legalities must be examined. The procedure for amending the state constitution provides that amendments will deal with only a single topic. After "13" was passed, it underwent legal challenges in the California Supreme Court based on this procedural requirement. The argument was that since "13" dealt with local property taxes and also limited the enactment of new or increased state taxes, it covered two topics rather than one. Therefore, it violated the amendment procedure and should be declared unconstitutional. "13's" supporters offered the counter argument that the amendment dealt with only one topic, that being taxes. Additionally, the point was made that the people had spoken and that the Court could not and should not stand between the people and what they had voted for. The question before the Court was one of a subjective interpretation. The Court ultimately decided in favor of the amendment saying in effect that only one topic, taxation, was covered in the amendment. However, if "13" had contained a serious attack on the mainstays of the state's revenues, the outcome of the Court decision could well have been different. As it was, the basis of the Court's decision may have been as political as it was legal because four of the seven justices faced reelection for 12-year terms in the fall 1978 elections. It is quite likely that a decision against "13" would have adversely affected their chances for reelection.

The overwhelming passage of Proposition 13 embarrassed a large number of the local government officials who opposed it. In the days immediately prior to the election, a great deal of press coverage was given to the "doomsday" budgets some local government officials had prepared. These budgets showed massive cuts in services and employees. They were based on the assumption that the state despite its huge surplus of funds would sit idly by and watch local government struggle to bear the burden of "13's" massive revenue cuts alone. These doomsday budgets were, in fact, part of the campaign against "13." When election day had come and gone, local government officials did what they knew they were going to do all along: they went to Sacramento to lobby Governor Brown and the legislature for state aid. Generally, the state legislators were content to let Governor Brown take the lead in setting up a program to funnel state funds to local government.

Jerry Brown accepted the challenge that implementing Proposition 13 presented with so much enthusiasm that he was christened "Jerry Jarvis" by some disaffected members of the California political community. His activities were concentrated in three major areas. First, he took a hard line in controlling state expenditures: cutting the state budget, advocating no pay raises for state employees, and imposing a hiring freeze for state agencies. Second, he began making concrete proposals for the distribution of excess state funds to local governments. Third, he endorsed the general concept of expenditure controls on both state and local government. These actions earned him the praise of Howard Jarvis and Paul Gann. They also earned him the displeasure of state employees. He was accused by some detractors of "political profiteering" in order to assure his reelection in the fall of 1978.

In the November elections he beat the Republican candidate, Evelle Younger, handily. But the question remained in the minds of some people: were his actions political profit making or was he genuinely responding to the desires of the voters as he interpreted them? From the point of view of the taxpayer, there is only one answer to this question. Proposition 13 represented the will of the majority of voting taxpayers in California. It was a direct action going over the heads of elected officials to make a fundamental change in the state's constitutional provisions regarding local government taxation. It was Governor Brown's legal and moral obligation to carry out the will of the people to the best of his ability. The voters of California approved of his actions and demonstrated this approval in the voting booth. Governor Brown's actions stand in sharp contrast to those of other government officials who hurriedly enacted new taxes before the June election or prepared ominous doomsday budgets intended to frighten voters out of approving "13."

## IMPLEMENTATION OF PROPOSITION 13

After the voters approved Proposition 13 the governor and the legislature were faced with the task of implementing the new constitutional amendment. Implementation had two aspects.

The first was to determine how the counties would distribute the reduced property tax revenues to the local governments within their boundaries. "13" provided only that this distribution take place "according to law." In June of 1978 no such law existed. Prior to "13," local governments levied their taxes based upon the property valuations made by each county assessor. Counties then collected the taxes and remitted to each local government the proceeds of the taxes that it had levied.

Within two months after the election, the legislature enacted a law providing that the reduced property taxes would be divided by the counties among the local governments on the same percentage basis that existed before the passage of "13." For example, if a given city received 10 percent of the total property tax revenues generated within the county before the election, then it would receive 10 percent of whatever property tax revenues were available after the election. This formula was good for only one year. It is expected that subsequent formulae would include adjustments for changing population patterns within the counties.

The effect of this implementation ruling was to effectively remove from local governments the power to set local property tax rates. The new maximum by constitutional mandate was 1 percent of the assessed valuation. Because the 1 percent was far below the previous tax rates, counties had no choice but to collect the 1 percent and distribute it on a prorata basis among the local governments. Local government officials no longer had the opportunity to agonize over what the local property tax rate should be. The voters had decided that issue for them.

The second aspect of "13's" implementation was political in nature. The state had a huge surplus of funds that would be used to bail local governments out of their newfound financial difficulty. That the bailout occurred was not surprising. But it was surprising that two issues plaguing California state government were for all intents and purposes resolved by the bailout formula. These issues were funding for education and the burden of rising welfare costs on local government.

Some years back the decision in the Serrano vs. Priest court case essentially required that funding for public education in California move away from its heavy reliance on the local property tax toward a more broadly based funding scheme. The bailout plan for all practical purposes met this objective by providing some 2.27 billion dollars in state funds to local school districts. These dollars brought the school districts' funding up to about 90 percent of what it would have been if "13" had not passed.[1] The end result was the maintenance of a reasonable level of school funding and the resolution of a difficult issue that the state legislature and local governments would have had to face sooner or later.

The second issue revolved around the rapidly rising costs of welfare programs being supported by the property tax. For a long time there had been pressure on the state to assume a larger share of the costs for these programs. This was accomplished in the bailout plan by earmarking the funds going to county governments for the support of various welfare programs. In all, counties received approximately 1.5 billion dollars. Of this amount, 1.1 billion dollars was earmarked for the support of welfare programs. This influx of state money brought counties' budgets as a whole to within 10 percent of what they would have been without "13."[2]

In summary, the state's hastily enacted bailout plan not only saved local governments from having to implement their doomsday budgets, but it also resolved two difficult problems that had been plaguing both the state legislature and local officials for a number of years. For the point of view of local government, all of this sounded like it was too good to be true. It was.

There was a price to be paid for the vast amount of state monies flowing into local government; that price was a further loss of local autonomy. In order for a local government to be eligible for state bailout funds, it had to comply with certain requirements relating to the amount of financial reserves the local government had on hand. Also, cities and counties were not allowed to reduce their levels of fire and police protection. From the point of view of the elected local government official, these restrictions were bad enough—a clear usurpation of local perogatives. However, the most offensive "string" of all related to the wages of local government employees. Salary increases could be granted only if they did not exceed the increases that were received by state employees. Governor Brown had decreed that state workers would receive no cost-of-living increases, therefore, no local government employees received increases. It should go without saying, that this was political dynamite causing no end of trouble with the powerful public employee associations in the state. No matter how distasteful these "strings" might be, most local governments had no choice but to give up a significant part of their autonomy in return for state dollars.

In addition to these direct implementation issues, there are a number of indirect implementation factors of interest. The framers of Proposition 13 neglected to make any provision for the control of the fees and charges enacted by local government. As a result, there was a flurry of activity resulting in many cities and counties increasing the fees and charges already in effect. The two areas that seemed to receive the most attention were fees or licenses associated with the construction and renovation of buildings and charges for the use of public recreational facilities. Traditionally, local government had maintained a set of fees and charges that did not usually reflect the true cost associated with the service or activity. These activities had been subsidized by general tax revenues. The increases in fees and charges had the effect of putting these activities on a basis that was more nearly self-supporting.

From the point of view of the taxpayer, this was a definite improvement. When it is possible for local government to establish a direct fee-for-service relationship, a number of benefits will result. Perhaps the most important is that the citizen knows exactly what is being received for the money paid out. This knowledge makes it possible for citizens to make more informed judgments about the efficiency and effectiveness of local government operations. Also, they are more likely to provide positive feedback on the quality of a service when they know they are paying the full cost of that service and they are not receiving something for nothing.

Even though "13" required that any increases in local taxes had to be approved by two-thirds of the voters, there was a flurry of new taxes and tax increases enacted by local governments between the June election and the effective date of "13," which was July 1st. The only taxes local governments could increase were a variety of excise taxes. Taxes on utilities seemed to be one of the most popular areas for increases during this grace period. Utilities had been adjusting their rates downward in order to pass their property savings tax along to the consumers. The reasoning may have been that these increased excise taxes would go unnoticed when added to the reduced utility bills because consumers would end up paying about the same as before "13." It is to the credit of many local governments that when the state bailout plan became effective, they placed a moratorium on the collection of these new taxes or repealed them all together.

Thus far the implementation of Proposition 13 has been discussed in terms of the legal changes it made in state and local revenue structures. But "13" must be viewed as more than a reduction of property taxes and a tightening of tax enactment procedures; it was a message sent by the people to their elected officials. This message was more direct and powerful than any that could have been transmitted through the normal procedure of election and reelection of public officials. However, to be effective some provision had to be made for a serious review of the manner in which government was operating. This review could not be accomplished during the hectic scrambling to save local governments from financial crises. It required a longer-term consideration of the value that government was giving citizens in return for their tax dollars. Concern over government's performance was the major message of the "13" vote. While it is true people were very unhappy with high property taxes, they were equally unhappy with the fiscal operations of the state that had resulted in a huge accumulation of surplus funds.

Governor Brown's response to this deeper message of Proposition 13 was the formation of a blue ribbon commission charged with the task of recommending solutions in response to the issues and problems raised by Proposition 13. The Commission on Government Reform was headed by the distinguished A. Alan Post, former long-time head of the state's legislative analyst office. Mr. Post enjoyed a wide reputation for competence and integrity. The other members of the Commission were appointed from a wide range of occupations and political view points.

In its initial meetings the Commission identified four major areas on which to focus its attention. They were: the effects and opportunities resulting from "13," the tax systems of state and local government, the expenditures of state and local government, and the organization of state and local government.

After deliberating for almost seven months, the Commission issued its final report in February of 1979. The report's recommendations can be condensed into three major points.[3] The first major recommendation was that the bailout of local governments should become a permanent component of the state/local government relationship. Specifically, the state should assume over 4 billion dollars in local costs for schools, health, welfare, and the courts. The second major recommendation provided for the augmentation of local revenue sources with an increased sharing of state sales tax revenue. This was to be in addition to the 1 percent add-on almost all local governments were using. The final recommendation was that state taxes be increased if necessary to maintain a reasonable level of local government operations.

The Commission's recommendations must have been a severe disappointment to those who had hoped the message of "13" had gotten across. What the Commission did in essence was to accept the loss of property tax revenues and proceed to construct a situation that would permit business as usual for the state and local governments. The only major change would be in the source of funds—state taxes rather than the property tax. Additionally, it could be assumed that if the state was going to take over full financial responsibility for schools, health, welfare, and the courts, there would be a corresponding loss of local autonomy and control. Conspicuously absent was the lack of any recommendation on how the magnitude of government operations might be reduced or any guidance on how the overall costs of government might be contained.

In essence, the report of the Commission seemed to ignore the fundamental point the people were trying to make with their vote on "13." Perhaps the answer to the Commission's failure to address the hard issues that were raised by "13" lies in the composition of its membership. Governor Brown had made an exhaustive effort to balance the Commission with representatives of all points of view. Perhaps it was because the Commission was so balanced that it was never able to reach a basic agreement on what it should do; specifically, whether or not it should address the hard issues of reducing government services.

In summary, the Commission provided an unfortunate verification of the model that was presented in the first chapter. The model explains the impossibility of restraining government costs and growth by ordinary means. It suggests that extraordinary action is necessary. Proposition 13 and the Post Commission prove the point. By passing "13," the taxpayers did reduce the bite of the property tax. However, in the areas that "13" did not directly deal with, "business-as-usual" was the order of the day. The whole thrust of the Commission's report was to find a way to maintain services even if it meant new taxes to replace the lost revenue of the property tax. The desires of the taxpayers for lower taxes and less government were entirely overlooked.

## CALIFORNIA AFTER PROPOSITION 13

California one year after the passage of Proposition "13" demonstrated that its proponents were a good deal more accurate in their predictions about the future than were the doomsday spouting opponents. Primarily because of the state bailout, the spending levels of local government have not been greatly reduced. The only major reduction has been the property tax revenue. In April 1979 the California Department of Finance issued a study of the impact of Proposition 13 on the budgets and programs of local government. The major points of that report are summarized in the paragraphs that follow.[4]

In the months following the passage of "13" local government revenues were about 1.4 percent below the level of the previous year. Without the state bailout funds, local revenues would have been down over 15 percent. Spending in cities, counties, and most special districts was up slightly over the previous year due mostly to the use of reserves and the deferral of some costs. The areas of spending hit the hardest were libraries, parks and recreation, and general administration. These discretionary areas of spending were forced to absorb more than their share of reductions because of the state mandates to maintain spending levels in the areas of police and fire protection, welfare, health, and the courts.

Counties as a group lost 49.2 percent of their property tax revenues, a decrease of approximately 1.4 billion dollars. For the fiscal year 1978-79 counties spent about 11 percent less than they had budgeted. Most of this saving was due to hiring freezes and postponement of capital expenditures. The number of full-time county positions fell by about 5 percent and the number of full-time employees was even lower because many authorized positions went unfilled due to hiring freezes. Another significant personnel factor is a developing shortage of skilled people in the areas of nursing, data-processing, and engineering. Also, because cost-of-living raises were denied during 1978-79, there is very likely to be strong pressure from public employee associations for significant salary increases. Personnel may be further reduced in order to finance these salary increases.

City revenue from property taxes dropped approximately 57 percent as a result of Proposition 13. The loss of 550 million dollars in property tax revenues was partially offset by 205 million dollars in state aid and 103 million dollars from new or increased taxes. Libraries, parks and recreation, and maintenance of the physical plant were the areas hardest hit by the revenue loss. Fire and police services were generally maintained at pre-"13" levels. Full-time positions dropped by about 3 percent and part-time positions dropped about 7.5 percent. Some cities reported trouble in recruiting employees for high-demand technical skill areas because of inadequate pay levels and job uncertainty.

Local governments overall managed to get through the first year without severe financial crises. The two major questions remaining for local government are how long the state bailout program can continue to be funded by the existing state tax structure and how necessary improvements and replacement of aging physical facilities will be financed. The prognosis for state revenues is good as long as the state's economy remains healthy because revenues from the state income tax and sales tax will continue to grow with inflation. The question of maintaining the physical plants of local government is not as clearcut. Politically speaking, the deferring of maintenance is one of the easiest budget reductions to make because it does not offend any powerful special interest groups. However, the cumulative effect of these "easy-way-out" decisions can be devastating. The experience of many older eastern cities (New York City in particular) gives ample testimony to the folly of these kind of actions. The maintenance of the physical plant is one of the major problems local governments have yet to face seriously. It will have to be addressed in the years ahead. The longer they wait, the harder the problems will be to resolve.

In addition to its effects on local and state government, "13" had some strong effects on the California housing situation. Perhaps the most visible is a growing trend toward rent control. During the campaign large property owners and landlord groups promised that savings in property taxes would be passed on to renters. By and large, this promise was not kept in the months that followed the election. As a result, angry renters' associations demanded and in some cases got rent control measures passed by city councils. It is still too early to determine what the long-term effects of Proposition 13 will be on the rental market.

A second factor influencing the housing market is the increase in the cost of new construction due to rapidly escalating costs for construction permits and the necessity for larger cost reimbursement payments by contractors to cities. With the shortage of property tax revenue, cities are now starting to insist contractors pay the full costs of the additional public services required by new construction. Contractors must pass these added costs on to the home buyer. The result is another jump in the already inflated California real estate market.

In assessing the impact of Proposition 13, the most important question to ask is how the taxpayers feel about their monumental action in June of 1978. Indications are they are not happy with the business-as-usual attitude that many local government officials have taken. A measure of this unhappiness is the ease with which Paul Gann was able to qualify his "Spirit of 13" initiative for the ballot in June of 1980. While 553,000 signatures were needed to place the measure on the ballot, Gann's organization was able to raise over 900,000 signatures, the third highest number of signatures in California petition history. The "Spirit of 13" is essentially an expenditure limitation measure linking increases in state and local spending to changes in population and the federal Consumer Price Index. The new "13" also requires state government to provide full funding for any services or programs it mandates to local government. This provision would ease a long standing grievance of local governments over having to pay local funds for state mandated programs. Although some prominent state officials have already endorsed the "Spirit of 13" initiative, it is still too early to tell how it will fare in the upcoming election. (Note: The initiative was passed by a large margin in the November 1979 election.)

In addition to Gann's "Spirit of 13" initiative, there are two other initiatives that may appear on the June 1980 ballot. One of these, sponsored by Howard Jarvis, would have the effect of cutting the state's highly progressive income tax in half. The other would abolish the 6 percent state sales tax. Both of these illustrate an approach similar to the original "13," making massive cuts in taxes to keep more money in the taxpayer's pocket. The fate of these three initiatives at the ballot box will be the clearest statement of how taxpayers feel about their government in "post-13" California.

As a lesson for taxpayers in other states, Proposition 13 is instructive in a number of ways. First, it obviously was effective in cutting down the burden of a single tax. Property owners received real financial benefits from the property tax reduction although these were somewhat offset by the loss of deductions against the federal and state income taxes. Second, it has been relatively *ineffective* in reducing the scope and expense of local government. The state's massive infusion of cash and the Post Commission's avoidance of the key issues of economizing in government served to blunt "13's" attempt to reduce overall government expenditures by a significant amount. Voters got only some spot decreases in discretionary programs such as libraries, parks and recreation, and consumer protection services. These were singled out for reduction because they lacked powerful interest groups to protect them and because the state required as a condition of its bailout that fire, police, health, and welfare programs be maintained at close to their pre-"13" levels. Maintenance levels for the physical plants of local government were also hard hit. These maintenance savings are false savings that will come back to haunt taxpayers in the future as the physical plants of local government start to deteriorate prematurely.

"13" had a number of side effects. First, it increased the importance of user charges in local government finances. In accordance with the benefit principle of taxation, this trend must be viewed as an improvement because it helps to establish a more direct linkage between the service government provides and the costs the taxpayer must pay. Second, "13" went a long way toward resolving the problem of school funding. Court decisions required that educational funding move away from its reliance on the property tax toward more broadly based levies. The legislature had been trying to accomplish this with little success. The conditions attached to the state's bailout plan proved to be a practical resolution to the problem.

The major lesson of Proposition 13 lies in the process of taxpayers taking matters in their own hands. If the situation in California is a typical one, then the lesson is clear and simple. Whatever taxpayers want changed, they must change through the ballot box. There is little evidence to indicate that elected public officials are willing or able to reduce government programs and costs without the direct mandate of the people. There are those that will criticize this direct approach because they argue elections are not decided by a rational judgment on the facts of an issue. Rather, they argue, elections are decided by mass media appeal, by high-priced public relations firms, and by the emotional self-interest of the public at any given time. There is an element of truth in this argument. To make effective and positive changes in government, taxpayers must be better informed about the way government operates. They must take the time to learn the facts on both sides of an issue. But most of all, they must look a little beyond their own personal economic interest in order to see the overall public interest.

## NOTES

1. California Legislature, *Report of the Assembly-Senate Conference Committee on Implementation of Proposition 13*, June 1978.

2. California Legislature, Senate Office of Research, *Summary of Legislation Implementing Proposition 13*, July 10, 1978.

3. "The Post Commission Report: Recommendations and Analysis," *Tax Revolt Digest*, March 1979, Special Report.

4. The California Department of Finance, Department of General Services, Documents and Publications, *A Study of the Local Government Impacts of Proposition Thirteen*, Volumes I to IV, April 1979.

# 6 THE PROPERTY TAX LIMITATION MEASURES OF 1978

California's Proposition 13 was passed in the spring 1978 election. Although there were other important provisions, its most significant impact was on the local property tax. This emphasis on the local property tax was duplicated in tax reduction measures on the ballots of eight states during the November 1978 elections. Like Proposition 13, many of these measures had provisions relating to state and local government affecting far more than the local property tax. Nevertheless, they were treated by the public, the press, and the politicians as primarily property tax measures. In six of the eight states, there were clearcut victories for the tax revolt movement. Only in the State of Oregon and in a Maryland county did property tax reduction measures meet defeat. Even in these two instances, there were circumstances indicating the voters were not content with "business as usual" government. The situation in each of the states will be examined in turn, starting with the first of four Proposition 13 "look-alikes."


## IDAHO

Idaho is not a state that stands out during a review of state and local tax burdens. In 1977 it ranked 34th in state and local expenditures per capita ($847.00) out of the 50 states. In terms of the local property tax as a percentage of personal income, Idaho is in a four-way tie for 25th place with 3.4 percent. Although state and local taxes increased 43.9 percent in the four year period between 1973 and 1977, this increase was only enough to earn the taxpayers of

Idaho a ranking of 19th out of 50, far behind number one Alaska's astounding 364.8 percent increase in taxes over the same period. From the picture given by these statistics, Idaho does not seem to be fertile ground for a taxpayer revolt. Yet in the fall 1978 elections, the voters approved by a strong 56 percent to 44 percent margin a virtual duplicate of California's Proposition 13. How can this apparent contradiction be explained?

The answer lies in two words that readers of this book have seen before: "discontent" and "accessibility." Despite the fact that taxpayers in Idaho do not have an exceptionally heavy state and local tax burden, they bear the same high federal tax burden as other taxpayers and, therefore, are subject to the same economic sabotage at the hands of inflation. They undoubtedly perceive that their standard of living is eroding and that their future economic prospects are not what they once were. In addition to these feelings of economic discontent, the voters had the opportunity to make a clear and unambiguous statement about the sector of government they were most familiar with, a level of government whose primary source of revenue is a painful and obvious tax. Given the provocation and the opportunity, Idaho taxpayers joined many others in making a clearcut statement of what they wanted. This is what they voted for.

1. Restricted property taxes to a maximum of 1 percent of market value except for taxes necessary to pay off existing indebtedness. The market value of property (assessed valuation) may not be increased by more than 2 percent per year and must be decreased if the consumer price index goes down.

2. Any legislation designed to change taxes in order to increase revenues must be passed by a two-thirds vote. No new property taxes can be imposed by the legislature.

3. Counties and municipalities may impose special taxes only by a two-thirds vote of all qualified electors.

Idaho voters favored the same tough provisions as the Californians: rigid control of the amount of property taxes paid. They did not opt for halfway measures such as controls on the tax rate or assessed valuation. The legislature was stripped of the power to create new property taxes. The rough treatment given to property taxes again illustrates the vulnerability of a tax that is visible and painful. And finally, the voters imposed an almost impossible requirement for the creation of new local taxes: a two-thirds majority of those registered to vote as opposed to a majority of those voting.

It is unclear at the present time how much money the taxpayers saved themselves. The State Tax Commission has estimated property tax revenues will drop at least 60 percent. In 1977 property tax revenues were about 211 million dollars. Therefore, the savings should amount to about 126 million dollars. All this may sound too good to be true. In a sense, it is. There are a number of serious questions regarding implementation that must be resolved before the taxpayers get their savings.

One question is: when does the measure take effect? The wording on the ballot specified October 1, 1979. That seems simple enough, how could there be a question? Easily! The tax year in Idaho starts on January 1st. Therefore, the legislature must wrestle with the question of when the new tax law takes effect. Proposals being considered range from a retroactive effective date of January 1, 1979 to January 1, 1980, which would not give the authorized tax relief until two years after the election.

There is a second question that the legislature must decide. In Idaho, as in other states, the counties are the unit of government responsible for the actual collection of the property tax. Before the election each local government added its tax rate to the amount the county collected. The tax rate determined the income the government received. The new tax reform permits only a 1 percent maximum. Therefore, the legislature must decide how the 1 percent will be divided. In all probability the 1 percent will be distributed on the same basis as the revenues received during the previous tax year. Therefore, those governments with the highest level of tax effort before the election will receive a proportionately higher share of the limited revenue. Those local governments with a lower tax effort will have to rely more heavily on state and federal aid or make more drastic cuts in programs and services.

A third question being considered is whether the state government should attempt to provide financial assistance to the stricken local governments. Unlike California, Idaho does not possess a large surplus of state funds. Therefore a state bailout of the local governments would mean either new state taxes or major cuts in state programs. Another alternative is to seek federal support for the local governments. This approach would be difficult because of Idaho's relatively small population and correspondingly small amount of political clout in Washington.

Of course, if all else fails, local governments can cut operations. This is what should happen. The taxpayers have asked for a tax cut, or rather, they have given themselves one. Therefore, they have the obligation to assist their local governments in determining the priorities necessary to convert tax cuts into budget cuts. The taxpayer who believes the loss of 126 million dollars out of 211 million dollars can be made up by increased efficiency and better management had better think again. The alternatives available to the Idaho taxpayer (as well as others) are discussed in a subsequent chapter. It is the responsibility of those organizations that led the fight for the tax cut to also lead the effort to get citizens involved with their local governments' efforts to decide how to respond to this massive loss of revenue.

## NEVADA

Taxpayers in Nevada voting in the fall 1978 elections found themselves in a unique situation. They were about to vote on a Proposition 13 look-alike measure. If it passed, it would not become an amendment to the state constitution as had happened in California; but rather, it would be an advisory message to the political leadership of the state. While sending messages to politicians via the voting booth is not unique, the ability to enforce the message is. In this case, the Nevada taxpayers have a very strong hand. The state's constitution requires that any amendment to the constitution added by the initiative process must be approved by the voters in two consecutive elections. Nevadans approved their tax cutting measure by an overwhelming three to one margin. They are now waiting to see if the legislature will respond to this message. If they are not satisfied with the legislative action in the fall of 1980, they have the opportunity to add the measure to the Nevada constitution.

The voters have spoken and given the legislature a chance to act. This is what they got. Governor Robert List took the lead with the state legislature and together they produced a $244 million dollar tax reduction package. The package is funded with a surplus in the state funds produced by the rapid growth of the state's two major industries—gambling and tourism. (In 1978 the state enjoyed a surplus of 168 million dollars in a budget of just over one billion dollars.) The tax cut package included the following major provisions.

1. A 27 percent reduction in property taxes as well as a provision for passing some of the tax savings on to renters. (A problem that California has yet to solve.)

2. The legislature urged the voters to eliminate the sales tax on food. They did by a four to one margin in a June election.

3. Expenditure limitations were placed on state and local spending. The basis for the limitations is the previous year's spending level plus provisions for increases based upon population growth, inflation, and emergency factors.

4. Part of the state's revenue from county real estate and gambling taxes was transferred to cities and counties to help offset the loss of property tax revenues. School districts are to receive increased state aid to help offset their revenue losses.

At this time it is not clear how Nevada voters are reacting to these changes. The "second-time-around" election in the fall of 1980 will give the verdict on how well the legislature and the governor have understood the desires of the taxpayers. Also, the taxpayers will have time to see if they like the reduced level of services they are going to have as a result of the tax cut package. State spending will increase only 10 percent, not enough to compensate for increased population and inflation. Education and welfare agencies are facing a significant reduction in their budgets and personnel. Even with state aid, local governments will probably have to reduce their operations and budgets. Taxpayers have the unparalleled opportunity to experience the benefits and costs of a modest reduction before making their final decision on major tax surgery.

Because of this two-step approval process and the time allowed for legislative action, the Nevada situation is a real testing ground for the power and longevity of the feelings fueling the taxpayer revolt. What happens on that election day in 1980 can, in part, be attributed to the economic conditions in the country. If inflation continues to run high, if major tax cuts are not forth coming from Washington, if the recession continues to deepen, there is a good chance that Nevada taxpayers will return to the polls angrier than ever—not necessarily with their own state or local governments, but with their overall economic condition. Thus, the issue at the polls will be confused. Are the taxpayers dissatisfied with what the legislature did? Or are they striking out at the closest available target they can find? Only time will provide the answer.

## OREGON

Native residents of the state of Oregon are well known for their aversion to anything that smacks of "California." In the opinion of some onlookers, this may have been part of the reason for the narrow defeat of the Proposition 13 look-alike, Measure 6, in the November 1978 elections. Measure 6, defeated by a close 52 percent to 48 percent margin, was identical to Proposition 13 except the maximum tax rate allowed was 1.5 percent of assessed value rather than 1 percent as in California.

A more likely reason for the close defeat of "6" was the presence of another competing measure on the ballot. Measure 11 was placed on the ballot by the state legislature under the leadership of the then incumbent governor, Robert Straub. Measure 11 provided a milder form of property tax relief and spending limits on the state general fund tied to the rate of growth in Oregon's total personal income. Measure 11 was defeated by a larger margin than "6," 55 percent to 45 percent. In a parallel election, Governor Straub was defeated by Victor Atiyeh, a state legislator who was a leading proponent of Measure 6.

Because both "6" and "11" were defeated, no tax reductions resulted from the election. Not because the people didn't want them, but because the tax issue got confused with a number of other factors. First, the presence of two separate measures on the ballot tended to confuse some voters. Second, Oregon pride could have played a significant role in the close defeat of "6."

Even more interesting is a comparison of the tax structures of Oregon and California. In contrast to California, Oregon has no state sales tax. Additionally, Oregon has an effective property tax relief program for senior citizens and low income home owners. These two groups, well treated in Oregon, were two of the major support groups for Proposition 13 in California. Another problem that contributed to the defeat of Measure 6 was the incompatability of its provisions (virtually copied from "13") with the Oregon constitution. The state attorney general was asked to give opinions on some 50 possibly contradictory points. Several of these major conflicts contributed to the legislature's reasoning in developing Measure 11 as an alternative. The tax revolt movement cannot count the Oregon election as a victory, but there are lessons to be learned from the experience.

Perhaps the first and most important point is enthusiasm does not substitute for organization. The constitutional conflicts in "6" almost certainly contributed to its downfall in the November election. Also, these conflicts encouraged the legislature to put the competing Measure 11 on the ballot, thus confusing the issue for many voters. Even the strongest proponents of "6" had to promise to ask the legislature to clean up the language enough to make it workable. A home-drawn provision would have been much better and would have not produced the strong anti-California reaction that may have been a significant factor at the polls. The second point to be considered is whether or not the property tax was the appropriate part of the tax structure to attack. It may have been that focusing on the limitation of state and local expenditures or on reductions in the income tax would have been more appropriate. If those who backed "6" and "11" could have agreed on a common set of reforms, the measures undoubtedly would have passed.

In the final analysis, too much enthusiasm, lack of organization, and competition were the factors that spelled defeat for the taxpayer revolt. It is too early to tell if the message of the revolt will be heeded by Oregon's state and local officials. If they choose to ignore it, it is quite likely that taxpayers will find a way to make their feelings known. And this time they may well be successful.

## MICHIGAN

If Oregon voters felt they were totally confused by having two tax cutting measures on the same ballot, they should have journeyed to the state of Michigan at election time. On the ballot were three separate constitutional amendments. All of them could make some claim to being tax reform measures. Only one of them was enacted.

Proposal J had many things in common with California's Proposition 13. It would have cut property taxes in half, but would have replaced some of the lost income with a 1 percent increase in the state income tax. Its supporters were characterized in the press as grass roots, tax rebels. "J" was almost universally opposed by local and state officials as well as business and organized labor. As might be expected in a state where business and labor working together are overpowering, "J" did poorly at the polls.

A second proposal, dealing primarily with education, "C" would have instituted a voucher system in lieu of the existing funding mechanism. The essentials of the proposal provided that parents would receive vouchers from the state they could use to send their children to the school of their choice, whether public or private. At best it was a roundabout method of property tax reform, and its critics called it a poorly disguised scheme to get public funding for private schools. It was soundly defeated by more than a three to one margin.

Proposal E was the lone winner among the three measures. The major provision of "E" was not related to property tax at all. Instead, it limited the amount of revenue the state could collect and spend to approximately 9 percent of the total personal income of Michigan residents. This was about equal to current levels of taxing and expenditure. Increases are allowed only as personal income levels increase in the state. "E" also limited increases in the local property taxes to no more than the national rate of inflation. The figure of 7.7 percent was used for 1978. Also, voter approval was required for the enactment of any new taxes by local government. A similar restriction applied to the state, except if revenues from a new tax were offset by a decrease in revenues from another existing tax. Finally, the state was required to pay for any new programs or services it mandated local governments to provide. Proposal E was supported by business groups and government officials. Its opponents were primarily labor unions and human services groups. "E" won by only a narrow margin on election day.

If the election was difficult for "E's" supporters, implementation was to prove even more so. The major problems were working out the details of controlling the property tax and deciding which local government programs the state would have to support financially. As late as six months after the election these issues still had not been resolved and taxpayers were still waiting for tax relief. It is ironic that Proposal E drafted by politicians and government officials seems as unworkable as the citizen-drafted Measure 6 in Oregon. The only difference being that "E" was passed and "6" was not.

Even when "E's" implementation problems are worked out, it is unlikely that taxpayers will get any real measure of relief because the controls on state spending and taxation as well as those on the property tax are based upon tax levels existing at the time of the election, and they can be adjusted upward with inflation and growth in personal income. The best taxpayers can hope for is that their future tax increases will be moderate.

Michigan voters allowed themselves to be convinced that a "moderate and reasonable" tax reform as defined by their government officials would actually give them some relief. They have yet to see any relief and it is doubtful that they will in the near future. Reflecting back to the model presented in the first chapter, there is no reason to believe that government officials are any more capable of reducing the scope of government spending and taxation by the initiative process than they are by the legislative process. While Michigan may not be counted as a victory for the taxpayer movement, it clearly demonstrates the need for taxpayers to take direct action if they are serious about reducing the scope and costs of government.

## PROPERTY TAX LIMITATION MEASURES
## IN OTHER STATES

There were four other property tax limitation measures put before the public in the November 1978 elections. Three of these passed.

The measure that failed was a local ordinance in Montgomery County, Maryland that would have drastically reduced the local property taxes. Its loss by a small margin may be partially explained by the fact that the affluent county has a large number of highly paid federal bureaucrats among its population. These are not the kind of people that would approve of drastic tax cut measures due to their "insider" view of government operations. Of the eight property tax reduction measures on the November ballot, only this one was clearly defeated without the confusion created by competing measures. The details of the three successful measures are described below.

### Alabama

The residents of the state of Alabama had to decide on a constitutional amendment designed to prevent large increases in the local property tax. Alabama already had one of the lowest property tax burdens in the 50 states. Although the measure limits the property tax on residences to 1 percent of the assessed value, this represents a small increase over the existing tax rate. The amendment was placed on the ballot by the state legislature in reaction to a court ordered reassessment of all residential property in the state. This reassessment could have resulted in massive increases in the property tax. Alabama is one instance where elected officials took effective action to limit large tax increases. It would have been very interesting to see if they would have been able to show the same ability when faced with the necessity for cutting taxes. As pointed out in the model presented in Chapter One, it is easier for elected officials to hold the line on spending and taxation than it is to make significant reductions.

### Massachusetts

Voters in Massachusetts approved a measure by a two-to-one margin providing substantial reductions in property taxes ranking among the highest in the nation. The measure struck down a court decision prohibiting separate assessment procedures for business and residential property. The way is now cleared for shifting part of the residential tax burden to business and commercial enterprises. Additionally, the measure provided for a $5,000 exemption in assessments for homeowners. The exemption reduces property taxes by eliminating the first $5,000 of assessed property value from the tax base. As a result of the reduced assessment the amount of tax owed is reduced.

Tax reform was also a factor in the gubernatorial race in which Edward J. King, a strong supporter of the tax reduction measure, defeated Republican opponent Francis Hatch by more than 100,000 votes. Although the Republican party has been traditionally associated with a conservative approach to government spending, it appears that, in this instance at least, party affiliation was not a clear guide in determining where the candidates stood on the issue. This message from Massachusetts is quite clear: Taxpayers cannot predict a politician's stance on tax reduction issues based upon party affiliation. Citizens who are serious about reducing taxes and government spending will have to be prepared to switch parties frequently to encourage the candidacies of officials who are willing and able to work for tax and spending reform.

### Missouri

Voters in Missouri passed a constitutional amendment giving the legislature the authority to reduce property tax assessments. The measure is designed to keep property assessments and, therefore, taxes from rising rapidly. The measure is unique because it makes no changes in the property tax directly, but rather provides authorization for elected officials to keep taxes from getting too high. In addition to passing this measure by a two to one margin, voters also turned down a number of bond issues that would have increased spending and taxation.

### THE PROPERTY TAX IN PERSPECTIVE

The election results of 1978 clearly demonstrate that property tax reduction was an important and successful part of the taxpayer revolt. The passage of Proposition 13 in California was clearly the catalytic factor in many of the November 1978 elections. Because the property tax is so obvious and painful a tax, it was a prime target for taxpayers who felt they had enough of big government and an increasing tax burden. While reduction of the property tax burden was clearly a prime target for taxpayers in 1978, there were more issues involved than just this single tax.

The election in California clearly showed that voters wanted more than a reduction in the propety tax. They wanted a slowdown in government spending and taxation. The question is: Did they get it?

Is attacking the property tax an effective means to reducing government spending and taxation overall? The answer to this question must be negative. Most of the response to "13's" passage was directed toward finding a way to replace the revenues that were lost. With the exception of Governor Brown's attempts to control increases in state spending, there was little evidence of elected officials giving more than lip service to the broader message conveyed by "13." The inaction of the Post Commission on the major issues had to have been a great disappointment to taxpayers. The majority of government officials proved themselves to be either unwilling or unable (for the reasons explained in Chapter One) to make any significant decreases in government operations.

To be sure there have been some reductions in budgets and services, but generally they were in those areas that lacked support from strong special interest groups such as libraries, and parks and recreation programs. The big spending areas of police, fire, welfare, health, and primary and secondary education were relatively untouched. The huge surplus the state accumulated through its progressive tax structure was used to keep most activities on a business as usual basis.

The gutting of the so-called discretionary programs (libraries, parks and recreation, and consumer protection) deserves special attention. These programs have no well-organized, well-financed support groups to defend them. Moreover, their activities are not directly related to the health and the protection of people or property. Therefore, they had to bear the brunt of whatever budget cuts were made. In many instances, their services were for all practical purposes eliminated. This is an unfortunate, but inevitable result of the taxpayer revolt.

Even though taxpayers never rose up and said, "let's do away with these services," the public officials saw that these areas would be the easiest to cut. The areas taxpayers were unhappy with such as welfare, general administration overhead, and health costs, were untouched compared to the cuts suffered by the so-called discretionary activities. As a result, even though citizens got their property tax cut, the major spending areas of government were not significantly affected. The areas that were affected were those providing valuable, but not critical, services to the majority of citizens.

In addition to inflicting drastic budget cuts, government officials failed to make provisions to continue these services by alternate means. Although some fees for recreational activities were raised, there was little or no systematic attention to the preservation of these services. If taxpayers want to continue these services, then some provision should be made for their financing either through user charges reflecting the actual cost associated with the service or by setting up these services as entrepreneural activities independent of the government units sponsoring them.

As separate entities, they would be out of the control of elected officials who seem to view them only as sacrificial offerings to irate taxpayers. They would offer their services to the public and the public would make the choice of whether or not they were willing to pay the cost associated with the service. The level of community support these activities received would determine the level of services they could offer. There is an additional advantage to the taxpayers in this kind of arrangement. Local officials would not be able to avoid reducing the budgets of the big-spending, well-defined programs by cutting those programs lacking powerful interest groups to defend them.

Thus far the discussion has focused primarily on the reduction of the property tax and related reductions in government spending. Little has been said about appropriate levels of property taxation and the services that property tax revenues should support. The previous examination of the property tax revealed that it is based primarily on the benefit theory of taxation; that is, those benefiting from a service should pay for it. The relevant question is what services of local government directly benefit the owners of real property. There are some obvious answers. Fire protection, zoning and land use planning, local road construction and maintenance, utility services including sewage, building and safety code enforcement, libraries, and parks and recreation programs are the services most commonly thought of as benefits to property owners and indirectly to renters. Some may question the exclusion of education from this list.

In earlier times, education was considered a beneficial service to property owners. However, the economic development of the United States over the last 30 years has demonstrated that the benefits of education accrue not only to the community, but to the state and the nation overall. The majority of the economic benefits of education go to the public at large and not to the local property owner. Therefore, according to the benefit principle of taxation, the property owner should not have to pay a majority of the costs of education. This position is reinforced by recent court decisions requiring educational funding to be accomplished through broader taxation of the public as a whole, rather than relying exclusively on the property tax.

Services that directly benefit property owners should be supported by property tax revenues unless they are funded on a fee-for-service basis. The decision of how to finance service should be made at the local level in order to take into account the desires and particular situation of the community. Taxpayers should not expect to get these services for free. Taxpayers must be willing to bear the cost of the services they want. In paying for services they have the right to expect government to operate with a reasonable degree of efficiency and effectiveness. Taxpayers have a right to expect their elected officials to represent their interests rather than being preoccupied with reelection. Lastly, the use of property tax revenues ought to be restricted insofar as possible to the provision of services directly related to property. For services with benefits more general in nature, revenues should come from taxes having broader base such as the income and sales taxes.

In the last two chapters the focus has been on the property tax as a vehicle for expressing taxpayer unrest. There is another approach that has not been discussed thus far. It is the limitation of expenditures made by state and local governments. The upcoming chapter will examine the experiences of several states with this facet of the taxpayer revolt.

# 7 NEW LIMITS ON STATE AND LOCAL EXPENDITURES

The taxpayer revolt is an indication of widespread dissatisfaction with the scope and quality of government operations. Specifically, taxpayers feel government is taking too much of their personal income through taxation. Additionally, they feel government is generally wasteful in its operations and that its inordinately high level of spending is a significant contributory factor to the fast rising inflation of the late 1970s and early 1980s.

The taxpayer revolt has focused on two major means of controlling and reducing the scope of government in American economic life. The most drastic of the two, tax limitation and reduction, has been discussed in the two previous chapters. The second means of controlling the scope of government activity is the topic of this chapter.

Government, like any other organization, has two sides to its financial structure: income and expenditure. It is the expenditure side of government that is the focus of attention here. Limitations on expenditure are designed to bring future relief to taxpayers by decreasing the proportion of income going into taxation. This can be achieved only if growth in government expenditures is slower than growth in personal income. Based upon the past patterns of growth in government expenditures and on the inherent difficulties facing government officials whenever they attempt to curb increased spending, it is safe to assume that unless effective expenditure limitations are enacted, government will continue to take a larger and larger portion of the earnings of every citizen. The only other way to control the growth of government is to force drastic reductions in the sales and income taxes. As of the end of the 1970s, expenditure limitation appears to be the most popular and practical of the two means of control.

## PRINCIPLES OF EXPENDITURE

Prior to a discussion of the means available to limit government expenditures, it is necessary to acquire a basic understanding of the principles of government expenditure. The first principle of expenditure is controllability. The naive citizen might make the assumption that all government expenditures are under the control of elected officials. This is simply not true. Every unit of government has certain expenditures it is required to make and which are beyond its control. These expenditures usually result from previous legal commitments made by the government. In terms of sheer size, the most important of these uncontrollable expenditures is the servicing and retirement of public debt. Almost every unit of government has debt outstanding in the form of bonds. Bonds represent money borrowed from private sources on which interest must be paid. Also, the principle or amount of money originally borrowed must be repaid. Expenditures for the payment of interest and principle are beyond the control of elected officials. These expenditures must be made or a fiscal crisis will occur and payment forced by court order. The only way these expenditures can be controlled is at the time the bonds are issued. Once issued, the expenditures imposed by the bonds are fixed.

A second type of uncontrollable expenditure involves payments to public employee retirement systems. Generally, these systems are funded on a shared basis, with the employee paying part of the cost and the government employer paying its share. While the details of the government payment will vary from system to system, in all cases the payments are expenditures that must be made. If they are not made, their payment may be enforced by court order. Control over these expenditures can only be achieved in two ways, and neither is a part of the regular budgetary process. Obviously, when the retirement system is created the structure of the benefits and the share to be paid by the employer determines what the future cost will be. Implementation of retirement systems should always be preceded by a thorough study of the long term costs likely to be incurred. From time to time, the benefit structure of retirement systems must be revised to take into account unanticipated factors such as growth in the number of employees and high rates of inflation. Revision of benefit structures offers an opportunity for the control of future costs of the retirement system. Other than these two instances, control over the expenditures required for retirement systems is beyond the capacity of the government official or the taxpayer.

A third type of uncontrollable expenditure is less clearcut than the first two. There are certain services that governments are required to provide by virtue of either constitutional provision or legal mandate. Usually these service requirements will not include specification of the quality and quantity of service. Because cost is directly affected by the quality and quantity of a service, it is not easy to determine what percent of the expenditures for a required service is uncontrollable. While everyone may agree a service cannot be eliminated, there is usually little agreement on the minimum required expenditure level.

Between expenditures that are uncontrollable and those that are fully controllable, there lies a middle ground composed of expenditures that do not fit easily into either of the first two categories. These expenditures are those supported by earmarked revenues from fees, charges, or excise taxes. Earmarked revenues may be used for only a specific purpose. Therefore, their collection creates an obligation for expenditure. This obligation is often not a legalistic one, but rather a matter of practical politics. While earmarked funds can be spent for no purpose other than the one specified, in many instances they do not have to be expended at all. However, not spending them will create an intolerable situation wherein money is being collected for a specific service not being provided. This occurs only on very rare occasions.

These areas of semicontrollable expenditures may often be identified by the existence of special financial arrangements such as revolving funds. A revolving fund is a device used to separate a group of revenues and expenditures from the general financial activity of a government unit. The revenues generated are used to make the expenditures necessary to provide a service. Reducing these semicontrollable expenditures usually requires a reduction or elimination of the source of the earmarked revenues. Reducing the yield of taxes or fees and charges is something that comes very hard to all government officials. Even if it can be done, it is a very time consuming and difficult process. Summarizing, semicontrollable expenditures are those requiring reductions in revenue in order to bring about any reduction in expenditure.

The preceding paragraphs have described expenditures that are not controllable or are not subject to direct control. To reverse the approach taken so far, how does one identify controllable expenditures? First, the legal basis for the expenditure should be examined. Is the expenditure required by law or is it merely permitted by law?

If it is to support an activity that the government *may* perform but does not have to perform, then the expenditure involved is likely to be controllable. A second point to consider is the source of revenues used to fund the expenditure. An expenditure funded from the general revenues of the government unit is not likely to be subject to the earmarking constraints discussed earlier. A third point for examination is the manner in which previous expenditure decisions have been made. Areas of controllable expenditure will be regularly examined as part of the legislative decision-making process. It is highly unusual for an expenditure area to shift from being controllable to uncontrollable.

General limitations of the expenditures of a state or local government usually apply only to those classified as controllable. Exceptions generally must be made for the funding of areas beyond the reach of the normal decision-making process. The effectiveness of expenditure limitation measures in reducing the tax burden is dependent on the percentage of a government's expenditures subject to control. A governmental unit having a very high level of outstanding debt or having a large assortment of earmarked revenues will be less effected by an expenditure limitation measure than a similar unit whose expenditures are highly controllable.

## TYPES OF LIMITATIONS

Just as there are different kinds of expenditures, there are also different ways to limit expenditures. Four of the most common means will be discussed here. Any of these types of limitations may be imposed through a constitutional amendment or by action of the legislative body. In the case of local governments, a charter amendment may serve the same purpose as a constitutional amendment. Limitations imposed by legislative action may be very ineffective because they can be changed or altered easily by legislative action. They do not provide the same kind of guarantee to the taxpayer as constitutionally mandated limitations. The types of limitation described below apply only to those expenditures that are controllable. They generally do not apply to expenditures classified as noncontrollable or to expenditures paid for from earmarked revenues.

The simplest type of expenditure limitation is one using a flat percentage of the previous year's budget to control increases. For example, an expenditure limitation measure allowing increases of 7 percent over the previous year's budget is considered to be a flat percent limitation because that 7 percent holds regardless of the rate of inflation, changes in population, or fluctuations in relevant economic indicators. The advantage to this approach in addition to being simple is that it offers the taxpayer a guarantee of holding down the size of government expenditure and of controlling increases in the tax burden. A disadvantage is that it may render governments incapable of responding to large increases in population. Increased population demands a higher level of government expenditure and also generates higher tax revenues without increasing any individual's tax burden. A flat percentage limitation is generally not a good idea for an area anticipating significant increases in population.

A second type of expenditure limitation is one linked to the inflation rate. Control on expenditure is exercised by limiting yearly increases to the adjusted rate of inflation for the previous year. Usually some generally recognized measure such as the Consumer Price Index is used to determine the rate of inflationary increase allowed. The idea is for existing levels of service to be maintained in the face of higher costs. Proponents of this approach to expenditure limitation use the assumption that increases in taxes will be held to the rate of inflation. Governments (with a progressive income tax) will soon find themselves accumulating cash surpluses because of the "inflation tax" phenomenon described earlier. About the only advantage to the taxpayer in this approach is that it offers some assurance that the costs of government while not less than the rate of inflation will not be any greater. The over-burdened taxpayer may find this to be a small comfort, indeed. From the point of view of the government officials and public labor organizations, this is a good kind of limitation to have (if there must be one at all) because it guarantees business as usual will continue to prevail except for fewer increases in programs and services.

A third approach to expenditure limitation involves tying budgetary increases to a percentage of the total personal income generated within the geographic boundaries of the governmental unit. The percentage chosen may either be the existing ratio of government expenditure to personal income or it may be some new figure decided upon by the public or the legislative body. For instance, if the first approach is used, government expenditures may amount to 8 percent of the total personal income generated in the area. This percentage must be maintained in future years. So if income increases, then government expenditure may increase by a similar amount. If personal income decreases, then government expenditure must also decrease. For every dollar increase or decrease in total personal income, government expenditure may increase or decrease by 8 cents.

If the existing ratio is not used, then some appropriate percentage must be decided upon. Although the potential for greatly reducing (or expanding) government expenditures exists with this method, it is quite likely whatever ratio is decided upon will closely approximate the current level of expenditure. The assumption behind this approach is that some optimum percent of total income ought to be utilized for government services. The main advantage to this approach is the taxpayer receives some assurances against the runaway growth of government expenditures. However, it is extremely unlikely this approach will result in any significant decrease in the tax burden.

There is a serious disadvantage to this approach when applied to state and large local governments. In times of severe recession or depression, personal income will fall in direct proportion to the severity of the recession or depression. This means government expenditures must also fall. Most economists say this is exactly the opposite of what government should be doing. In bad times, the government is expected to provide an economic stimulus by providing jobs and various forms of direct assistance. An expenditure limitation tied to personal income would prevent this kind of action. Overall, there does not appear to be any particular advantage to this kind of an approach over the other two discussed thus far. Probably the only reason this approach has any popularity at all is that limiting expenditures to a percent of total personal income has a basic appeal because of its political payoff if used properly.

The final type of expenditure limitation to be discussed is an approach linking the amount of money spent to the amount of revenue available to the government, in other words, a "balanced budget" approach. Most state and local governments are prohibited from operating at a planned deficit in their budgetary projections. These prohibitions do not prevent the accumulation of large surpluses such as happened in California or from actually ending the fiscal year in the red if revenue projections were faulty. The main advantage to the taxpayer in the balanced budget approach is that it guarantees governments will not operate at a "profit," accumulating large surpluses of funds that properly belong in the taxpayer's pocket. On the national level, there are other advantages to the balanced budget approach because the federal government has no limit on deficit spending other than a legislatively imposed debt ceiling that Congress continually finds reasons to increase. In most instances, the balanced budget approach offers the taxpayer no promise of decreased tax burdens or of limiting government spending. Therefore, for taxpayer groups to advocate the balanced budget makes sense only at the national level or for the sole purpose of eliminating huge surpluses of funds.

No matter what form limitation takes, it is almost always accompanied by an emergency provision that can be used to authorize expenditures above the maximum level permitted by law. These provisions are necessary in order for governments to be able to deal with extraordinary circumstances such as flood, earthquake, tornado, and other disasters. While necessary, these emergency provisions may also be the source of efforts by government officials to circumvent expenditure limits. In some instances, these emergency provisions are structured so loosely that they are constantly in use to provide extra spending authorization for routine items. When this practice occurs, taxpayers have no protection from uncontrolled growth in government spending and taxation.

Another point should be made about expenditure limitations. An increasingly important part of state and local government revenues comes from intergovernmental transfers of funds, or subventions as they are sometimes called. Since these revenues are generated from outside the jurisdiction of the government unit, should they be subject to the expenditure limitation? On the surface, the answer to this question may appear to be an easy "yes." In actuality, it is very difficult for governments to turn down "free" dollars. These dollars represent an opportunity for the state or local government to provide an increased level of service to its citizens without a direct increase in the tax burden. Even the most disillusioned taxpayer might find it difficult to turn down a tempting offer such as many of these subventions provide.

There is a negative side to these "gifts." Perhaps the most important negative aspect of these subventions is some of them have provisions requiring a gradual takeover of the service or program by the local government. Second, subventions may have conditions the receiving government must conform to in order to be eligible for the funds. These conditions will tend to reduce the autonomy of the government and its decisionmakers. Therefore, subventions can increase the percentage of government expenditures that is uncontrollable. In view of these negative side effects of subventions, it is clear that funds of this type should be included within any expenditure limitation provisions.

In terms of applicability, there are some distinct differences in applying expenditure limitations to state and local governments. Many of these differences stem from the fact that local governments are political subdivisions of the state and thus are subject to many laws and regulations.

One of the most significant differences involves the practice of mandating. By mandating, states require local government units to provide some particular kind of program or service. In some instances the state will also provide the funds to support the mandated activity. In other instances local governments have to find the funds to pay for the activity on their own. Regardless of the source of funding, mandating can easily lead to conflict with local government expenditure limitations. For instance, if a state decided to turn over all unemployment programs to local government and provided the necessary funding, this increased level of expenditure would probably exceed any limit on increases the local government might have. This kind of conflict can cause no end of trouble for the local government, and yet nothing will have been accomplished for the local taxpayers because their tax burden is not affected at all.

Mandating can also affect state expenditure limitation because it can be used as a means for states to avoid their own expenditure limits. What the state can do is require local government to operate a certain program, provide the funds required for the program, and thus allow the program and its funding to "escape" from the expenditure limitation. This kind of escape has implications for the state taxpayers who may be relying on the expenditure limitation controls to lessen the growth of their tax burden. The state can still use its taxes to pay for the program, but the program escapes the expenditure limit by being mandated to local governments who either have to absorb it within their limit or exclude it from limitation provisions. This escape process is even easier in a situation where the state government has an expenditure limitation, but the local governments in the state do not.

Another problem local governments have in applying expenditure limitations relates to their relatively small size. Many smaller size governments have a difficult time predicting extraordinary population changes that might effect their expenditure limitation. Also, smaller governments with their limited resources may have difficulty dealing with emergency situations because they are less able to absorb these unanticipated costs in their budgets and expenditure limits. States generally can be more accurate in their population predictions and have a greater ability to absorb the cost of emergency operations.

Still another problem arising from expenditure limits on local government involves the very process of adopting the limits. In general, local government operations are governed one of two ways, either by a charter granted by the state or by a set of general laws passed by the state. Local government charters usually have provisions for changes that can be made by the local citizenry. Such a change is not unlike changing the constitution of a state. Local governments governed by a set of general laws present problems of implementation. These general laws may not provide the flexibility for citizens to enact their own expenditure limitations. If this flexibility does not exist, the limitations can only be imposed by changing the general laws governing all local governments in the state. This approach obviously presents problems because of the wide differences in needs and resources to be found in the local governments within a given state. In general, expenditure limitations have a better chance of being effective at the state rather than at the local level. Taxpayers seeking relief in their tax burdens at the local level are probably better off using limits on taxation.

Thus far, expenditure limitations have been discussed only in the abstract. There have been a number of states using expenditure limitation measures for quite some time. Other states recently passed such measures in the November 1978 election. In the following paragraphs, the experiences of some of these states are examined.

## ARIZONA

In the November 1978 election voters approved a constitutional amendment limiting state spending to 7 percent of the total personal income reported in the state. The measure was placed on the ballot by the legislature. The legislature also enacted implementing legislation prior to the election. As a result there have been few implementation problems. The amendment creates an Economic Estimates Commission having the responsibility for estimating the total personal income figure for each fiscal year. This figure determines what the level of state spending will be. The enabling legislation provides a specific definition of "state spending" encompassing only state tax revenues. This definition is reproduced below.

> ...means the revenue of the state for its own use from licenses, fees, and permits, and from state taxes on property, income, transaction privilege and use, excise, fuel, luxury privilege, insurance premiums, estates, gifts, motor carriers, pari-mutual, compensation insurance, watercraft licenses, bingo receipts, boxing and wrestling receipts and all other state taxes levied and collected for its use. State tax revenue does *not* include federal, private or other grants, gifts, aids, and contributions, nor trust and agency funds, intrastate service funds, bond funds, endowment earnings, nor revenues from sales and services, dividends, interest, nor gifts collected by the state for distribution to counties and incorporated cities and towns. (emphasis added)[1]

Using this definition, the expenditure limitation applies only to the expenditure of state tax monies yielded by taxes, fees, and charges. It does not include the expenditure of funds coming from subventions or earmarked taxes going into trust or agency funds. The definition used in the implementing legislation clearly indicates the purpose of the limitation amendment: to control the spending of state tax revenues and thereby control the tax burden on the citizens of the state. The amendment also provides for changes in the expenditure limit in the event programs are moved out of state government to local or federal jurisdiction or if programs are picked up by the state government from local government. These transfers only cause changes in the limit if the taxes of the other government unit involved are adjusted accordingly. A sample statement from the amendment is given below.

> If, by order of any court or by legislative enactment, the costs of a program are transferred from a political subdivision of this state to the state, the appropriation percentage limitation may be commensurately increased provided the tax revenues of the affected political subdivisions are commensurately decreased.[2]

This example demonstrates the intent of the legislature and the people to control the tax burden within the state. If the state expenditure limit is to be increased by the transfer of a program from local government, then the local government must decrease its tax burden accordingly. Ideally, there will be no change in the overall tax burden.

This amendment appears to accomplish its intended goal of limiting increases in the state tax burden. However, this measure does not reduce the current level of taxation because the 7 percent level is approximately what the state of Arizona was spending prior to the election. If tax control rather than tax reduction was the goal of Arizona citizens voting for the measure, they appear to have gotten what they wanted.

As discussed earlier, limitations tied to personal income can create a problem in times of recession or depression unless provisions are made for exceeding the limit. The Arizona amendment has such a provision. The legislature, by a two-thirds majority of the membership in each house, may override the spending limit set by the Economic Estimates Commission. Although the intent of the override provision is for emergency use only, there is nothing in the amendment preventing the legislature from voting overrides whenever it chooses. Although it could be argued that such irresponsible behavior is controlled by the threat of defeat at the polls, the argument is difficult to accept because it means a full two-thirds of the legislature would have to be turned out of office. This would be an almost impossible task and, of course, legislators are aware of this. Therefore, the threat of being turned out of office is not strong enough to prevent irresponsible legislative behavior.

A more realistic type of override provision is one requiring a vote by the electorate to override the expenditure limit. Legislators might well argue that such elections take too long to provide an adequate response to emergencies. Because most emergencies requiring an override are likely to be of an economic nature and thus gradual in development, there is no reason to believe the few months required for a special election would constitute an undue delay. The choice between the two override provisions ultimately rests on the amount of trust taxpayers have in the actions of their government officials.

In Arizona it may be possible to get a preview of the legislature's actions regarding the use of the override provision by examining what has happened with the expenditure limitation measures in force for Arizona local governments since 1921. In that year state lawmakers made Arizona the first state in the union to adopt expenditure limitations for local government. The legislature decreed that city and county budgets could not increase by more than 10 percent from year to year. This limit is much more restrictive than the recently passed state limit because there is no provision for either inflation or increases in population. The total personal income guide used in the state limitation accommodates the effects of inflation as well as population growth.

Given the high rate of inflation and population growth in Arizona over the last 60 years, it should come as no surprise that local government officials are very adept at finding ways to get around the limit. One of the major means of getting around the expenditure limit has been to persuade the courts and the legislature to exclude certain types of budgetary expenditures. At the current time only about one-half of the local government budget in Arizona is subject to the expenditure limitation. Another means of evasion has been for the legislature to enact special one-time exceptions to the limit. For example, in 1972 the expenditure limit was raised to 15 percent for one year only. In the fiscal year 1977-78 local governments were allowed to spend all of the revenues they had collected. This was undoubtedly done to allow the local governments to get rid of an accumulated surplus of tax revenues. Of course, each of these exceptions raised the base for the next budgetary year. Therefore, the effects of these exceptions are more longlasting than the deceptive "one-time" level indicates.

Another means for local governments to get around the limit is to declare a "fiscal emergency" and petition the Arizona Tax Commission to allow the spending limit to be exceeded. One county in Arizona has done this for ten consecutive years. In addition to these highly visible methods of evasion, there are a multitude of accounting and budgeting techniques that can be utilized to avoid the expenditure limitation. Is this preponderance of evasive activity a forerunner of what is to come at the state level?

This question can be partially answered by examining the similarities and differences between the two expenditure limits. Both have formal means of exceeding the limit that are relatively easy to implement. Both can be exceeded by legislative action, although in the case of the state limit a two-thirds majority of both houses is needed. The expenditure limitation measures are also different because the local limit is very inflexible and nonresponsive to the pressures of inflation and population growth. Also, it has existed for almost 60 years. This long time period makes the pressures of inflation and population just that much more severe. The state limit, on the other hand, is very flexible in terms of inflation and population growth.

Will state officials act as the local government officials have acted in regard to expenditure limits? It is too early to tell, but Arizona taxpayers should not be surprised if the legislators enact the emergency override provision when the 7 percent limitation figure starts to interfere with business as usual in state spending and taxation. The key point about the evasion of the local governments is that they were helped at every turn by the legislature, and it was the legislature's own enactment they were evading. If legislators as a group tolerate this kind of disregard for their own actions, why should taxpayers feel that they are going to be reluctant to circumvent the will of the citizens whenever they feel a need to do so? If this should happen, the simplest remedy would be to change the override provision to require a vote of the electorate rather than a vote of the legislature. Arizona will provide an interesting test of the question of whether curbing the growth of government can be entrusted to the legislative process or if it must be accomplished through direct action of the taxpayers.


## NEW JERSEY

In 1976 the New Jersey state legislature passed two laws placing limits on state and local spending. During this same session the legislature enacted a state income tax over the opposition of some tax-payer groups. Additionally, the legislature has a long history of failing to act on property tax reform measures that it has promised to the taxpayers at various times. This background information is important for a complete understanding of the impact of the New Jersey limitation provisions.

The state limitation is tied to changes in the per capita personal income for the state. The increase in per capita personal income in one year sets the limit for the percentage increase in state expenditures for the following year. This formula allows for the impact of inflation as reflected in personal income, but does not allow for the effect of population increases or decreases because the use of the per capita figure cancels out the effect of any population changes. As long as the state population remains relatively stable there should be no significant problems, but if there are significant population increases, the state government will find itself running short of funds. On the other hand, if there are significant decreases in population, the state will find itself with surplus spending capacity.

The types of expenditures subject to the limitation are defined by the section of the law reproduced below.

> "Expenditures" or "appropriations" means all amounts appropriated by the state in the general appropriation law and all other laws appropriating money for any purpose in any fiscal year, exclusive of money appropriated and paid or to be paid by the state as the state aid to counties, municipalities and local school districts or on behalf of counties, municipalities and school districts, or other instrumentalities: and exclusive of all expenditures of money received by the state from the federal government, and of money derived from or expended in payment of any interest or principle on, any general obligation bond issues approved by the legally qualified voters of the state at any general election.[3]

Generally, the limitations do not apply to uncontrollable expenditures related to state bond issues or to subventions from the federal government or those paid to local governments. The transfer of functions to or from state government is provided for by adding or subtracting the amount of the expenditures involved from the previous base year. For example, if the state takes over a service provided by local government in the fiscal year 1982, then the amount of funds the local government spent on that service in the fiscal year 1981 is added to the state's 1981 expenditure base. This 1981 expenditure base is then adjusted either upward or downward by the percentage change in the state's per capita personal income.

Exceptions to the limitation provision may be made only by vote of the people. The vote required for passage of an override provision is extraordinary because a majority of all registered voters is required, not just a majority of those voting in the election. This kind of requirement for an override is obviously much more stringent than the two-thirds majority of the legislature required in Arizona. It is not likely that the override provision will have to be used unless there is a startling increase in the state's population or unless there is a sharp drop in the per capita personal income in the state caused by a severe recession or depression. If either of these cases were to occur, there would certainly be plenty of time for an election to be held.

The expenditure limitation imposed upon the local governments is different in almost every respect from the state limitation. The primary limitation on expenditure increases is a flat 5 percent from year to year. This is ordinarily a very restrictive kind of a limit, but in this case its power is reduced by a long list of exceptions to the 5 percent limit. There are ten different categories of exceptions for municipalities and six different categories for counties. Some of these exceptions are described below.

1. Property tax revenues generated from increases in the total assessed valuation due to new construction or improvements are not subject to the 5 percent limit and become part of the base for the next fiscal year.

2. Capital expenditures funded by any means other than property tax revenues are not subject to the 5 percent limit.

3. Expenditures mandated by either state or federal law are not covered by the limit. The importance of this provision is that the state can unilaterally override the expenditure limit by requiring the local government to perform new functions.

4. Revenues derived from new or increased service fees or from the sale of municipal assets are not subject to the spending limit.

5. Expenditures for the payment of interest on bonds or the retirement of the bonds are not subject to the 5 percent limit.

6. Certain expenditures made by contractual arrangement for one or more of the following purposes are not subject to the limit: public improvements for water, sewer, solid waste, parking, senior citizen housing, or any similar purpose.[4]

The end result of this long list of exceptions to the limitation coverage is that only expenditures coming from property tax revenues on existing property or improvements are subject to the 5 percent limitation. This seems to be an indirect and convoluted means of controlling the property tax. If this is the major purpose, and it appears that it is, then it would be much simpler to limit the amount of property tax to a percent of assessed valuation such as in California. Of course, this would be a much more severe (or from the point of view of taxpayer, effective) limitation on the property tax than the expenditure limit scheme New Jersey is trying to employ.

Exceptions to the 5 percent limit must be granted by the vote of the people. In 1977 there were three successful override elections. In 1978 four out of 14 were successful. In 1979 13 out of 32 elections resulted in increased expenditure limits. There is another kind of override permitted for the purpose of meeting physical emergencies. The text of this provision is provided below.

> A local government unit may make emergency appropriations, after the adoption of a budget, for a purpose which is not foreseen at the time of the adoption thereof or for which adequate provision was not made therein. Such an appropriation shall be made to meet a pressing need for public expenditure to protect or promote the public health, safety, morals or welfare or to provide temporary housing or public assistance prior to the next succeeding fiscal year.[5]

This kind of emergency provision makes a lot of sense for local government. It provides a means for governments to act quickly and react to physical emergencies threatening the welfare and safety of the citizenry. Abuses of this provision are fairly easy to identify, especially in a local community. Also, they are easily remedied at the next local election.

From the point of view of the citizen, both the state and local provisions are ineffective in controlling the tax burden. The state limitation is tied to a personal income factor very responsive to inflation. About the best taxpayers can hope for is for the cost of their state government to stabilize in relation to their incomes and not increase. The override provision is a good strong one requiring a two-thirds vote of the electorate. This should be some consolation to the taxpayer. The local government limitation provision is riddled with so many exceptions that it cannot be properly identified as an expenditure limitation at all. It is really nothing more than an indirect means of controlling the spending of property tax revenues. If its purpose is indeed to provide property tax relief, as the political history of the issue seems to indicate, it is a poor means compared to some of the more direct measures enacted in other states. Time will tell how effective these legislatively enacted expenditure limitations really are.

## HAWAII

In the November elections of 1978 citizens of Hawaii approved a constitutional amendment by a two to one margin placing a limit on the expenditures of their state government. This limitation is tied to the rate of economic growth of the state. Compared with other definitions of state expenditure, the one used by Hawaii is a model of simplicity and understandability. It is reproduced below.

> ...the legislature shall establish a general fund expenditure ceiling which shall limit the rate of growth of general fund appropriations, *excluding federal funds received by the general fund*, to the estimated rate of growth of the state's economy as provided by law...(emphasis added)[6]

All funds are included in the ceiling except for federal funds received by the state. This kind of definition without extensive lists of exceptions gives citizens a clear statement that the role of state government will not increase in relation to overall economic activity within the state. This approach is much preferred to some of the previous ones discussed wherein long lists of exceptions create so much confusion that the average citizen has no idea of what expenditures are limited.

The amendment contains an override provision permitting the legislature to spend above the ceiling. The override must be passed by a two-thirds majority of the membership of each house and the bill must specify the reasons for the action taken as well as a dollar amount of the excess spending. The requirement for written reasons and a specific over-expenditure figure gives some assurance the legislature will act responsibly when and if it exercises this override option.

In addition to these basic expenditure limitation provisions, the amendment takes two other actions making it unique among the measures examined thus far. First, the amendment requires a mandatory tax refund or tax credit be given to taxpayers when for two years running there is a general fund surplus of 5 percent or more. While this provision does not actually make the expenditure ceiling more effective, it does at least create the impression that the legislature is serious about controlling and perhaps even reducing the tax burden.

The action required by the amendment is actually a form of balanced budget provision. It provides for the formation of an independent body, the Council on Revenues, charged with preparing estimates of revenues for each fiscal year. These estimates are transmitted to the governor and to the legislature and are also made public. If the governor or the legislature intend to recommend or pass appropriations exceeding the estimated revenue, they must make public a statement giving the reasons for the excess and also the dollar amount of the excess spending. The provision exists as a safeguard against either the legislature or the governor attempting to spend revenue surpluses rather than allowing them to accumulate for eventual repayment to the taxpayer.

From the point of view of the taxpayer, the entire amendment is well written and seems to be a workable means of implementing a curb on the growth of state spending. There are only two areas that might be strengthened. The first is the override procedure. There is no reason why an override should not require a vote of the people rather than merely legislative action. Controlling legislators through the electoral process is a difficult and unsure business. It is much better for taxpayers to reserve for themselves the power to exceed the spending limitations they have enacted. The second area needing clarification is the manner in which the level of economic growth is determined. This should have been spelled out in the amendment. Such a general requirement could be easily interpreted in a way that imposes no spending restraint at all. Even if the manner of determining the rate of economic growth were clearly spelled out, the best the taxpayers could hope for would be no further increases in their tax burdens. It is unlikely that this provision will provide any real tax relief for those who voted for it.

## COLORADO

In the November 1978 election Colorado voters turned down a plan limiting state spending increases to the rate of inflation in the state. On the surface this might appear to be a defeat for the tax-revolt movement. It was in fact, just the opposite. The reason being that in 1977 the state legislature enacted two measures that limited spending and taxation much more severely than the defeated ballot measure would have.

The statutory limitation on state spending passed in 1977 is short, simple, and to the point. It is reproduced below.

...state general fund spending shall be limited to seven percent over the previous year. Any amount of general fund revenues in excess of seven percent, and after retention of unrestricted general fund year end balances of four percent of revenues, shall be placed in a special reserve fund to be utilized for property tax relief. The method of distribution of such relief shall be determined by the legislature...[7]

In addition to limiting expenditures to a seven percent increase, the measure also provides that excess funds be set aside for use in reducing the property tax burden. The flat percentage limitation is the strongest form of limitation in times of high inflation. For instance, the replacement measure defeated on the November ballot would have tied future increases to population growth as well as to annual rates of inflation. With inflation running in double figures during the late 1970s, state spending could have increased by about 12 percent per year instead of the 7 percent provided for in the 1977 statute.

There is, however, one major flaw in the statute. It does not contain any provision for override expenditures in cases of emergency or recession. Because there is no special provision calling for an electoral decision or an extraordinary majority of the legislature, the statutory limit can be amended or even eliminated by simple majority vote. The taxpayer has little or no guarantee that this expenditure limitation will be in force for its projected life. Colorado has a "sunset" law that limits the lives of all new laws automatically. The State Government Limitation Statute will expire with the end of the 1982-83 fiscal year unless renewed by specific action of the legislature.

In addition to the limitation on state spending, the legislature also passed a statute limiting the taxing ability of local government. A 7 percent limit is applied to increases in the property tax levies of all local governments. Therefore, the total amount of tax collected in any one year cannot exceed the previous year's collection by more than 7 percent. The only exception to this 7 percent limit is the revenue necessary for the payment of the interest and principal on outstanding bonds. This kind of limit provides an absolute guarantee that property taxes cannot increase by more than 7 percent per year (except for required bond payments). The term "levy" refers to the amount of tax a person owes; therefore, changes in the assessed valuation or the tax rate cannot be used to increase the tax liability as long as the amount of tax that can be collected is limited. The only exception to the 7 percent limit is that the assessed value of new construction or improvements to property may be taxed at the prevailing rate. These exceptions become part of the base for the subsequent year's revenue limit.

Local governments have two means to override the 7 percent limit. One is to apply to the state's Department of Local Affairs for permission to levy more than a 7 percent increase in property tax revenues. If permission is granted, the amount of the increase is deducted from the 7 percent increase allowed in the subsequent year. This provision insures that governments will seek overrides only when it is absolutely necessary because they cut down the increases available in future years. The second means of getting an override requires approval of the voters. Passage of the override requires a simple *majority of those voting.* This requirement is much more liberal than the override provisions of many other states in which a majority, either simple or two-thirds, of *all registered* voters is required.

Both of the 1977 provisions are stronger in their ability to control taxation and expenditure than are the provisions of other states. The measure defeated in the November 1978 balloting would have greatly liberalized these controls by permitting government expenditures to keep up with the rate of inflation. This would have meant business as usual for government officials in the state. The existing limits of 7 percent in a time of double digit inflation actually forces cuts in government spending every year that the rate of inflation goes over 7 percent. For the taxpayer, this is going to result in a steadily decreasing tax burden and in all likelihood a steadily decreasing level of government services. This decrease in tax burden and services will be accelerated by the increases in population Colorado is experiencing in the late 1970s and early 1980s. Needless to say, these limitations are going to cause a number of problems for state and local officials in the years ahead.

## TEXAS

In the November balloting Texans aligned themselves with the citizens of other states who voted for limitations on state government spending. A huge majority (85 percent) of the voters approved a constitutional amendment tying increases in state spending to the rate of economic growth within the state. The measure defined "state spending" as appropriations from state tax revenues. This definition excludes from the limit revenues coming from subventions, fees and charges, and miscellaneous income from state enterprises. The measure also contains a provision for emergency override appropriations; a simple majority of the membership of both houses of the legislature is required. The override appropriation measure must state the reasons for the override.

The Texas limitation measure is quite lax in terms of its protection of the taxpayer. The limitation does not cut current spending, but instead maintains the current level with adjustments for inflation. The override provision is among the most lenient of all the states, requiring no extraordinary majority of the legislature nor a vote of the people. The flexibility of the expenditure ceiling probably explains why there are so few limitations on the types of appropriations included within the limit. Also, there are no provisions for returning surplus tax revenues to the citizens. Overall, the measure will probably prove to be of doubtful value in controlling the growth of Texas state government.

## TENNESSEE

The state of Tennessee currently has a constitutional limit on the growth of appropriations of state tax revenues. The limitation is based upon increases in the estimated growth of Tennessee's economy. The emergency override provision is almost identical to that of Texas, requiring only a simple majority of both houses of the state legislature. The override measure must state the amount of the override in dollars and the percentage rate by which the expenditure limit is exceeded. In the same measure, there is a requirement for the state to share the cost of any new programs or services it requires local governments to undertake. The size of the state's share is not specified.

There is nothing unusual in Tennessee spending limitation provisions. What makes the situation worthy of note is the manner in which the limitation was enacted. In 1977 a limited constitutional convention approved the basic idea. In January 1978 the state legislature approved implementing legislation for the amendment. On March 7, 1978 the voters passed a referendum adding the limitation measure to the state constitution and thus activating the implementing legislation passed earlier. This three step process demonstrates the wide acceptance the measure enjoyed in the state. However, the weakness of the provisions in terms of the flexibility of the limit and the ease with which the limit can be overridden probably explains why government officials and the taxpayers were able to agree on the measure. Whether or not the measure proves to be effective in limiting the tax burden remains to be seen.

## ILLINOIS

In discussing the limitation of government spending and taxation, a strong point has been made to the effect that these actions must be taken directly by the citizenry because elected officials either are not capable or are not willing to vote significant decreases in levels of government activity. Government officials might reply to this argument by saying that there is great danger in the electorate taking matters into its own hands: "People do not understand how government really works and elections can be easily influenced by public relations techniques and mass media campaigns." They might also state that the essence of representative government requires that policy-making powers reside in the hands of the elected officials rather than the people. Lastly, public officials will strongly maintain that they are responsive to the will of the people. In order to provide a comment on this argument, some recent occurrences in the state of Illinois will be examined.

First, it must be stated that the structure of government in Illinois discourages not only direct action by the people, but responsiveness by powerful political parties. The people of the state of Illinois do not have the means at their disposal to make changes directly in the constitution or laws of the state. What they can do is to vote in "advisory" referenda. In the November 1978 balloting the people of Illinois by a margin of four to one passed a referendum expressing their desire for mandatory limits on government spending and taxation. Governor Thompson, running for reelection, supported the measure. Can it be assumed government officials got the message?

In the same month as the election the state legislature voted itself a 40 percent pay increase. The Chicago City Council and the Cook County Board both voted themselves a 75 percent pay increase. These irresponsible actions created an uproar by the public unmatched in Illinois political history. Enraged citizens started a "tea bag" campaign against local and state officials. New and used tea bags arrived by the thousands to symbolize taxpayer anger. Newspapers conducted contests for the "best angry letter." As a result of these protests, the pay raises were eventually spread over a two to three year period. A contrite Governor Thompson explained his failure to effectively oppose the legislative salary increases as a mistake. (He was on a vacation when the legislature passed the pay raise bill. His absence resulted in an automatic veto, which was overridden by the legislature in one day. If he had been present, he could have held the bill captive long enough for public pressure to have some effect on the legislators.)

The essence of this story is that Illinois taxpayers have no effective recourse against the legislators who acted so blatantly against the will of the people. Voters can only wait until the 1980 elections to contend with Illinois' peculiar election laws, which strongly favor incumbents.

To be sure, Illinois is not representative of state government overall. But what happened there illustrates why it is important for citizens to have a direct means of influencing the actions of their government. The working coalition of elected government officials, government employees, and special interest groups makes it impossible for the citizenry to be assured that government will be responsive to their wishes even when a clear message is sent. Because of the manner in which representative democracy has evolved in the United States, it is necessary for citizens to take direct action if they are going to put controls on the seemingly inevitable rise of government spending and taxation.

## CALIFORNIA REVISITED:
## THE "SPIRIT OF 13" INITIATIVE

Paul Gann and a large number of taxpayers in California seem to be unhappy with the way the local and state governments responded to the "message" of Proposition 13. As a result, Californians will have the opportunity to enact a comprehensive limitation of state and local spending, probably in the June 1980 elections. All current indications are that the spending limitation initiative will pass easily. Gann easily obtained the 553,000 signatures needed to place the measure on the ballot and, in fact, a total of 900,000 signatures were obtained.

The limits placed on state and local spending would be similar to those enacted in other states. Increases in appropriations from year to year would be linked to population increases and rises in the cost of living. Exceptions to the limitation include for state government, subventions to local government (these are counted within the local government limit), payment of the principal and interest on bonded indebtedness, expenditures of federal funds, refunds of taxes, and payment of benefits for retirement, unemployment insurance, and disability. The only exception from the limit allowed for local government is the refund of taxes.

For both state and local government, there is a provision for emergency override of the limits by legislative action. However, the "excess" spending must be "paid off" within the subsequent three years by downward adjustment of the spending limit. The limits may be revised upward or downward by vote of the people. These changes remain in effect for four years unless there is another vote to extend them. Governments are prohibited from charging fees for services in excess of the actual costs of the service. The last major provision is that surplus tax revenues at either level of government must be returned to taxpayers through a downward adjustment of rates during the two years after the surplus.

The "Spirit of 13" initiative, if passed, will be one of the most comprehensive expenditure limitation measures in existence. Although it allows for liberal increases in government spending through population and inflation adjustments, it has stringent override conditions and requires excess taxes be returned to the taxpayers. In contrast to the original Proposition 13, the measure exercises control over virtually all aspects of state and local government spending. It does not have the "loop holes" used by local government officials so readily when "13" became law. One of its most significant features is the provisions for a mechanism to adjust the spending limit by the direct action of the people. This potential for direct action should encourage elected officials to be very scrupulous in carrying out the will of the people in limiting the spending of government. If the "Spirit of 13" passes, it will prove to be a valuable working model for voters in other states to follow. (Note: The "Spirit of 13" passed in the November 1979 election.)

## CONCLUDING COMMENTS

The main purpose of this chapter has been to describe the basic principles of limiting government expenditures. Additionally, existing expenditure limitation measures have been examined. While there is no one best way to limit government activity, there are certain principles that can and should be applied when taxpayers are seeking means to limit the spending and taxation of a particular state or local government.

First, taxpayers must decide whether they want to reduce the spending of government or whether they will be content with limiting any future increases in the size of government relative to the rest of the economy. If the latter is the intended goal, then limits tied to increases in population, inflation, or some measure of economic activity are appropriate. However, if tax reduction is desired, then limits on increases in government spending must be structured to allow increases less than the rate of inflation or growth in personal income. The most popular way to accomplish this is through the use of flat percentages (current ones in force range from 5 percent to 7 percent) well below the rate of inflation.

Second, attention must be given to the definition of the expenditures to be limited. Generally speaking, the more exceptions there are to the limit, the less effective the limit is likely to be. Exceptions that make sense from the point of view of the taxpayer are those for the servicing and retirement of bonded indebtedness approved by the voters, funds for tax rebates or other refunds, and appropriations of federal dollars. Any other exceptions should be reviewed with a very critical eye. Also, provisions must exist to control the transfer of services from one level of government to another. Any expenditure escaping the limit of the state government should be part of the local government limit and visa versa.

Third, emergency or override provisions should be structured so that the reasons for and the dollar amount of the override are clearly spelled out. Any overrides permitted by legislative action should be "repaid" by a reduction of the allowable percent of increase in future years. Also, legislative overrides should require an extraordinary majority for passage, at least two-thirds of the membership of the legislative body. The electorate should have the opportunity to enact overrides and also to adjust either upward or downward the percent of allowable increase in expenditures. The experience of several states indicates it is very important for the citizens to retain the ability to directly adjust the spending limitation. This potential for citizen action has a very positive effect in keeping legislators committed to the purposes of expenditure limitation.

The last major point is that there must be specific provisions made for the return of excess revenues to the taxpayers. The form of these tax refunds should be determined by the nature of the taxes supplying most of the revenue surplus. For instance, a surplus from a progressive income tax should be returned in a different manner than a surplus from a sales tax. Generally speaking, in instances where there appears to be a continuing surplus, the tax rates should be adjusted downward so that continual rebates are not necessary.

The final question to be addressed is: which is the preferred approach to reducing tax burdens, tax limitation or expenditure limitation? The answer to this difficult question depends upon the goals to be accomplished. In the case of California's Proposition 13, there was a clear need and desire to remedy the heavy burden of the property tax. This was accomplished, but the overall level of government activity seemingly was not affected. There has not been an attempt so far to limit a variety of taxes in order to cut down the size of government. Again using California as an example, the "Spirit of 13" initiative will try to limit the size of state and local government through expenditure control. The unanswered question is: would controls on state revenue from the sales and income taxes be a better approach? The big disadvantage of this approach is that it leaves the way open for the implementation and use of new taxes as well as large increases in fees and charges.

In the last analysis, the question boils down to one of control by limiting spending or control by limiting revenue. The best answer to this question in any given situation depends on the circumstances involved. The key variables are: the attitudes of the majority of the taxpayers, the tax structure of the state, the amount of direct control citizens are able to exercise, and the political history and traditions of the state. Taxpayers who want to limit or reduce government activity are going to have to devote a good deal of time and effort to understanding all of these influential factors. The more the taxpayers know about the situation, the better able they will be to work their will on government.

## NOTES

1. Article 5, Section 1, Title 41, Chapter 3, Arizona Revised Statutes.
2. Arizona State Senate Concurrent Resolution 1002, 1978. Subsequently passed by the voters of the State of Arizona as a constitutional amendment.
3. Article 2, State Expenditures Limitation Act, New Jersey, 1976.
4. Article 6, Sections 3 and 4, Local Government Expenditure Limitation Act, New Jersey, 1976.
5. Ibid, Article 6.
6. General Fund Expenditure Ceiling, Constitutional Amendment, State of Hawaii.
7. Statutory Limitation on State Government, 24-75-201.1, State of Colorado, 1977.

# OTHER RESULTS OF
# THE TAXPAYER REVOLT

The three preceding chapters have examined the 1978 elections that made the taxpayer revolt a reality. In the states and localities where spending and tax limitation measures passed, taxpayers have gained some measure of relief from a growing and oppressive burden. There is one further dimension of the anti-tax movement that merits further discussion. This involves the federal tax structure. There have been no "Proposition 13s" at the national level because there is no legal device for the public to use to "send messages" to Washington. If there were a national initiative or referendum process, tax reform at the national level would be a relatively simple matter of taxpayers organizing for a single, national election issue. Because this simple, direct approach is not available, other means must be used. These alternative approaches are the major subject of this chapter.

## REFORMING THE FEDERAL TAX STRUCTURE

There are basically two means available to change the national tax and expenditure structure: legislation passed by both houses of Congress and amendments to the United States Constitution. To accomplish anything by either of these two methods requires political action on a massive scale. Presidential elections are only a starting point because, as the last ten years of Presidential leadership has clearly demonstrated, the power of the Presidency does not extend throughout the legislative process. The President may initiate legislation, he may lobby and bring pressure on Representatives and Senators, and he can veto legislation he disapproves of, but he does not have the ability to create laws or fashion constitutional amendments.

Additionally, pressure must be exerted in every election for the House of Representatives and the Senate. (There are over 1,400 separate campaigns in a six-year period that require the attention of citizens interested in reducing their tax burden.) Citizens must be organized in every state to bring about changes in the federal tax structure.

While most people are familiar with the process by which Congress creates law, the process of adding amendments to the Constitution is not so familiar. The amendment process starts in one of two ways. Only one of these methods has ever been used—that of Congress initiating amendments, which must then be ratified. The other method, involving a federal constitutional convention, has never been used. Article V of the United States Constitution describes the process of amendment.

> The congress, whenever two-thirds of both houses shall deem it necessary, shall propose amendments to this constitution, or, on the application of the legislatures of two-thirds of the several states, shall call a convention for proposing amendments, which, in either case, shall be valid to all intents and purposes, as part of this constitution, when ratified by the legislature of three fourths of the several states, or by conventions in three fourths thereof, as the one or the other mode of ratification may be proposed by the congress: provided that no amendment which may be made prior to the year one thousand eight hundred and eight shall in any manner affect the first and fourth clauses in the ninth section of the first article: and that no state, without its consent, shall be deprived of its equal suffrage in the senate.

For Congress to propose an amendment, a vote of two-thirds of both houses is necessary. The proposed amendment must be ratified by three-fourths of the states either by action of the state legislature or by action of a special state constitutional convention. The method of ratification that the states must use is determined by Congress when it passes the proposed amendment. The alternate method of proposing an amendment involves the legislatures in two-thirds of the states passing resolutions asking Congress to call a federal constitutional convention. When two-thirds of the states have made such a request, Congress must issue a call for a federal constitutional convention.

In late 1979 and early 1980 steps were taken by taxpayer groups to utilize all three methods of reforming the tax structure (one legislative and two forms of constitutional amendment). The National Taxpayers Union (NTU) mounted a drive for a federal constitutional convention. The National Tax Limitation Committee (NTLC) pushed for Congress to adopt a proposed constitutional amendment. The American Tax Reduction Movement (ATRM), headed by Howard Jarvis, pushed for legislative relief from the heavy federal tax burden. The following paragraphs describe some of the details of these three anti-tax efforts.

## The Constitutional Convention

The approval of 34 states is required to force Congress to call a federal constitutional convention. In March of 1979, 27 states had already adopted constitutional convention resolutions. These states are: Alabama, Arizona, Arkansas, Colorado, Delaware, Florida, Georgia, Idaho, Kansas, Louisiana, Maryland, Mississippi, Nebraska, Nevada, New Mexico, North Carolina, North Dakota, Oklahoma, Oregon, Pennsylvania, South Carolina, South Dakota, Tennessee, Texas, Utah, Virginia, and Wyoming. These 27 states represent ten years of work by the National Taxpayers Union.

The purpose of the NTU is embodied in their National Tax Reduction Plan. The Plan has three main features. It calls for a balanced federal budget, substantial reductions in federal income tax rates, and a significant lowering of the capital gains tax. The rationale for the NTU's advocacy of a constitutional convention is that the threat of a convention is required to force Congress to act to reduce taxes and spending. If Congress fails to act, then the necessary amendments can be approved for national ratification at the convention. There is good reason for Congress to resist a constitutional convention. The delegates to the convention are selected in accordance with the laws of each of the 50 states. Most of the states have requirements for an electoral process. There is no assurance that members of Congress would be delegates to the convention. The creation of a convention is a direct loss of power for Congress.

The possibility of a constitutional convention creates uncertainty for groups other than Congress. The delegates at the convention have the power to approve amendments for ratification dealing with virtually any aspect of government. They would not be limited to considering only the balanced budget amendment. Opponents feel this wide potential for action is a very strong argument against a convention because it could open the door for fundamental changes in our form of government and even the possibility of tampering with the Bill of Rights.

Proponents of a call for a constitutional convention feel there are some changes that might well be considered in our system of national government. One change might be the provision for a form of national initiative or referendum allowing voters to have a direct input into the policies and practices of the national government. Such a process could take one of three forms. It could be advisory, thus indicating the general sentiments of the voters, but not having the force of law. It could be a legislative initiative, wherein the issue decided upon would become law. It could be a constitutional initiative similar to the one in the state of California, which allows voters to have the opportunity to amend the constitution directly.

Evaluating these alternatives purely on the basis of effectiveness for tax reform, there is no doubt the constitutional initiative has proven to be the most potent weapon in the taxpayer revolt arsenal. However, a national constitutional initiative would be a clear break from a national tradition of slow and deliberate change in the United States Constitution. (In contrast, state constitutions are known for their detailed treatment of a large number of specific issues. This specificity requires more frequent change than do the broad general principles of the national constitution.) In the event a federal constitutional convention should be convened, the creation of a process for national advisory referenda might be a distinct possibility. However, the primary item on the agenda would undoubtedly be a balanced budget amendment to the Constitution.

## The Constitutional Amendment Proposed by Congress

The National Tax Limitation Committee (NTLC) was founded in 1975 and played a major role in the taxpayer revolt of the late 1970s. NTLC was active in over 30 state elections supporting initiatives and referenda aimed at controlling the taxation and spending of state and local government.

On the national level, the NTLC waged an aggressive campaign to induce Congress to propose a constitutional amendment curbing the spending and taxation of the federal government. The means of limitation was the requirement that the federal budget be balanced every year. Simply stated, the amount of money appropriated could not exceed anticipated revenues in any given year. The balanced budget would not only stop the growth of the national debt with its huge interest payments, but would actually reduce it. The NTLC contends this limitation of government would result in a reduced rate of inflation and a stronger economy. Much of their campaign effort was directed toward individual citizens to encourage them to put pressure on Congress. The essence of their approach to the taxpayer is embodied in the following quotations taken from NTLC literature used in a direct mail campaign during the summer of 1979.

> If we don't stop the free-spending politicians from squandering our tax dollars and inflating our currency, we will have a financial crisis that will make the depression look like child's play.
>
> Think about this. If we don't stop these politicians soon,
> * inflation will continue its upward spiral, wiping out our hard earned savings;
> * our dollar will continue to weaken—jeopardizing the fiscal integrity of the entire western world;
> * businesses will stagger, jobs will be lost—everything that we have all worked for could collapse around us.
>
> The time to stop this outrageous waste of our hard-earned tax dollars is now. We've got to *force* the politicians to make cuts!
>
> And to do this, we must force our Tax Limitation Amendment through the maze of Congressional committees it must struggle through before it can be voted on by the U.S. House and Senate.
>
> We have to build enough pressure that free-spending Congressmen and Senators, as much as they might like to, cannot and *will not* ignore us. This is why it's so important that you do your part.
>
> Please don't let a single day go by. Take the postcards I have enclosed, sign them and mail them today.

These three quotations capture the main points of the NTLC argument: politicians are incapable of doing anything but spending, runaway spending by government in addition to imposing a heavy tax burden has caused inflation, and direct action by the people is required if changes are to be made in this situation. The postcards referred to were preaddressed to the Senators for the state in which the recipient lived. The message on the postcards was preprinted and is reproduced below.

> Dear Senator:
>
> Inflation is on the rise, my standard of living and the value of the dollar are falling, and the American economy is dying on its feet.
>
> The *only* cure for these problems is an *immediate* reduction in taxation, spending, and the incredible *waste* at the federal level!

I beg you to support and pass an amendment to the U.S. Constitution that will limit the amount Congress can spend, and the amount of my hard-earned money that Congress can tax away from us.

Sincerely yours,

---

The message borne by the postcards is essentially the same as that of the accompanying literature. The use of preprinted postcards represents a compromise in political strategy on the part of the NTLC. Using preprinted cards will have the effect of increasing the number of cards mailed as opposed to asking people to write postcards on their own. However, the fact that they are preprinted will decrease their impact in the minds of the senators receiving them because they are obviously part of an organized campaign and not a spontaneous "grass-roots" movement. The benefit to NTLC from a large return is that it shows the organization has the ability to mobilize a large number of voters. This ability translates into influence with public officials at election time. In essence, the postcard campaign is as much an effort by NTLC to increase its political power as it is an effort to inform elected officials of what taxpayers want.

There is another piece of NTLC literature of interest here. It is a petition to the President of the United States. Recipients of the mailing were asked to fill it out and return it to the NTLC. The accompanying literature states that all the petitions returned will be presented to the President by the NTLC leadership. Of course, as with the postcards, the presentation of the petitions fulfills two functions: communication of taxpayer unrest and demonstration of the political clout of the NTLC. The text of the petition is reproduced on the next page.

The content of the petition is almost identical to that of the preprinted postcards. Both pieces of literature ask for tax and expenditure limitation on the federal government. The argument is these actions are necessary if inflation is to be reduced and a heavy tax burden lifted from the shoulders of the working public. While the message of these materials is specific enough to gain public support, it is not specific enough to guide the development of concrete proposals. Presumably, specific proposals would be worked out between the leadership of the NTLC and those Representatives and Senators who support the concept of a constitutional amendment to limit federal spending and taxation.

Organizations like the National Tax Limitation Committee are filling a gap in the governance system as far as the tax reform issue is concerned. Elected officials have proven themselves incapable of limiting spending and taxation. At the national level, citizens have no means of making a direct statement of their concerns or of making policy. The NTLC and similar groups provide a means for mobilizing the latent unrest of the citizenry, transforming it into political pressure that can be brought to bear on elected officials. Without organizations of this type, there could not be a tax revolt at the national level.

PETITION
for an
Amendment to the Constitution of the
United States of America

WHEREAS, taxes levied by the Federal Government have become so excessive as to cause a severe burden to every working American and

WHEREAS, Federal spending has created massive inflation which is robbing America of its prosperity;

WHEREAS, our tax dollars are being squandered on many wasteful, unnecessary and poorly managed programs:

NOW, THEREFORE, the undersigned citizen of the United States hereby petitions the Congress to adopt an Amendment to the Constitution of the United States that will:

 CUT, LIMIT AND CONTROL FEDERAL SPENDING AND THE AMOUNT OF TAXES WHICH CAN BE IMPOSED ON UNITED STATES CITIZENS NOW AND IN THE FUTURE.

 Signature _____
Please print:
Name _____

Address _____

City _____ State _____ Zip _____

## The Legislative Approach to National Tax Reform

The American Tax Reduction Movement (ATRM), founded by Howard Jarvis of Proposition 13 fame, is another national organization dedicated to easing the burden of the U.S. taxpayer. It plays the same "middle-man" role as the National Taxpayers Union and the National Tax Limitation Committee. While the NTU and the NTLC both advocate a constitutional approach to national tax reform, the ATRM is working on a legislative approach. It is sponsoring a proposal called the American Tax Reduction Act of 1979. The major provisions of this proposal are set forth below.

    I. Reduce Federal income taxes for everyone in the United States by 25%.

   II. Reduce Federal spending by 20%, 5% per year until the spending cuts are completed.

  III. Reduce capital gains taxes to a maximum of 15%.

  IV. "Index" income tax rates to eliminate the process whereby citizens pay higher rates solely because of inflation.

   V. Eliminate the budget deficiency, and apply all budget surpluses to reducing the National Debt.

  VI. Limit government spending to a maximum of 18% of all spending in the U.S. (the current level is more than 22%). [1]

Of the six specific proposals, three pertain directly to changes in the personal income tax. Two of the six are a form of expenditure limitation, calling for an absolute reduction in the amount of federal spending and limiting the size of government expenditures to 18 percent of all spending. These proposals are far more specific than those previously discussed. They share a common background with many of the tax reform measures approved in the states. The most significant feature is the promise of specific kinds of relief from taxes. Jarvis' Proposition 13 offered a specific reduction in the property tax of about 50 percent for most people. Similarly, this proposal offers a cut in personal income taxes of 25 percent as well as an adjustment of the rates for inflation and a drastic decrease in the capital gains tax rate to 15 percent. For taxpayers worried about their economic future, these tax breaks offer good news. In addition to personal relief, the proposal attacks problems facing the country such as inflation, balance-of-payments deficits, and the threat of a severe recession. In the preamble of a petition circulated by the ATRM in the summer of 1979, the rationale for the proposal is clearly spelled out.

WHEREAS, the tax burden being imposed on the American people has exceeded our ability to pay, and

WHEREAS, inflation caused by deficit government spending has caused incalculable harm to the economy of the United States and to the budgets of its citizens, and

WHEREAS, waste and inefficiency is rampant in every aspect of government and that government can easily cut its level of spending without eliminating any vital service, and

WHEREAS, taxpayers have seen their tax bracket increased year after year due solely to inflation rather than real increases in income, and

WHEREAS, excessive capital gains taxes has forced capital spending and business investment to dangerously low levels in the United

States, resulting in millions of fewer jobs and opportunities for all, and,

WHEREAS, the strength of the dollar has constantly fallen in international markets, other nations with balanced budgets and lower taxes, and

WHEREAS, the great free enterprise system which built this nation into the most powerful country on earth is threatened by excessive government interference, bureaucratic meddling and taxation.[2]

The seven clauses of the preamble hit just about every major problem facing the United States in the late 1970s. The overall message is clear: not only are cuts in taxes and government spending good for the individual, but the consequent reduction in the magnitude of government operations will have a host of positive economic effects benefiting every person in the country.

The American Tax Reduction Act campaign uses the same formula that worked so well for Mr. Jarvis' Proposition 13 campaign. Unfortunately, the national government is much better insulated from the direct action of the people than state and local governments in California. There is no direct initiative process. Mr. Jarvis and ATRM must work indirectly trying to persuade Senators and Representatives to support the tax reduction proposal. It is extremely unlikely that this or any proposal will come through the complex committee system of Congress with its hard-hitting provisions intact. Passage through both houses without crippling amendments would be equally difficult. In order to accomplish its goal, ATRM must be prepared to lobby and pressure Congress for more than just a year or two. It will have to display great staying power and will have to be willing to accept some compromises in its tax reform program. Compromise and negotiation are the trademarks of the national legislative process. Unless ATRM and similar organizations can create political pressure equivalent to that generated during World War II and the Great Depression, it is unlikely they are going to be able to bring about any revolutionary changes in the taxing and spending structure of the United States government.

## ⌐WHAT TAXPAYERS CAN DO

Despite the lack of any direct influence on the taxing and spending policies of the federal government, concerned taxpayers should not become discouraged. Although the decision-making processes in Washington are not conducive to revolutionary change, they are capable of gradual, evolutionary change. It is possible for taxpayers to work constructively for a reduction in their tax burden and for a limitation on the size and spending policies of the federal government.

~There are two issues that deserve the support of the tax-paying public. The first is direct participation by the public in the resolution of national policy issues. This participation is best achieved by the initiative or referendum process proven so successful at the state and local levels. The question of what type of initiative process is one every voter will have to decide individually.

Three levels in the initiative process have been discussed: advisory, legislative, and constitutional. The advisory initiative gives citizens the least amount of influence and the constitutional initiative the most. Going up the scale from advisory to legislative to constitutional, the potential for drastic change increases and so does the need for responsible, informed, non-selfish judgments by the electorate. The constitutional initiative process gives the people the power to change the basic structure of government by means of a single election. The legislative initiative gives the people the power to make sweeping changes in the laws subject only to constitutional limitation.

The question each voter must ask in determining what type of initiative to support is: "How much trust and confidence do I have in the collective judgment of the American people?" The more confident a person feels about the "collective wisdom" of the American people, the stronger the initiative process that should be favored. Regardless of what level of participation any one individual sees as most desirable, it is in the interest of all taxpayers to support at least an advisory initiative.

An objective analysis of the national political system will yield the unmistakable conclusion that when it comes to reducing government spending and taxation, the wishes of the majority of the taxpayers do not carry much influence. The best the public can hope for under the current system is a great deal of tax-cutting rhetoric and perhaps a few short term, "quick fix" tax cuts. Neither of these confronts the real problem of uncontrollable taxation and spending by the federal government. Representative government has shown itself incapable of instituting real curbs on spending and taxes. Citizens have no choice but to work for an opportunity to make a direct input into the process of controlling the national finances. The level of direct participation desired is a question each citizen will have to answer individually.

The second issue requiring citizen support is not a procedural issue like participation, but rather a substantive issue—cutting taxes and spending. Here again, citizens have a decision to make. This time the question is: how severe of a tax cut do they really want and what services are they willing to give up in return? There is no doubt that the federal government operations could be improved by proper management and elimination of redundancies. There are also areas that could be reduced or eliminated without appreciable loss of service to the public. However, the savings in these areas are not likely to be enough to make a significant reduction in each individual's tax bill. The only logical alternative is a significant cut in services, unless another rationale is used. That rationale maintains that tax cuts and reduced government spending would stimulate the economy to the extent that government would receive sufficient revenues to provide necessary services. Also, this would allow government workers whose jobs were eliminated to be absorbed into the private economy rather than ending up on unemployment or some other type of government support. In short, a drastic cut in the size of government would be an economic benefit for all citizens.

The substance of these opposing views can be summarized in a few short sentences. Assuming that citizens want to reduce their tax burden, should they approach the issue with the view that significant cuts in taxes must mean significant cuts in services, or should they embrace the more optimistic view that significant cuts in taxes will lead to increased economic activity with little or no loss of important government services and a better economic situation for all? There is no way for anyone to know with certainty which of these predictions is likely to prove the most accurate. The economic results of Proposition 13 in California have not developed to the point where a clear judgment can be made. There have been no massive layoffs of government employees and, by and large, vital government services have not suffered. On the other hand, the state's huge surplus is being used to keep local governments close to pre-"13" spending levels and the impact of deferred capital expenditures is as yet to be felt. Also, there is a great deal of difference between cutting the local property tax in California and making significant cuts in the federal income tax. The only reasonable conclusion to be drawn about large scale reductions in the federal income tax is that no one knows for sure what will happen when and if such cuts are made.

To summarize, taxpayers who are fed up with the heavy federal tax burden should strongly support the creation of a nationwide initiative process to give people a direct and strong voice in the national government. They should also lend their support to one or more of the organizations seeking to pressure Congress into significant tax reductions. Finally, if taxpayers have an opportunity to influence their own Senators or Representatives, they should express their high degree of dissatisfaction with the performance of elected officials in controlling spending and taxation.

While working to change the federal tax structure is a long-term project, more immediate results can be achieved at the state level. Many states have an initiative process that allows citizens direct input into state government. (State legislators are much more accessible to the average citizen than their federal counterparts. Significant progress can be made in relatively short periods of time to curb taxation and limit spending. In addition to the examples already examined, citizens in other states have made progress towards tax relief. These are described briefly in the next few paragraphs.)

Voters in North and South Dakota achieved some degree of tax relief in the November 1978 elections. In North Dakota a measure mandating significant cuts in the state income tax passed by an overwhelming two to one margin. At the same time, South Dakotans made it more difficult for their state legislators to enact new taxes or raise the rates on existing taxes. A measure raising the majority needed to pass tax increases from simple to two-thirds was approved by a narrow margin.

In Wisconsin citizens received one-time tax relief from the state legislature as well as an adjustment in income tax rates. This legislative action came on the heels of a gubernatorial campaign in which both candidates refused to endorse a Proposition 13 approach to tax reform. Because of the anti-tax presence during the election and the state's bulging surplus of almost one billion dollars, legislators were under pressure to provide some tax relief lest Proposition 13 strike in Wisconsin. This is what they did: an eight week moratorium on withholding payments for the state income tax, a one-time property tax relief payment of $100 for homeowners and $40 for renters, and an adjustment in the income tax to reduce rates and create wider brackets in order to compensate for the "inflation bite." The purpose of the tax refunds was to use up part of the state's surplus revenues. These refunds also served the purpose of cooling off the anti-tax fever. The adjustment in the state's progressive income tax not only eased some of the pain of inflation, but also will help to prevent the state treasury from accumulating another problem-causing surplus. Elected officials are beginning to realize that surplus revenues tend to magnify citizen unhappiness with high taxes.

The track record of the tax revolt in the states clearly indicates taxpayers can do something about taxes if they get angry enough and are willing to invest some time and effort. The key in state tax reform is to work for long lasting effects rather than onetime rebates that have only a temporary effect on the overall tax burden. In fact, concerned citizens should do everything in their power to avoid the onetime tax rebate because it lessens the amount of pressure that can be brought to bear on governors and state legislatures. The effect of a $50 or $100 tax refund is insignificant compared to an adjustment of income tax rates such as indexing the tax brackets in order to reduce the "inflation tax." The existence of a large surplus in state treasuries is a strong addition to any anti-tax campaign because it demonstrates the basic inability of government officials to reduce taxes.

To summarize, political action at the state level pays high dividends. Pressure can be brought on elected officials, and if there is an initiative process, it can be used to achieve tax relief. The other factor to be considered is that basic changes in the governmental structure may be needed in order to achieve tax relief. This will lengthen the amount of time required, but may well pay other dividends in terms of improving the operation of the state government overall.

Illinois is a case in point. After a strong showing of anti-tax feeling on an advisory referendum, the legislature ignored taxpayer sentiments in granting themselves a large increase in pay. As a result of this affront, taxpayers are organizing to change the means by which state representatives are elected. The current system makes it difficult to displace more than one incumbent from any given district. When and if the electoral system is changed, it will be much easier to bring pressure on legislators to support tax reform programs.

Local government is the point where citizens can have the greatest impact on their tax burden and on how the government functions in meeting their needs. Local government is accessible to the average citizen. Local government officials, especially in small and medium size districts, are usually known to a large number of citizens. Generally, local government operations are easier for citizens to understand than state or national operations because the functions of local government involve activities and services with which most people are familiar. The structure of local government often provides for a means of direct citizen participation in decision making. In many areas in New England the town meeting is an institution that gives every citizen the opportunity to express an opinion. In other parts of the country citizens vote on whether or not bond issues should be authorized for the construction of physical facilities. Still other local governments operate under state laws that provide the opportunity for people to vote on a wide number of substantive issues. Also, local government officials at least give lip service to the idea that citizens should be encouraged to participate in local government affairs to the maximum extent possible. All of these factors combine to make citizen action at the local level one of the most productive ways to reduce the overall tax burden as well as improve the quality of service government provides. In addition to making positive contributions to the local community, this kind of involvement can serve as a training ground for talented, motivated taxpayers to move into statewide or even national politics.

When a person decides to get involved in local government for the first time, there are a number of questions that probably need to be answered. What are the first steps to take? How much does one have to know about the way the government runs? What do local governments do and where do they get their money? What problems are local governments facing as a group and how can the symptoms of these problems be identified in any particular local government? The answers to these questions may be difficult to find. Word-of-mouth information is often inaccurate. Books on the subject of local government are usually texts designed for an academic audience, containing little of practical value to the concerned citizen. The remainder of this book is devoted to answering the questions listed above and others like them. It is designed to provide the reader with the basic knowledge of how local government works. The material is presented with the assumption that the reader is interested in getting better value for the tax dollar. Whether a person is merely interested in getting a little better service from some local government agency or is strongly committed to working for a significant reduction in local property taxes, the information that follows should prove to be extremely useful.

## NOTES

1. Petition, American Tax Reduction Movement. Los Angeles, California, 1979.
2. Ibid.

# PART III
## The How and Why of Local Government Spending and Taxation

# 9 THE FUNCTIONS AND SERVICES OF LOCAL GOVERNMENT

Local governments are the most diverse part of the three-layer system of government. The federal government functions under one constitution and one set of laws. State government has fifty different variations, each with its own set of laws and its own constitution. Local governments are creatures of the state in a legal sense. They derive their rights, powers, responsibilities, and authority from state government. Different states have different means of governing the activities of local government. There are three different means normally used by states to regulate the activities of local governments: charters, constitutional provisions, and statutes.

Charters are a form of birth certificate for local government. A charter is a statement of what an individual local government is authorized to do: what services it *can* perform, what services it *must* perform, what taxes it can collect, what its structure will be, what role citizens can play in its operation. In short, the charter of a local government is a guide for all of its actions and activities. The charter functions for local government in a manner similiar to a constitution for a state government. Local government charters are all unique. Even within the same state it is very unlikely that any two will be exactly the same. Different states provide for charters to be created for local governments in different ways. Some are authorized by state constitutions. In other states statutes provide that charters will be granted when certain conditions are met. Generally speaking, local governments operating under a charter are subject to less state regulation than local governments operating under constitutional provisions or statutes.

In some states the constitution specifies what the structure of local government shall be. Different types of local governments are identified and each type has its own set of operating provisions. In some states there are sets of rules and operating procedures that citizens of a local government unit may vote to adopt. Generally, these optional provisions have the effect of giving citizens more control over the activities of the local government as opposed to having them controlled by state statute.

As an example of the multiplicity of local governments existing within a single state, the State of Illinois proves a useful case in point. Article VII of the Illinois Constitution deals exclusively with the structure of local governments in the state. Article VII contains a basic definition of local governments in Section 1. This section is reproduced below.

> "Municipalities" means cities, villages and incorporated towns. "Units of local government" means counties, municipalities, townships, special districts, and units, designated as units of local government by law, which exercise limited governmental powers or powers in respect to limited governmental subjects, but does not include school districts.

The subsequent sections of Article VII define specific aspects of the governance of the different types of local government existing in the state. Four of the 12 sections make special provisions for counties. One section deals with school districts. Another section deals with the powers of "home rule units." In addition to addressing specific aspects of local government operations, the constitution specifies which local government operations are governed by the actions of the Illinois state legislature. This is the reason for the definition provided above in Section 1. In summary, the local government provisions of the Illinois constitution serve two general purposes. First, they serve to define general categories of local governments in order to facilitate the control of local activities by statute. Second, the provisions describe the manner in which specific aspects of local government shall operate.

Statutes are the third means that states use to control the operations of local government. Statutes generally cover all those areas of local government operation the state has an interest in that are not covered in the constitution. Statutes can cover a wide range of subjects from the type of welfare services a local government must provide to the budgeting procedure that must be used, including specific dates for the fiscal year. Statutes are also the means states use to mandate services or programs to local governments. The state legislature can require a local government to carry out a specific program, although it does not have to provide funding for the program. This practice of mandating without financing has been remedied by some of the tax reforms approved during the 1978 elections.

Fortunately for the taxpayer interested in local government, it is a great deal easier to understand the legal basis of one single local government unit than it is to understand local governments in their total complexity. The first question is whether or not the local government operates under a charter. If it does, then a copy of this document can be easily obtained. If it does not, then the taxpayer must find out what exact category the local government belongs to in terms of constitutional and statutory provisions. Usually a single telephone call to the local government office will yield this information. Once the legal definition of the local government is determined another telephone call, this time to the office of a state representative, will usually yield a copy of the relevant laws and a copy of the state constitution.

The next task is to go through these materials and identify which articles and sections pertain to the local government under study. (While this search process is not difficult, it can be tedious and somewhat time consuming. It is a very worthwhile project for a local taxpayer association or for citizen groups to undertake.) As a result of this search process, the taxpayer will have identified the legal basis for the local government. This legal basis will describe the most important powers, responsibilities, and operating procedures of the local government; it will not describe every detail of compliance with state statute and regulation.

An understanding of the legal basis of the local government provides a start in examining the specific structures and functions of interest to the taxpayer.

## TYPES OF LOCAL GOVERNMENT

While the specific operating characteristics of local government are determined by the legal basis of each individual unit, some broad generalizations can be made. Local governments can be put into one of two categories based upon the extent of the services and programs they provide. *General* local government units are those authorized to provide a wide range of services to citizens within a particular geographic area. Cities, towns, and counties are the names for general local government units with which people are most familiar. *Special* local government units provide limited, specialized kinds of services. These are commonly called special districts. Autonomous school districts fall into this category.

In addition to these two classifications, there is another type of local government unit worthy of mention. Some local governments assist in the creation of special kinds of units that are entrepreneurial in nature; that is, they are set up to operate a specific kind of facility and derive the majority of their revenues from the operation of these facilities. These units may be completely autonomous from the governments that created them or they may still have a connection such as having their boards composed of elected officials from the founding local government unit. Examples are utilities owned by local governments or special purpose authorities such as those operating seaports, airports, or municipal athletic facilities.

Primary local government units such as cities and counties often have the power to create other kinds of local units to assist them in providing services. These units do not qualify as local governments in a legal sense because they generate no revenues and operate at the will of the primary local government unit. Examples are such bodies as planning commissions, library commissions, and parks and recreation commissions. These units often serve an advisory function to the elected officials of the unit that created them. These commissions and boards provide an excellent opportunity for citizens to get involved in a particular type of local government operation. Although this increased participation is an advantage in some ways, it can be a disadvantage in other ways. For the citizens pursuing a specific goal or objective, these advisory boards and commissions may be nothing more than an additional obstacle to overcome.

In addition to the types of local government already identified, there is one more form worthy of mention. Some areas of the country have regional government units designed to provide a specific service in an area overlapping two or more primary local governments. Regional units exist to meet needs beyond the scope of primary units either in geography or financial capability. A good example is the rapid transit districts serving large metropolitan areas including any number of cities, counties, and school districts.

In spite of the large number of different types of local government units, the city or town is the form of local government citizens are most likely to have an interest in because these units provide most of the local services. The exception to this general rule is the instance of unincorporated areas where county government carries the responsibility for providing all the basic services. In order to ease the difficulties of generalizing about the diverse structures and functions of local government, the focus of the following discussion will be on city and county government.

Just as the national and state governments have three branches, so do local governments. Cities and counties have their own court systems operating in areas of jurisdiction specified by state law or by state constitutional provisions. Cities and counties elect officials to carry out a legislative or lawmaking function similar to state legislatures and the United States Congress. It is in the executive function that local governments are unique. The executive function of government at any level involves the implementation of policies initiated by the legislative branch. The executive is responsible for the management function of government involving personnel, budgeting, and other administrative concerns. Local governments as a group have three different means of carrying out the executive function.

The first means of operating the executive function is to merge it with the legislative function. Under this system elected policymakers are also responsible for the management of a part of the local government structure. The commission form of government in cities is a good example of merged functions. Typically, commissioners are elected in conjunction with a specific function of government such as fire or police. The commissioner is responsible for the leadership and management of these programs. (An example might be a commissioner of public safety who is responsible for fire and police operations.) In addition to these executive functions, the commissioner also sits on the legislative body of the city, sometimes called the city commission. There, with the commissioners from the other departments, ordinances are passed, budgets are adopted, and taxes are levied. The obvious disadvantage to this arrangement is that each commissioner has a special interest in one part of the budget, the part pertaining to the commissioner's own department. This special interest makes it very difficult for the commissioners as a group to give first priority to the overall interests of the city and its citizens. In addition to a lack of concern for the overall interests of the city and its citizens with this system, it is difficult for taxpayers to identify accountability for overall taxes and services because each commissioner has only a partial responsibility for city operations.

In conclusion, when the executive function is merged with the legislative function, two things happen. First, there is no central executive to provide leadership and management for the city as a whole, thus there is no one whom the citizens can hold responsible. Second, the legislative function suffers because each member of the legislative body has a particular special interest that many times predominates over the overall public interest. This kind of special interest thinking deprives the city and the citizens of a legislative process that focuses on the interests of the city as a whole. As a result of these problems and the prevalence of corruption in the commission form of government, it is slowly but surely being re-placed by other forms of local government.

The second means of carrying out the executive function in local government involves a separation of the executive from the legislative function. This is usually carried out by having a single official who is elected with responsibility for the overall leadership and management of local government operations. The most common title for this type of offical is "mayor." Mayors are often elected by the entire population of the local government, while legislative officials are usually elected from wards or districts. The office of mayor in this type of local government (mayor-council form) is in many respects similar to that of governor or president. The offices are similar because they both have responsibility for the overall leadership and the effective management of the government. The differences among the three offices lie in the relationship with the legislative branch of government. Very often mayors have a more direct and frequent contact with legislators than do governors or the president. It is not unusual for mayors to chair the meetings of the legislative body and, in some instances, they may even have the right to vote as a member of the body. Additionally, most mayors have a veto authority similar to that of governors and the president.

The advantages of the mayor-council form of government lie in the clear separation of the legislative from the executive function. The mayor holds and accepts primary responsibility for the overall management of the city. Citizens rightly look to the mayor for leadership, giving praise when things go right and assigning respon-sibility when things go wrong. Because the mayor and the legislative body have separate and independent roles in the government, they can serve as a check and balance on each other thereby avoiding the temptation for easy graft and corruption that became the hall-mark of the commission form of government. The second clear advantage to the mayor-council form of government is that the legislative officials can devote all of their time and energy to rep-resenting the interests of the voters who elected them. Similarly, the voters have a right to expect the officials to make a concentrated effort to determine what the citizen interests are in their districts and to work toward achieving them. In short, the members of the legislative council can spend all their efforts on policymaking, rather than dividing their time between administrative and legislative duties as in the commission form of government.

The third means of carrying out the executive function of local government involves the appointment of a chief administrative officer or city manager who carries the overall responsibility for the management of all government operations. All of the city employees report to this person, and the manager in turn serves at the pleasure of the city or county council. The council-manager form of government may have a mayor as part of the council, but this person is usually chosen from among the council members rather than being elected-at-large. Typically, mayors operating in this form of government have little or no real power. This is because they have no overall leadership responsibilities or authority. They also lack a political power base because they are elected from a single district within the city or county and thus do not have the power that comes from winning a city-wide or county-wide race.

The advantages and disadvantages of the manager-council form are to some extent dependent on the attitude and values of the persons making the judgment. From the point of view of professional public managers and those members of the public who value efficiency and effectiveness in government over all else, the presence of a professional and highly educated manager as the key executive in a local government is a definite asset. Because all city employees work for the manager and not the elected officials, the chances of undue political pressure and corruption are lessened. Elected officials are assured that the policies they make will be carried out efficiently and effectively by a neutral and objective public servant who is not at all concerned with "politics," but only the good management of the local government. Superficially at least, this list of advantages sounds like the epitome of good local government.

There is, however, another side to the story. This side is the point of view of the average citizen. To be sure, efficient government serves an interest of the people. But there are other interests of the people that must also be served. The foremost of these is responsiveness. In order for any government to be responsive, the people must be able to exercise control over their representatives in government. In the council-manager form of local government, the people have no representative in the executive function. To be sure, they do have representation through legislative officials. Theoretically because the legislative officials can hire and fire the manager, the interests of the people are communicated to and honored in the executive function. However, this is not usually the case. The manager is interested in doing a good job. This means efficient and effective services. It also means providing the maximum level of service possible. Maximum service for the manager translates to high taxes for the citizens. Because managers do not have to face the citizens during elections and because they report to the council and not the people, they are shielded from pressures that serve to communicate the people's need for a reasonable level of taxes and services.

One might well ask given this situation,why can't elected officials control the actions of managers so the people's priorities and not the managers' are served? The answer to this question lies in the model discussed in the first chapter of this book. Elected officials must make and fulfill promises if they are going to be able to hold onto their offices. To do this, they must have the active cooperation of the manager for the simple reason that the manager knows how the government works, knows how to get things done, and most importantly knows where to get the money to pay for new programs. Given this situation, it should come as no surprise that the legislator-manager relationship is not one of the typical employer-employee. In any case, the manager can be fired only upon a majority vote of the council. The astute manager builds relationships with all members of the council by giving them what they want and by suggesting projects for which money can be found without obvious increases in taxes. These suggestions are easily converted to the coveted "record of achievement" that is the basis of many successful campaigns. This kind of relationship makes it impossible for the check and balance system to operate between the executive and legislative functions. In the commission form of government this lack of a check and balance caused graft and corruption; in the manager-council form it causes a lack of responsiveness and continuous increases in spending and taxes.

In order to evaluate any particular unit of local government in terms of its three basic function, a number of things must be considered. First, while the form of the government is an important starting point, one must go beyond the form and look at the substance of what actually occurs. The political history of a government and the character and power of the people who run it are at least as important as the formal system. Each local government has its own unique way of getting things done. The comments made in the previous paragraphs are not intended to be final judgments on the quality of different types of government, rather they are a starting place for concerned citizens to evaluate the quality and responsiveness of their own government. Using these ideas as a base, citizens should consider the political history of the community and the personal record of the elected officials. Individual judgments must be made about the responsiveness of the government and its officials, both elected and appointed. The values of upper level managers must be examined to determine their attitudes toward conserving tax revenues and other resources.

While the technique of analyzing the executive role is a useful one for the concerned citizen, there are other considerations that must be taken into account. These include an understanding of how local government functions, that is, how it translates resources into programs and services, and understanding of the major types of services local governments provide. These considerations are the next topics to be considered.

## HOW LOCAL GOVERNMENT WORKS

For many people the question, "How does local government work?" is answered in a civics class or perhaps a class in political science. The answer presented usually involves a lot of legal references and a good deal of jargon. These kinds of responses are not useful to citizens who want to have some influence on the quality and quantity of services they get in return for their tax dollars. To provide a useful answer to the question of how local government works requires a more complex model than those usually found in introductory classes. The model must of necessity place a good deal of emphasis on the financial processes of local government. The financial processes are the means by which tax dollars are translated into services. Because this is the prime function of all governments, it is the point of greatest concern to taxpayers who want to improve the value they get for their tax dollar.

An examination of how local government works must start with the question of what do local governments do? What do they produce? There are three types of productive outputs associated with local government. They are services, goods, and regulation. Examples of local government services include health, welfare, education, and police services. Local governments also produce goods such as roads, buildings, and capital equipment such as that used in publicly owned utilities. Regulation as a type of productive output of local government requires a further explanation. The ultimate goal of any government is to serve the overall public interest. There are instances when the activities of individuals or organizations might work against the good of the general public. Regulation by local government is designed to discourage activities that are not in the public interest and to encourage other activities that are beneficial to the public. Because regulation contributes directly to the overall goal of local government, it qualifies as a productive output.

The answer to the question of "How does local government work?" may be addressed by identifying those processes enabling local governments to carry out their productive functions. Five distinct processes can be identified.

1. The identification and pricing of areas of production in response to the needs of the local community. In carrying out this process the techniques of budgeting and planning are used.

2. The raising of sufficient revenue to carry out the necessary production functions. Within this process taxation and revenue administration are the main areas of activity.

3. The allocation of available resources to the production of goods, services, and regulation. This process focuses on the political decisionmaking mechanisms of the local government, especially the legislative and executive functions that have already been discussed. Additionally, other groups such as public interest groups, taxpayer associations, special interest groups, and labor organizations play significant roles in carrying out this decision-making process.

4. The management of the fiscal and human resources used in the production function. Management of these resources often involves the use of such advanced techniques as management by objectives, zero base budgeting, and human resource accounting.

5. The process of auditing and reviewing production expenditures is used to assure the efficiency, the effectiveness, the honesty, and the public accountability of local government actions and the participants in those actions.

The five processes that allow local governments to generate productive outputs are arranged in the model presented in Figure 9-1. For each of these broad processes, there are a series of component parts which combine to make the processes operate. These parts are discussed in detail in the following paragraphs.

### Identification and Pricing of Productive Outputs

Part I includes the two major functions of planning and budgeting. Planning involves the identification of problems falling within the jurisdiction of the local government. Based upon the identification of problems, programs are generated describing a series

FIGURE 9.1
Process Model for Local Government

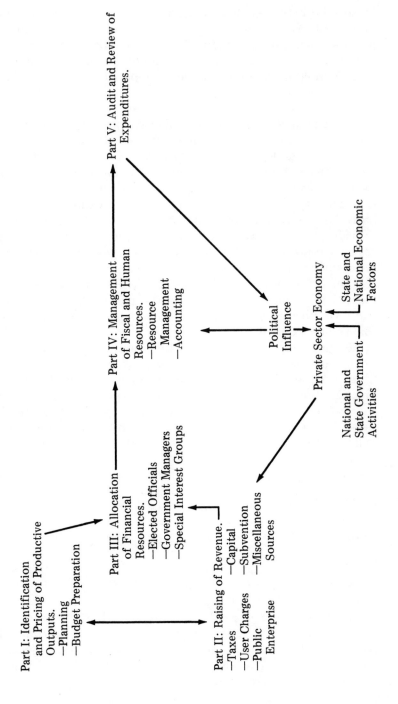

of specific activities that, if carried out, should solve the problem. The problems and the programs to solve them are transmitted to the political decision makers for final action. Essentially, the planning function is one of sensing and examining what is happening in the local community. Problems and opportunities, when identified, start the planning process.

The planning function can be carried out by a number of different people. The public can identify problems and bring them to the attention of the local government officials. Elected officials from either the legislative or executive branch can identify problems and suggest solutions. The planning function can also be carried out by the managers who work in the various departments of the local government. The planning efforts of these various groups form the basis for determining the type of services the local government will provide. There is one other source of problems and programs that should be mentioned. The legal structures governing the operation of local government sometimes require that certain programs be carried out. In planning terms, this means officials at the state level have identified problem areas that are the responsibility of government and have decided that local government is the appropriate place for them to be handled.

Budget preparation involves the forecasting of costs for (or the pricing of) new and existing programs. The costing of programs is usually done by local government managers. Budgeting involves breaking the programs down into their component parts: personnel, equipment, supplies, office space, and contracts. When the costs of these components are added together, the result is the budget estimate for the program. The costs of the various programs being considered are combined and thus the overall budget is created. Programs and budgets are submitted to the legislative body. Decisions are then made on which programs will be funded and on what the overall level of spending should be.

### Raising of Revenue

There are six major sources of revenue for local government: taxes, user charges, revenue from public enterprises, capital funds, subventions, and miscellaneous sources.

Taxes are defined as those charges on the public for which no direct service is rendered. Chapter Four presented a comprehensive picture of the most common taxes used by local governments.

The second major source of revenue is user charges. User charges are defined as charges against the public for which a direct benefit is obtained. Examples might include charges for building inspection, for the use of recreational facilities, and for garbage collection. These are direct user charges, but there are also indirect charges such as city taxes on motor fuel. These taxes are earmarked for road improvement exclusively. Therefore, even though they are technically defined as taxes, they actually function as indirect user charges because of the earmarking of their revenues.

The revenue raised from public enterprises usually represents a fairly small percentage of overall local government revenues. The most common type of public enterprises sponsored by local government include utility services and sports and exposition authorities. Public enterprises charge fees for their products and services much the same way the private enterprises do. Their costs and revenues are usually separated from the general funds of the local government. They are created to provide specific services without using any tax revenues. Ideally, the money they take in should cover their expenses. If they fall short, general revenue funds must be used to bail them out. If surplus revenues are accumulated, they are operating at a "profit," which means they are charging too much for the services they provide. The goal of public enterprises is to break even. However, they are sometimes encouraged by the local government to operate at a "profit" so that these surpluses can be used by the local government for its own purposes. This is an undesirable practice because it places a hidden tax on people using the services of the enterprise. To repeat a point previously made, hidden taxes are undesirable because they prevent taxpayers from determining whether or not they are getting good value in return for their tax dollar.

Capital funds are those funds utilized for the specific purpose of large-scale construction activities. There are two common forms of debt instruments used to secure capital funding. These are revenue bonds and general obligation bonds.

Revenue bonds are usually linked to a specific project. The promise of repayment of principal and payment of interest is based upon revenues generated by the project exclusively. Local governments sometimes issue a special kind of revenue bond to encourage industrial or commercial development. These are called industrial revenue bonds. They are actually sold for and repaid by a private enterprise under the auspices of the local government. They are attractive to businesses because the interest earned from these bonds is not subject to federal income tax as is the interest earned from corporate bonds. Therefore, the bonds can be issued at a lower rate of interest, thereby saving the private enterprise a substantial amount of money. Industrial revenue bonds are an inexpensive means local governments can use to attract industry and commerce.

In contrast to revenue bonds, general obligation bonds are issued for a broad, general purpose and their repayment (both of principal and interest) is guaranteed by the general taxing power of the local government. Normally, general obligation bonds carry a lower rate of interest than do revenue bonds because of their higher assurance of repayment. Most local governments are required by law to seek voter approval before issuing any general obligation bonds. This is because they are guaranteed by tax revenues, which voters will have to provide. Additionally, many states limit the amount of general obligation bonds a local government can have outstanding to a certain percentage of the government's total assessed property valuation. This limitation exists because the property tax, as the largest source of local government revenue, will be the primary means of repayment of the bonds.

There is a third type of debt instrument used by local government. Strictly speaking it is not a source of capital funds, but it is a type of borrowing so it should be mentioned here. Tax anticipation notes are used to provide operating capital for local government. They are necessary because tax and other revenues are not received on a regular basis. They are usually received only a few times each year. Therefore, tax anticipation notes are utilized by some local governments to even out their cash flow. These notes are repaid once tax funds become available.

Subventions are a broad category of revenue encompassing all types of fund transfers between governments not directly related to an exchange or provision of services. Local governments receive a significant amount of funds from the federal government, usually in the form of categorical grants in aid, block grants, or revenue sharing funds. In contrast to most other types of federal aid, revenue sharing funds are distributed to all local and state governments on a formula basis using population as a major component. These funds are relatively free from "strings" and therefore place few additional restrictions on the perogatives of local government. States also provide subventions to local government in many of the same forms used by the federal government. The 1978 tax revolt caused a rapid rise in the amount of state funds going to local government in a number of states. In some instances, such as California, the state governments used their surplus funds to replace lost property tax revenues. In other instances states were forced by the voters to start reimbursing local governments for programs costs incurred as the result of carrying out programs mandated by the state. There is every reason to believe that subventions will continue to grow in importance as a source of local government revenues.

The category of miscellaneous revenues sources includes such items as interest from the cash balances maintained by local governments in short term investment accounts. Also in this category are revenues received as the result of payments from public enterprises and from revolving funds. After an initial capitalization, revolving funds operate out of their own current revenues and thus do not constitute a drain of the general operating funds of the local government. An example of a revolving fund can be found in the funding of municipal tennis courts where the fees paid by the users pay for maintenance and upkeep. In this way the courts can be operated at no cost to the local government.

Revenues from all sources must be budgeted in much the same way as costs for programs are estimated. Revenue forecasts are used to determine how much money will be available for use during the upcoming year. Most local governments are required by law to pass a budget in which projected program costs do not exceed projected revenue. These requirements are known as "balanced budget" laws.

## Allocation of Financial Resources

The process of allocating available revenue to program budgets is the part of the local government model most open to the influence of groups outside the government. It is open because the decisions are made by the elected legislative officials in open meetings. The amount of revenue available and the program spending proposals are both open to public scrutiny.

Most local governments have an executive budget process. This means the proposed budget is submitted to the legislative body by the head of the executive branch of the local government. Depending on the form of government, the person presenting the budget may be the mayor, the city manager, or each of the commissioners. The presentation consists of two parts, the revenue side and the program spending side. At the end of the decision process these sides must balance.

But before that happens, there are many decisions to be made. Program costs will have to be reduced. Some proposed new programs will have to be eliminated. Perhaps some new sources of revenue will have to be developed. Local government almost always suffers from a shortage of revenues to carry out desired programs. Therefore, the nature of the decisions to be made is always the same. It is a question of allocating too few resources among too many competing programs. The big question in the minds of most officials is: "How can we get enough money to do everything that we have to do?" Officials are under a great deal of pressure to provide programs to meet needs. There are election promises to keep. There are special interest groups who want programs to serve their particular needs. Local government managers have their own pet projects for which they seek budgets. The pervasive attitude is "too much to do and not enough money to do it with." The universal assumption of local government officials is that more revenues are needed.

Needless to say, the point of view of the taxpayer is somewhat different. The major interest of most taxpayers in local government is the tax they must pay. The number of citizens who worry about the level of service they receive from local government is generally quite small. Citizens who are concerned about government services almost always focus on only one service or, at most, a few services that are of direct benefit to them.

It is this basic disparity of values that is the underlying reason for the taxpayer revolt. In economic hard times citizens feel taxes more and want to do something about the ones they can see. This makes local government the prime target for the taxpayer revolt. While the dynamics taking place in the third part of the local government model explain why there is a tax revolt, they are not sufficient by themselves to explain to concerned taxpayers what they can do to try to reduce government spending and taxes. Knowledge of all parts of the model is essential to make taxpayers effective advocates for their point of view.

## Management of Fiscal and Human Resources

After the approval of the budget, resource management becomes a primary concern. This area may be conveniently categorized into human resource management and fiscal or monetary resource management. Both of these areas of managerial concern have a common goal; that is, to carry out the production of goods, services, and/or regulatory activities with a maximum of efficiency, effectiveness, honesty, and concern for public accountability. The management of human and fiscal resources often utilizes sophisticated management systems such as zero base budgeting, program budgeting, human resource accounting, and others.

The rationality of these management systems is geared toward efficiency and effectiveness. It is not always compatible with the political rationality of the resource allocation process. Elected officials are often more concerned about meeting the needs of special interest groups and keeping their campaign promises than they are about efficiency and effectiveness.

The result of this clash of rationalities is a good deal of conflict between elected officials and management officials of local government. This conflict is well hidden from the average citizen for two reasons. First, many of its manifestations take place in situations other than public meetings where there are no outsiders present. Second, in order to understand this conflict, the citizen must understand the conflicting points of view of the managers and the elected officials. The citizen who is interested in trying to reduce taxes has a direct interest in this conflict. The advocacy of efficient and effective operations can result in reduced taxes as long as the savings achieved in any given area are not used to fund programs in some other area. Managers usually feel that monies they save through increased efficiency and effectiveness should be used to improve existing services or add new ones. It is at this point that the manager and the taxpayer may part company on their views. Taxpayers want savings passed on to them in the form of reduced taxes. In short, the manager and the taxpayer are allies when it comes to fighting for efficiency and effectiveness against elected officials, but they go in different directions when it comes time to decide what to do with the savings.

An important subcomponent of managing resources is the accounting function. The accounting function is basically one that provides information and monitors the expenditure of public funds. Information gathering serves not only as a data base for the subsequent audit and expenditure review, but also is a valuable input for planning and budget preparation in future years. The accounting function can be one of the major resources for taxpayers to use in trying to reduce their tax burden. As citizens they have a right to most of the operating information used in local government. There are very few areas such as personnel files that can legally be closed to public scrutiny. Knowing what information to ask for and understanding how it fits into the overall operation of the local government can prove a valuable asset to taxpayer groups fighting to curb spending and taxes. (The details of information gathering are covered in a subsequent chapter.)

## Audit and Review of Expenditures

Audit and expenditure review is a process by which the management and expenditure of public funds is examined to insure that regulations and legislative intent have been satisfied. Traditionally, audit and expenditure review has been concerned with fiscal accountability; that is, seeing if funds were expended in accordance with duly established regulations and policies. Recently, there has been a trend toward progam auditing and review. The emphasis of program auditing is to ascertain whether or not the program is effective in meeting the goals set during the legislative process of budgetary approval.

Fiscal and program reviews are as important to the taxpayers as they are to elected officials. They serve as checks and controls on the activities of the local government managers. They offer assurance of honest and judicious use of public funds and also provide useful evaluations on the effectiveness of programs. This information is particularly useful in helping elected officials and taxpayer groups to identify programs that are in need of improvement or that are candidates for elimination. Taxpayers may find themselves allied with elected officials in using audit information. However, as in the case of the alliance with government managers, there will be a parting of the ways because of the divergent purposes of the two groups. Politicians are interested in finding ways to cut funds from existing programs in order to create new programs—new programs that will satisfy special interest groups and help keep campaign promises. Taxpayers want to discover wasteful and unneeded programs so tax dollars can be saved.

## Interaction with the Private Economy

The productive output of local government has an influence on the amount and type of revenues that are available. The private economy of the local community serves as a processor, taking the productive outputs of the local government and combining these with the productive outputs of the state and federal governments. There is an amalgamation with the economic factors within the local community, and the outcome is a level of economic activity that determines the yield of the local government's revenue activities. Additionally, the actions of the private sector economy serve as a major input to the planning process. Thus, there is a complete loop from the planning activities and revenue structure of the local government to the production of goods, services, and regulation interacting with the private economy, back to the planning and budgeting processes.

To summarize the main point of the model, local government does not operate in a vacuum isolated from the other levels of government or from the private economy of the community. Changes in the local government are reflected in changes in the community. Similarly, changes in the private economy will affect local government's revenue and spending needs. The same concept of interdependence holds true within the structure of local government itself. Changes in one part of the governmental system will bring about other changes. It is important to review these interdependencies when changes are contemplated. As a case in point, California's Proposition 13 placed heavy controls on the introduction of new local taxes, but did nothing about new fees and charges. Taxes and charges are both a part of a single process within local government: revenue generation. That many local governments enacted heavy sets of new fees and charges would not have come as a surprise to California taxpayers if they had considered the possible effects of "13" in terms of the model just presented.

Second, in using the model as a means to understand the operations of local government, it is important to realize the difference in the value systems of the people involved in the decisionmaking processes. Managers, elected officials, special interest groups all have a far different set of values than the taxpayer who wants more service for the tax dollar and who wants to limit taxes to the minimum amount necessary. There are times such as those discussed earlier when taxpayers will find it beneficial to work in consort with one or another of these groups, but the time will always come when the difference in goals and values will force a parting of the ways. As nice as it would be to say that all groups working together will achieve a common purpose, taxpayers must realize that this cannot happen for them. Conserving tax dollars and curbing government spending directly oppose the goals of the other groups.

Thus far in this chapter the legal basis of local government has been examined, different types of local governments have been described, and a model has been presented describing local government operations in a very general way. The last task of this chapter is to briefly discuss the multitude of different services offered by local governments.

## SERVICES OF LOCAL GOVERNMENT

The services local governments provide are subject to a number of limitations. The first is an affirmative limitation from state government. Local governments are mandated to provide certain services by the state either from their own revenues or with state support. Because they are creatures of the state, local governments must provide the services specified. Each of the 50 states has its own set of mandates local governments must follow.

The second limitation also comes from the state government and is negative in the sense that local governments are prohibited from providing certain kinds of public services and from using certain kinds of taxes and other revenue devices. These prohibitions occur because the services and revenues are those the state government itself operates with. The term commonly used to describe these prohibitions is "preempted." For instance, local governments in many states are not allowed to license motor vehicles. In these cases, the state government is said to have "preempted" this service (and the associated revenues) for itself.

Local governments are also subject to limitations from the federal government. The federal government derives its power from the states. The original colonies gave up some of their autonomy in order to create the federal government. This loss of autonomy allows the federal government to be the sole provider of some services such as national defense and the sole collector of some kinds of revenues such as tariffs on international trade. There are areas of service in which the federal government preempts state government. These preemptions also apply to local government by virtue of the fact that local governments are subordinate units of the states.

Although limitations differ from state to state, there are services that are common to the different types of local government units. Some of these are described below.

Cities and towns are general purpose governments providing a wide variety of essential services. These services are provided either directly by city personnel or by contract with other government units (usually counties) or private industry. Cities are responsible for fire protection, police protection, emergency health services, planning and zoning functions, building and safety inspections, maintenance of roads, the licensing of certain businesses and professions, and other traditional functions. Cities may also operate public enterprises such as transit systems, ports, parking garages, and recreational facilities. All of the services provided directly to the public are called "line" services. The term "line" means these functions are the primary business of the organization. In addition to "line" functions, cities also have "staff" functions. A "staff" function is one that supports the operation of the primary functions. Examples of staff functions are personnel departments, finance departments, internal auditors, garages for the repair of city vehicles, and accounting departments. In addition to the goods and services, cities also provide regulation as a productive output. The city attorney's office and other departments regulate a wide range of activities, from limiting the hours cocktail lounges may be open to issuing permits to cab drivers.

Counties are also general purpose governments offering basically the same services as cities to those geographic areas in the county not within the boundaries of a city or town. In addition to these services, they may provide services on contract to cities and towns. Police services are a popular contract service. Counties also provide some unique functions cities do not. The best example is in states where the counties have responsibility for the assessment of property and the collection of property taxes. Cities and other local governments receive their share of the property tax revenues from the county offices. The boundaries between city and county services are determined by the laws and constitution of each state. Another type of service reserved for counties in many states is the administration of state welfare programs.

In addition to the general purpose governments, all states have special purpose governments existing to provide a limited set of services to citizens within a defined geographic area. Perhaps the best known example of limited governments are school districts. In areas where cities and counties do not provide educational programs, special districts fill this function. Other types of special districts are mosquito abatement, water conservation, flood control, and transportation. Special districts are set up for a number of reasons. The primary reason is to provide a service to a geographic area encompassing several counties and towns. Flood control districts are a good example. Special districts may also be set up for revenue purposes. Most special districts have the ability to levy a property tax. In states where there is a maximum property tax rate, special districts are a device to provide a service that could not be funded out of existing revenues.

The list of services local governments provide is long, and listing them all is impossible. Chances are that activist taxpayers are only interested in one particular local government. Therefore, the job of finding out what kinds of services the government provides is quite simple. The easiest way to get the information is to obtain an organization chart of the local government. These charts depict all of the major functions and departments. They are a quick handy reference to the activities of local governments.

## CONCLUSION

This chapter has served as an introduction to the structure and services of local government. It provides taxpayers with the basic information necessary to begin to understand the complexity of government organization. This information should be used as a means to understand how any particular local government functions. A point of particular importance is the divergence of the values and goals of elected officials, government managers, special interest groups, and the taxpayer. The taxpayer is the only one that has a continuing interest in curbing government spending and taxation. The other groups are generally interested in spending and expanding programs because this expansion provides a payoff for all of them, although for each in a different way. This divergence of goals does not mean taxpayers should not work with these groups when the opportunity arises. It means taxpayers must be aware that at some point there is going to be a parting of the ways.

# 10     THE FUNDAMENTALS OF THE BUDGETARY PROCESS

The budgetary process is the heart of local government operations. It is the means by which elected officials decide what the programs and services of the local government shall be and what the revenue requirement will be. Because of its importance in local government operations, the budgetary process must be thoroughly understood by the taxpayer who wishes to influence taxing and spending policies. This chapter will describe all of the essential aspects of the local government budgetary process.

Budgeting in any type of organization is essentially a decision-making process performing the function of allocating resources (dollars) among competing demands (programs). Despite high tax levels, local governments almost always find themselves in the position of having more demands for funds than they can satisfy. In this situation, local government officials have the responsibility to make the best possible use of the resources available.

The first question to be addressed is: What is meant by a "best" decision? A "best" decision is one that satisfies all demands presented to the decision maker and does so with a minimal amount of resources. It should be obvious that such decisions are few and far between and are almost always impossible for local officials to achieve. However, what a decision maker can do is to make a "good" decision. A "good" decision is one that uses existing resources to meet the needs of the community by carrying on activities and providing services in a reasonably efficient, effective, and economic manner while fulfilling the legal and ethical requirements that apply to local government officials. The key terms in this definition are efficient, effective, economic, and legal and ethical requirements. Each of these is defined in the paragraphs that follow.

## EFFICIENCY

An efficient decision is one that provides a fixed amount and quality of service at the lowest possible cost. To measure the efficiency of a given program, two types of information are necessary. It must be possible to determine the quanity as well as the quality of the service provided. And it must be possible to determine what the costs are.

The activity of providing police assistance in response to telephone calls is a good means to examine the concept of efficiency. In this example the specific measure of efficiency is the time necessary for a police unit to respond to calls for assistance. The specific measurement is the time elapsed betweeen the receipt of the call at the police station and the arrival of the police on the scene. For the purpose of the example, assume the average response time desired is four minutes, plus or minus thirty seconds. The average response time is calculated on a monthly basis and acceptable performance is determined to be somewhere between three and one-half and four and one-half minutes.

Applying the concept of efficiency to this example, the question is how can this predetermined level of service (i.e., a three and one-half to four and one-half minute average response time) be provided at the least possible cost. Three alternative means of providing this service are: use of a one man unit, use of a two man unit, or use of a motorcycle unit. In terms of efficiency, the choice between the three alternatives is made on the basis of which one costs the least while providing service that meets the predetermined standard. In basing the decision on efficiency, there is no attention given to what happens after the unit reaches the scene of the incident. Also, the concept of efficiency is not served by lowering the level of service below the predetermined standard. The essential question is simply which of the three service alternatives costs the least and is capable of achieving the minimum average response time required?

To summarize, the efficiency criteria in decision making focuses on the question of which alternative will provide a predetermined level of service for the lowest possible cost.

## EFFECTIVENESS

To be effective is to provide a service that actually carries out the function or accomplishes the goal for which the service was provided.

The previous example of response time to calls for assistance can be used to demonstrate the concept of effectiveness. In understanding effectiveness, the first step is a consideration of the goals the activity is designed to fulfill. The overall goal of responding to calls for assistance might be two-fold:

1. To reduce the incidence of crime in the area.
2. To protect the lives and property of citizens.

Dispatching officers in response to calls for assistance achieves this goal by fulfilling the objectives of apprehending suspects and providing emergency assistance.

The next question to be asked is how does response time affect the accomplishment of the overall goal. Or more specifically, how does response time contribute to apprehending suspects and providing emergency assistance? It would be natural to assume that the faster the response, the more effective the service. This may not always be a correct assumption. For example, although a faster response time is achieved by using motorcycle units rather than two-man units, a single officer may not be able to deal with the situation as effectively as two officers, even though the officer might arrive sooner. Therefore, while efficiency is achieved by having the least expensive unit arrive on the scene within the predetermined time, effectiveness is not achieved if the motorcycle unit cannot handle the incident as well as the two-man car unit. In this instance, efficiency is gained at the expense of effectiveness. The conclusion drawn from this example is that the achievement of both efficiency and effectiveness may not be possible in some situations. Decision makers will have to decide which of the two criteria they value more.

## ECONOMY

Economy is defined as spending the least amount of money possible to provide the absolute minimum required level of service. Again the example of response time can be used. Local government officials might determine the minimal level of service required by law is to respond only to emergencies involving a threat to human life and to reports of crimes in progress. Based upon this definition of minimal service, officials may choose to cut down the number of personnel on the police force in an attempt to save money. This savings is possible because the police will have to respond to fewer calls. In this instance the concept of economy involves no consideration of the effectiveness or efficiency of the service provided.

It should be noted that economy is often used in a very broad fashion by elected officials and others involved with local government. Many of these people who speak in public about the need for economy in government would probably say that the definition given above is not what they really mean. The common definition used for economy is a combination of efficiency, effectiveness, and economy. But in order to clearly understand the consequences of decisions made by local governments, taxpayers must have more than a general understanding of the meaning of these terms. It is important to identify and separate out the factors of a decision that influence efficiency, effectiveness, and economy. The quality of the decision must be judged on how well it fulfills *each* of these three separate criteria. Taxpayers must then decide for themselves which of the three criteria they value most in any given decision.

## LEGAL AND ETHICAL REQUIREMENTS

The fourth concept involved in making "good" decisions goes beyond the managerial and economic considerations of efficiency, effectiveness, and economy. The operations of local government and the conduct of local government officials are both subject to the legal constraints of the federal government, federal and state constitutions, state statutes, and local laws and regulations. Beyond these legal requirements, there are also ethical requirements imposed on the decisions of local government officials by the expectations of their constitutency, the expectations of society, and their own system of moral values.

Jails provide an example of legal requirements affecting a budgetary decision. The legal minimum requirement for jails might be to maintain the inmates within the bounds of the institution. This legal requirement might also include providing a minimal level of subsistence in terms of food, shelter, clothing, and medical care. Any decision made regarding the jail must be within the guidelines of these legal requirements. For instance, a work release program might not be tolerated if it violated the fundamental legal requirement of security, i.e., insulating inmates from the rest of society. Programs involving the lessening of security could be attacked as failing to meet the necessary legal requirements of that particular decision. Therefore, a good decision is one that meets the existing legal requirements for the service being provided.

The ethical requirement of a good decision may be based on a number of different foundations. One of these might be codes of conduct. Many professional organizations have codes of conduct they urge their members to abide by. Police officers, attorneys, nurses, and professional managers are all local government employees likely to have their own codes of conduct they feel they must follow. Additionally, many local governments have their own internal codes of conduct designed to guide the actions of both elected and appointed officials. A less tangible, but very important source of ethical requirements is the expectations citizens have for the performance and conduct of their local government and its officials. While these expectations may not be clearly spelled out in each decision situation, it is the responsibility of the public official to learn and understand what these expectations are. A final foundation for ethical requirements in decisions comes from the official's own set of moral values. In summary, the ethical requirements in any situation must be satisfied for a decision to be qualified as "good." In the 1970s there have been too many examples where public officials seemed to act as though there were no such things as ethical components to government decisions.

Examination of the four criteria for local government decisions provides a means to evaluate decisions made as part of the budgetary process. However, there is a great deal more in the budgetary process than the decisions emerging from it. There are different types of local government budgets; there are also different methods of budgeting. Budgets must also mesh with other local government operations. It is important for taxpayers to understand these dimensions of local government budgeting because they describe the essence of how things get done. Managers and elected officials in local government generally understand these aspects of the budgetary process. If taxpayers are going to be successful in combating the spending habits of these individuals, they must have an equal knowledge of these vital processes.

## TYPES OF BUDGETS

Local governments often have two types of budget documents: the operating budget and the capital budget. The operating budget may be referred to as an "annual" budget. The term annual suggests the repetitive character of the items in this budget. These items normally are one year or less in duration. They represent the recurring expenses necessary to run and maintain a local government operation. Examples of items in the operating budget are salaries, contractual services, commodities, and various kinds of supplies.

The second type of budget is known as the "capital" budget. The capital budget includes items that are unique and unlikely to be repetitive from one year to the next. These items are usually tangible and clearly identifiable. Often their costs are of such magnitude that they will require extraordinary types of financing such as the sale of bonds or the use of grant money from state or federal governments. Specific items in the capital budget may require formal approval from state or federal agencies and may have a major impact on the future financial decisions of the local government. Examples of items in the capital budget include construction of new parks and recreational facilities.

A question often asked by taxpayers is why have two different types of budgets? The answer lies in the different issues represented by the budget. Expenditures requested in operating budgets are normally based upon precedent; that is, they are extensions of continuing activity, and the legitimacy or desirability of these expenditures is rarely questioned. A good example is an item in the operating budget for police salaries. In contrast, an item in the capital budget is usually presented for the first time. The question at issue is whether or not the activity should be undertaken. An example is the construction of a new or improved health facility. The discussion and debate will focus more on the need for the health facility rather than on how much it is going to cost over a period of years. However, in the case of the operating budget, the discussion of police salaries is centered on the amount of increase that should be given rather than on whether or not police salaries should be paid at all.

Categorization of items into either the operating budget or the capital budget may also serve to identify different types of conflict in the decision process. Items in the operating budget usually provoke discussion and conflict on the basis of how much more or how much less money will be allocated for the upcoming year as opposed to the previous year. Usually, the survival of the budget item is not at stake. Again the example of the police salaries serves well. The nature of conflict over salaries will usually be on how much of a raise is to be given or what kind of fringe benefits are to be added to the compensation package. On the other hand, conflict over capital items tends to be very clear and takes the form of an either/or situation: should we build a new city hall or should we not?

The decision processes for operating budgets and capital budgets may differ in terms of who is required to participate in the decision. Normally with the operating budget the participants are: the government managers, elected officials, and the citizens who live within the boundaries of the local governmental unit. On the other hand, capital budget items may require the participation of state and federal officials for the purposes of approval and review. This requirement for outside approval and review places additional constraints on the decision-making capacity of the local government. For instance, application for a grant to construct a new correctional facility may involve other related expenditures on the part of the local government that must be made as a condition for receiving federal or state funds. As the number of participants in the decision-making process increases, it is quite likely that the complexity of the decision will increase. It is logical to assume that complex decisions related to capital budgeting should receive a good deal of consideration and that all of the consequences of involving outside funding sources should be carefully identified, reviewed, and considered. Whenever outside funding is used, there is always a chance that conditions will be attached to the funds that may hamper the freedom of action of the local government and its officials.

Thus far, budgeting has been viewed as a process used to allocate scarce resources among conflicting demands. There is an additional type of budgeting that does not involve the decision-making process. This is cash budgeting. Cash budgeting is the balancing of revenues and expenditures over the fiscal period. It is somewhat akin to an individual balancing a checkbook. There must always be enough money on hand to pay the expenses incurred. The ability to balance revenues and expenditures on a cash basis is often affected by the accuracy of the revenue projections and the cost estimates. Budget documents normally specify to the dollar what expenditures will be made. Unfortunately, revenues can only be estimated and cannot be specified down to the last dollar. Therefore, many local governments maintain a surplus of funds from year to year as a cushion to use in meeting expenditures when actual revenues are lower than anticipated. While cash budgeting is an important function of the financial management of local government, it is not an integral part of the budgetary decision process.

## METHODS OF BUDGETING

Local governments use a wide variety of budgetary formats to make spending decisions. While the formats may vary from government to government, there are only four basic methods of budgeting commonly used by local governments. When an individual understands the essentials of each of these four methods, the interpretation of any particular budgetary format is made a great deal easier. The four methods of budgeting are presented in an ascending order of complexity with each one building on the concepts of the previous methods.

## Line Item Budgeting

Line item budgets are also referred to as item of expenditure budgets. The budgetary format focuses on the costs of particular items. Items are simply listed with their associated costs, such as "desk—$250," "secretarial salaries—$12,000," and so on. Costs are usually grouped together by department or major function. A line item budget tells how much everything will cost, but it says nothing about what services will be provided or what needs will be met. However, this type of budget does provide for budgetary accountability and forms the basis for regular financial audits and the operation of the other three methods of budgeting.

## Performance Budgeting

A performance budget presents financial information in the form of costs for performing units of work. An example is presenting a police budget so that costs are shown in terms of miles of streets patrolled or number of calls for assistance answered. These costs per unit of activity are based on a line item treatment of the costs. The basic concept of performance budgeting is to provide the local government official with the opportunity to make a decision based on the number of work units desired. An example is to make a decision to provide police patrol services for 6,000 miles of road as opposed to a higher figure of 7,500 miles. If the cost per mile of patrol is $10.00, then the difference between the two choices is $15,000. Choosing the lesser quantity of miles to be patrolled might result in a reduction in the number of patrol cars and police personnel needed.

The advantage of the performance budget is that it allows decision makers to decide how much of a given service they want to fund. Reducing the number of miles patrolled gives a clear indication of what benefits are being sacrificed for a reduction in spending. If a line item budget were the only budgetary form used in this case, there would be no way to know what services would have to be foregone if $15,000 were cut out of the police budget.

The information provided by the performance budget is extremely valuable to taxpayers trying to curb government spending and taxation because it provides the information necessary to determine the trade offs between reduced revenues and reduced services. One last point about performance budgets: because all the information of the basic line item budget is included, performance budgeting is an excellent means of assuring budgetary accountability. In addition, the audit process can be expanded to include verification of the number of work units performed. The ability to perform this type of check makes it possible for elected officials and taxpayers to be certain they are getting all the service that they paid for.

## Program Budgeting

In a manner similar to performance budgeting, program budgeting relies on the basic information of the line item budget. The main difference between program budgeting and other budgeting methods is that costs are grouped along the lines of programmatic activity rather than along the lines of organizational units or subunits. For example, a program budget for a correctional facility would have a total dollar figure attached to it as well as a breakdown of the costs using a line item budget format. Thus the program budget shows the type of activities undertaken with the associated costs. Decisions can be made about what programs will be funded and how much money will be allocated for each This is in contrast to a line budget where decision makers are faced with a long list of separate items each with its cost, but with no clear idea of what will be accomplished if the items are approved.

The use of a program budget provides decision makers with the opportunity to choose the kinds of services they wish to provide and to select the programs they believe will best carry out the goals of local government. In essence, program budgets present decisions in terms of what will be accomplished, rather than merely in terms of costs for specific items. The successful use of the program budget relies heavily on the ability to aggregate cost data by programs rather than on the basis of organizational units. Therefore, sophisticated accounting systems are required before program budgeting can be successfully applied.

Program budgeting can be a powerful tool for both elected officials and taxpayers. It provides a means to see the results of spending tax dollars. Decisions can be made on the basis of "What do we want to accomplish?" rather than "How much is the right amount to spend for a new fire truck?" Program budgets allow a comparison of benefits received for dollars spent. This type of comparison is important if government operations are to be efficient and effective. But most of all, a workable program budget allows taxpayers to evaluate the benefits of programs against the cost in tax dollars.

## Zero Base Budgeting

Zero base budgeting is a form of budgeting requiring a comprehensive review of all expenditures planned for the coming fiscal year. The object of this review is to determine which services and budget items are no longer necessary and, therefore, can be eliminated. This is in contrast to the operation of most budgeting systems where decisions usually focus on how much more is going to be spent on each item. In other systems, the previous year's budget is viewed as a base for the formulation of the new budget. The questions addressed are: "How much must be added for inflation?" "How much must be added for new personnel?" the question of "Do we actually need to continue this service or function?" is rarely asked. The purpose of zero base budgeting is to ask this question in a serious and systematic manner. The ideal of zero base budgeting is that all expenditures are reviewed every year eliminating those no longer necessary. Unfortunately, this happens only in theory. In actual practice, zero base budgeting turns out to be not unlike the more traditional forms of budgeting in that decisions focus on how much should be added or subtracted from last year's budget.

Zero base budgeting often turns out to be percentage budgeting; that is, a percent of the previous year's budget is regarded as fixed (i.e., 85 percent); any requests for funds above this amount are subject to strong scrutiny, and decision makers focus their attention on decisions in this critical area. The advantage of zero base budgeting for the elected official is it forces government managers to come in with lower budgets, which can be raised if a good case has been made that additional services are needed. From the point of view of the taxpayer, zero base budgeting can be a good means to help government determine which services are the most essential, thereby minimizing the loss of important services when massive tax cuts or expenditure limitations are imposed.

The four methods of budgeting described are only different means for carrying out the basic activity for which the budgetary process exists: the allocation of scarce resources in the best manner possible—in essence, to reach a "good" decision in the spending of the taxpayer's dollars. The suitability of the more advanced methods of budgeting for any particular local government depends on the amount of technical expertise available, the financial condition of the government, and the knowledgeability of the elected officials. It is always better to use simpler methods of budgeting, doing them well, than to attempt a budgeting process beyond the capability of those involved.

Taxpayers can use a simple criteria to judge any budgeting process: does it provide the information necessary to determine how tax dollars are being spent and to evaluate the services received?

## HOW BUDGETS ACTUALLY WORK

Thus far the types and methods of budgeting have been examined. The actual step by step process of budgeting has not been described. As previously stated, every unit of local government has its own unique way of budgeting. Fortunately, there are some basic steps in the budgetary process that are, or should be, contained in every local government budget cycle. These steps can serve as guide posts for the taxpayer who wants to understand how tax monies are allocated.

### Setting Policy

A budget is a document affecting the policies, programs, and goals of the local government. Therefore, the ideal place to start in building a budget is to review existing policies and programs. As an aid to organizing this review, five important points can be identified.

First, there should be a review of local government finances. This review should include an assessment of revenues and expenditures generated within the local government unit. It should also include a review of the role played by external sources of funds. This would include the availability of grants, revenue sharing funds, and other types of financial aid from the state or federal governments.

Second, there should be a review of local and regional economic conditions. The focus of this review is to identify any major changes in the economic environment that might affect the financial resources available to the local government unit or that might create conditions requiring an extraordinary expenditure of funds. Examples are the establishment of an outlying shopping center, the opening or closing of a factory, or the construction of a major state project in a nearby area such as an interstate highway or airport.

The third area of review is major program changes. This should be an attempt on the part of local government officials to ascertain if there are significant changes in the kinds of services citizens expect of local government. An example is a strong and vocal desire on the part of the citizenry for increased levels of police protection. Major changes in program emphasis are best considered at this point in the budgetary process rather than at a later point when decision makers are concerned with balancing the budget. Early consideration of program changes will save a good deal of wasted time and effort. It would be inconsistent with the central theme of this book not to suggest that as part of this review public officials should also be considering what programs can be reduced or eliminated rather than looking only for areas of expansion.

Fourth, the employee-management relations of the local government should be reviewed. Factors to be considered in this review include: the level of militancy among organized groups of employees, the extent of the organization of the labor force in the local government, and any significant action on the part of the courts or the state legislature that might affect the organization or collective bargaining ability of the local government employees. The final question to be asked is: "What are the likely effects of changes in the labor relations area on the budget?" This point is extremely important because, for most local governments, personnel costs are the single largest budgetary item.

The last area of review concerns national economic trends. Of most importance is the effect of inflation on the cost of local government operations. Particular points to be noted are the costs of commodities, the cost of utilities, and the effect of inflation on any major building projects.

Carrying out reviews in the areas described provides significant information that is quite likely to affect the policies and programs of the local government. The importance of making policy changes before the detail work of budgeting begins cannot be overstated.

## Estimating Expenditures

Once the major policies of the local government have been identified, the next step is to estimate the expenditures required to carry out these policies. These expenditure estimates take into account relevant information not covered in the previous review. Generally, estimates of expenditure will be carried out along the lines of existing budgetary categories. The most common budgetary categories used are personnel requirements, contractual services, materials and supplies, equipment needs, and, in some cases, contingency accounts. Cost estimates for capital budget items are separate and apart from the budgetary process that creates the annual or operating budget. The method of budgeting used will determine the exact format for the estimation of costs: either line items, performance, or program.

## Reviewing Expenditure Estimates

The review of expenditure estimates will ordinarily involve three separate groups of people: department representatives, centralized budget or administrative staff, and elected officials or their representatives. The purpose of reviewing expenditure estimates is to reach a tentative agreement among all three parties on what the expenditure program of the local government will be. The term, agreement, is perhaps too strong. Elected officials have the final authority to decide what the expenditures will be. However, a communicative process involving the other local government officials is undoubtedly helpful in carrying out the programs in the most efficient and effective way possible.

## Estimating Revenues

Preparation of revenue estimates occurs simultaneously with the preparation of expenditure estimates. The first step in estimating revenues is a consideration of the overall constraints on the revenue producing capacity of the local government. There may be legal prohibitions against deficit spending. There may be legal restrictions on tax rates. There may be adjustments pending on existing tax bases. (This area of concern might also include changes such as those brought about by measures like Proposition 13.) Also, consideration should be given to bills pending before the state legislature that could add or take away sources of revenue for the local government. The actual estimating of local government revenues should take into account a number of things: first, the local and regional economic conditions affecting the taxes of the local government; second, the administrative procedures necessary for the collection of taxes or other types of revenue for the local government. Another concern in revenue estimating should be a review of the possibilities for matching grants and other forms of intergovernmental financial aid. Particular attention should be given to matching grants because they usually require specific amounts and kinds of appropriations from local government.

## Making Budgetary Forecasts

Budgetary forecasting involves the prediction of revenues and expenditures beyond the current year. Forecasting is normally done for a four or five year period. The purpose of forecasting is to try to determine whether there will be significant changes in the level of expenditures required or the revenues available in coming years. Particular emphasis is given to those changes requiring adjustments in the current year's budget. Simply stated, budgetary forecasting is an attempt to look into the future to determine if there are adjustments that should be made in the current budget to accomodate possible future events. An example is the discovery that a community development grant program will last for only three more years. This would involve a reduction in the amount of funds coming to the local government and a need to develop other sources of funds to take up the slack.

## Preparing the Budget Document

"The purpose of the budget document is to present to the legislative body and the public a comprehensive picture of proposed operations for the budget year, expressed in both verbal and statistical terms."[1]

The details of the budget document vary with the practices and the legislative requirements of each local government. Generally, the following components usually make up the budget document. They are: a budget message, summaries of expenditures and revenues, detailed estimates of revenues and expenditures, supporting data, and, where necessary, drafts of new revenue and appropriation ordinances. Once complete, this budget document is submitted for public hearing and review.

## Reviewing and Adopting the Budget

The procedure for the review and adoption of local government budgets is usually spelled out in the state statutes governing the operation of local government. Additionally, local governments almost always have their own ordinances that specify the steps to be followed in adopting a budget. (Most local governments have short summaries of their budget process that are available to interested citizens.)

## Executing the Budget

There are two main steps in the execution of a budget once it has been adopted. First is the allotment process. Funds are normally not disbursed to departments in one lump sum at the beginning of the year. Instead they are apportioned out on a quarterly or monthly basis. This process of allotment serves as a control on department spending to assure that the funds available will last for the entire year. Allotments are sometimes made more frequently toward the end of the year to insure that departments do not engage in last minute spending sprees to use up their budgets before the end of the fiscal year.

The second step in the execution of the budget involves the use of management and accounting controls. This is the audit and review process referred to in the model of local government operations discussed earlier. These controls are used to assure that public funds are spent only on authorized programs and in a manner that meets all of the requirements and procedures set down by the local government. These controls also offer taxpayers the assurance that their tax dollars are being spent in a way that can be verified at a later date. This assurance is very important when there is suspicion of dishonesty or incompetence on the part of public officials.

## CONCLUSION

This chapter has looked at budgeting in local governments both from a theoretical point of view and from a practical point of view. Taxpayers concerned about understanding the way local government operates cannot afford to ignore this important function. The budgetary process is the means by which tax dollars get turned into public services. Or, to put it another way, the budget process turns revenues into expenditures. Taxpayers who are concerned either about the amount of taxes they pay or about the quality of services they receive must understand this process in order to know what kind of changes they should advocate in order to achieve their objectives. Government managers and elected officials make it their business to have a thorough understanding of how these processes work. The taxpayer who does not have a comparable understanding will have a very difficult time in combating the spending tendencies of these two groups.

In summary, a budget means different things to different people. To the citizens of a community, the budget is an economic document that has significant influence on the economic and social life of the community and all of the people in it. To the elected officials, the budget is a political document that can be used to fulfill campaign promises and on which political futures depend. To public employee groups, the budget is a means to increase their salaries and general economic well being. To special interest groups, the budget is the means by which their special needs can be met. To the government manager, the budget is an expression of professional competence and success. And, last but not least, to the taxpayer, the budget represents services purchased with tax dollars.

## NOTE

1. Lenox L. Moak and Catherine W. Killion, *A Manual of Techniques for the Preparation and Consideration, Adoption and Admistration of Operating Budgets* (Chicago: Municipal Finance Officers Association, 1973), p. 14.

# 11     GETTING TO KNOW YOUR
## LOCAL GOVERNMENT:
### QUESTIONS TO ASK

The previous two chapters have been devoted to describing the operation of local government in a general way. Of necessity, this description has lacked specific details because the wide diversity of local governments in the United States makes it impossible to provide specifics that apply to all of the local governments taxpayers might encounter. The intent of this current chapter is to remedy this deficiency.

Even though taxpayers support local government through their tax dollars, they are outsiders when it comes to having any real knowledge of the financial situation of the government. Normally, they have no way of knowing if the revenues the local government is receiving are sufficient to provide necessary services. A revenue surplus or a revenue deficit can go equally unnoticed. Also, it is difficult to determine just what services local governments offer and, more importantly, what these services cost.

Without this basic revenue-cost information, it is impossible for taxpayers to make an informed judgement about the efficiency and effectiveness of government operations. To go one step further, unless taxpayers have some knowledge of these areas, they cannot evaluate the consequences of potential tax cuts, curbs on expenditure, or limitations on taxation in general. To go back to the situation in California with Proposition 13, voters had no way of knowing what would happen if they voted to cut property taxes. Would the prophets of doom be correct in their charge that local government would collapse with a cessation of vital services and thousands of public workers unemployed? Or were "13's" proponents correct in saying that the loss in property tax revenue would not affect services or put thousands of people out of work? Time and events proved that the proponents of "13" were more nearly correct in their predictions than were its enemies. In a situation as complex as that in California with thousands of local government units as well as state government involved, no one could say with certainty what would happen.

While the techniques offered in this chapter will not give the average taxpayer the ability to predict what might happen in the event of a state-wide tax reform they will give taxpayers sufficient means to acquire an excellent understanding of the financial condition of small to medium size local governments. This understanding is a necessary precondition to taxpayers trying to evaluate their local government. Is it doing a good job with the revenue it has? Are taxes too high for the level of services being produced? Is there a legitimate need for a tax increase? What will happen if property taxes are decreased by a given percentage? These are all questions that require financial information to answer. Ultimately, each taxpayer will have to make an individual judgement about these questions when the time arises, either by voting on initiatives and referenda or by deciding which candidates to support in local elections. These individual judgements are likely to be more accurate when they are based on an adequate understanding of the local government involved.

This chapter is organized in the following manner. The initial section deals with the question of how responsible the local government is in terms of the needs and desires of its citizens. A series of items will be presented that can help the individual make a judgement about the capacity of the local government to be responsible. Second, there will be discussion of guidelines that can be used to evaluate the overall financial policies of a local government. These guidelines provide a sense of how well the local government can be expected to function in providing cost-effective services and in conserving tax dollars. The third and fourth sections provide a detailed list of expenditure and revenue categories that are typically used in most local governments. This list provides a guide to the taxpayer in obtaining financial information from a particular local government. When this information is complete, it will indicate the approximate financial position of the government and will provide a guide for use in determining the financial consequences of proposed tax reforms or reductions. In short, it puts the taxpayer on an equal footing with local government officials when it comes to discussing changes in the taxing and spending structure of local government.

## CRITERIA FOR RESPONSIBLE GOVERNMENT

Local government has a dual responsibility to its citizens. There is a primary responsibility for accountability for public funds. As the term is used here, accountability means that the local government is able to demonstrate to its taxpayers that it uses funds in a manner that is honest, is in accordance with all applicable law and regulation, and is verifiable. In this instance, verifiable means it is possible to determine how all funds were used after they have actually been expended. Accountability is important to the maintenance of public trust in local government and its elected officials. Public trust is a necessary precondition for local government to effectively provide the services the community needs. If taxpayers can determine that a local government is fulfilling its responsibility for accountability of public funds, this allows them to accept with some degree of confidence the facts and figures local government provides in regard to its fiscal operations. If, on the other hand, it can not be established by taxpayers that a local government is fulfilling its responsibility in this area, then taxpayers have a right to expect local government to be able to demonstrate through its organizational structure and operations that it is accountable for the use of public funds. If government can not demonstrate this to the satisfaction of the taxpayers, then they have a right to demand a change of this situation from their elected officials. One of the primary responsibilities of an elected official in local government is to make absolutely certain that accountability can be demonstrated to the full satisfaction of the taxpaying public.

The second area of responsibility involves the purposes for which public funds are expended. The area of accountability covers only the manner in which public expenditures are made. Taxpayers must be assured that public funds are used only for the purposes for which they were intended. Another way to state this is that the local government must be able to demonstrate it is carrying out the legislative intent of its elected officials. The nature of representative government requires "purpose" accountability. Citizens elect local officials because they expect the officials to represent their interests in the operations of local government. Officials are judged on the basis of what they do in office to protect and enhance these interests. However, elected officials have primarily legislative responsibility; they do not usually have direct control over the implementation of the policies they make and the programs they approve. Implementation is usually the province of the executive and managerial personnel of local government. Public officials have to be certain that what they decide is actually carried out. From the point of view of the taxpayer, local government must be able to demonstrate it has the mechanisms to assure that legislative intent is carried out in all matters of public policy. If local government can not do this to the satisfaction of the taxpayer, then it has lost credibility as a form of representative government. Without assurance that legislative intent is carried out, taxpayers can not accept at face value the actions of their elected officials because they have no assurance that the decisions of the elected officials are carried out.

It is not enough for taxpayers to know that local government can demonstrate accountability for the use of public funds. Taxpayers must know how to determine whether or not the local government has the *mechanisms* to provide this accountability. The following paragraphs present a series of questions designed to help taxpayers discover the capacity of any given local government to give assurance of its accountability. These questions should be presented to local government officials and their answers should be carefully evaluated along the lines indicated.[1]

1. *Is it possible to fix responsibility on a specific individual for the expenditure of all public funds?*

For any expenditure made by local government there should be one individual who is clearly responsible for that expenditure. As it is used here, responsible means authorizing the expenditure and, by doing so, confirming that the expenditure is a proper one in terms of the purposes it is intended to serve and that it conforms to all of the application regulations. Additionally, the authorization is a guarantee that the expenditure and its purpose can be verified at a later date should the need arise. If the response to this question is mixed, if there is uncertainty as to who is actually responsible for all expenditures or even any particular expenditure, then the taxpayer has cause to be concerned about the responsibility of the local government and its officials. Every single expenditure a local government makes should have an easily identifiable official responsible for that expenditure. Taxpayers should not accept an answer of "I don't know" or "It's either official X or official Y." Unless there is a single individual responsible for each and every expenditure, there is no recourse for the taxpayers should something go wrong. If taxpayers receive a negative answer to this question, they should demand action from their local officials. They should demand a system be established in which there is individual responsibility for each and every expenditure. Elected officials should be as concerned as taxpayers about remedying a situation that deprives them of certain knowledge that what they have decided is actually carried out. Without this individual responsibility, it is not possible for citizens or elected officials to know who is responsible for the successes and failures of the local government operation. The whole essence of the representative form of government is specific responsibility for the actions of government. Taxpayers can not and should not accept less.

## 2. *Is the local government's financial reporting system comprehensive?*

The taxpayer interested in the financial affairs of local government will soon discover they are exceedingly complex. Perhaps the most confusing part of all is the multiplicity of funds local governments use to run their financial affairs. This multiplicity of funds presents problems of understanding for elected officials and taxpayers alike. It is safe to say that the only people involved in local government who can easily understand the finances in all of their complexity are the professional managers and finance officers. There is one device that can serve to cut through some of this confusion and present an integrated view of the local government's financial condition. This device is a reporting system that presents an overall view of the local government's finances in a format relatively easy for the ordinary person to understand, regardless of whether that person is an elected official or a taxpayer.

A comprehensive reporting system should consolidate the financial condition of the local government's various funds and accounts into a single statement that, at the minimum, gives the following information: the amount of money authorized for expenditure in each of the major functional areas, the amount of money expended to date, the amount of money obligated for expenditure, but not yet paid out, and the amount of money remaining for use in the fiscal period. This information should be duplicated for the revenues as well. How much revenue has been received to date? How much more is expected during the current fiscal period? Is either a surplus or deficit anticipated? These questions and others like them should be easily answerable from the information provided in the comprehensive financial reporting system.

If a local government does have a reporting system that can provide the necessary information, then the taxpayer can feel secure in knowing it is possible to accurately ascertain the financial condition of the local government at any given time. This kind of accurate information can serve as a check on the statements of elected officials in regard to the feasibility of acting on taxpayer requests. For example, if taxpayers want a downward adjustment in property tax rates and elected officials assert this is not possible because of the poor financial condition of the local government, taxpayers will be able to verify this statement for themselves. It will be possible to determine where tax monies are being spent and in what areas reductions in spending are possible. A comprehensive financial reporting system serves as a check on the statements government issues to its citizens.

If, on the other hand, a local government does not have such a system, the taxpayers can only rely on faith: either faith their local government officials are telling them the truth or faith the officials are biasing the truth in order to serve their own ends. It is an unfortunate part of today's society that the second article of faith seems to be the most prevalent. The inevitable result of distrust for local officials is a deterioration in the quality of local government services and, very probably, an increase in the cost of those services. Another possible result is a mindless revolt by taxpayers that prevents government from carrying out essential services for the economic and social well-being of the community.

If taxpayers find their local government does not have an adequate financial reporting system, they should bring immediate and strong pressure on local government officials to institute such a system. They should not allow themselves to be talked out of their position by arguments that financial affairs of government are too complex for the common person to understand. This argument is not acceptable because local government has the responsibility to communicate to the people it serves in a language they can understand. Local government officials who can not or will not do this, do not deserve to continue to "serve" the people who elected them.

*3. Is there a means for independent professional verification of the financial reports generated by the local government?*

The previous question underscored the importance of simple, comprehensive reporting of the financial affairs of local government. In addition to having this information, taxpayers must have the strongest possible assurance that the reports are accurate and honestly prepared. The best way to get this assurance is to have the reports audited by competent people, independent of those running the day to day affairs of the local government, who have the public interest at heart. At the local government level, this function is best filled by an independently elected official whose job is to audit and verify the financial and operating reports the local government produces.

While almost every government has some kind of audit procedure, there are certain criteria that must be met if the desired result is to be achieved. First, the people doing the audit must be professionally competent or employ a professionally competent staff. Second, the people must be totally independent of other elected officials. Third, the people must be performing the audit with the public interest as a primary concern. The easiest way to meet these three conditions is for a local government to have an independently elected auditor with sufficient staff resources to do a comprehensive review of all financial and operating reports. The auditor's staff must also be independent of general local government operations. This means separate hiring and firing procedures. Obviously the characteristics of the individual holding the office have a great deal to do with whether or not an adequate review takes place. But regardless of who is in office, if it is not properly structured, its function cannot be performed no matter how well-intentioned the holder of the office might be.

While an independently elected auditor is not the only possible way to meet the conditions set up by this question, it is certainly the best way. Appointed auditors or "independent" firms hired from the private sector may well provide a competent professional judgement and they may even have elements of independence, but they are not as independent as a separately elected official and there is no reason to believe that the interest of the public will take precedence over their own personal interests. The elected auditor has as his or her personal interest, the interests of the citizens overall.

Most local governments could respond to this question with some kind of affirmative answer. But, it is up to the taxpayer to evaluate the verification system. If the taxpayer is satisfied the local government does have a means for independent and professional verification of its financial reports, then the reports themselves can be accepted as reasonably correct. Therefore, the taxpayer can rely on them in making judgements about the operations of the local government, about the performance of public officials, and about the feasibility of plans for tax reductions or service improvements. If, on the other hand, the taxpayer is not satisfied, the usefulness of the local government's financial reports is diminished. If this occurs, then it becomes the obligation of the taxpayer to work toward the creation of a reliable verification system. Without it, taxpayers will have a very difficult time making the changes they want in local government's spending and taxing habits. Finally, if taxpayers are not convinced that there are adequate means to verify the financial reports of local government, then distrust in local government will develop with negative consequences for the community and its citizens.

### 4. *Is there a means for citizens to appeal the financial actions or regulations of the local government?*

The three previous questions have examined the manner in which the local government conducts its financial affairs overall. The thrust of these questions is to fix responsibility, to communicate financial information, and to provide a means to verify that information. None of these three functions provide any means of recourse should a substantial question come to light. Responsible local government requires that there be a means of appeal from the financial action it takes. Two types of financial actions require appeal: first, actions affecting an individual taxpayer such as assessement of property for tax purposes or the taking of property for the public good, second, actions taken by local government that appear to be questionable in their legality or propriety. In either case, local government is acting in behalf of its citizens. The presumption is that it is carrying out the will of its citizens. Should a doubt arise in either case and citizens feel strongly enough to protest, there should be a means of appeal allowing the issue to get a fair and impartial hearing.

Unfortunately, local governments as a group do not have a commonly accepted means for implementing this appeals process. Virtually all local governments using the property tax have a means for appealing assessments. Some governments have a means for citizens to appeal other actions. The office of ombudsman is a form of this appeals process. Ombudsmen are independent officials whose responsibility is to represent the interests of citizens against the actions of the government. They are, literally, the people's advocates. They can act in behalf of individuals or in the interest of the public as a whole.

A typical answer to this question will not be a clearcut yes or no. Taxpayers will have to evaluate the answer they receive from a given local government unit based upon their knowledge of local conditions and the political history of the community. If they decide there is not an adequate appeals process, then this should become an issue to raise with elected officials. Appeals are important because they provide a check on the power of local government and they serve to balance the rights of individuals against the rights of the local government acting on behalf of the people. If the answer received is that there is no need for this kind of appeals process, then taxpayers should regard this as the strongest possible message that such a process is very badly needed. It means that officials do not want to be bothered with having to worry about their actions being challenged. Such officials have no place in public office because they are either dishonest, incompetent, or indifferent to the rights of the people they are supposed to represent.

## HOW TO EVALUATE THE FINANCIAL POLICIES OF LOCAL GOVERNMENT

The evaluation of the financial policies of local government must logically start with a definition of financial policy. In the broadest sense of the term, financial policies are plans that guide the operations of local government in generating revenues and incurring expenses. The question might well be asked: how are financial policies any different than budgets? It is true that both financial policies and budgets are plans, but there are several significant differences between the two. The first difference is one of time. Budgets ordinarily cover only one fiscal period, usually the fiscal year. Financial policies cover a much longer time span, with many aspects of financial policy continuing indefinitely until they are eliminated or altered. The second difference is one of scope. Budgets usually focus on specific expenditures of a relatively short duration. Even capital budgets have a relatively short time span, perhaps five or 10 years at the most. And, of course, capital budgets pertain only to items whose acquisition, life, and financing stretch over more than one year. Financial policies are much broader in scope than budgets. Financial policies are assumptions and decisions about the operations of government that determine in part what type of expenditures will be made and what revenue sources will be used to finance them. Policies serve as guidelines, not necessarily rules, for the formulation of budgets on a year to year basis.

The question might be asked: why is it important for a local government to have financial policies? They are important because they bring stability to the operations of local government and they provide a means of accomplishing long term goals whose scope and time period are far beyond that of a single budgetary period.

Using a family budget as an analogy is a helpful way to illustrate this point. Consider that the budgetary period for the family is one month as opposed to the fiscal year used by local government. Suppose the family sets as one of its goals the accumulation of enough money to provide for a down payment on a house. A naive family might reason as follows: "The house we would like requires a down payment of $10,000. We currently have $4,000 in cash. We can save another $5,000 in four years. By that time we should accumulate about $1,000 in interest on our savings, giving us the $10,000 needed." What's wrong with this reasoning? Everything! First, $10,000 will not buy the same house four years from now. So either a smaller house will have to be purchased or more money is needed. Second, the family can currently afford the payments for the house they want, but will they be able to do so in four years? Third, has there been any consideration of income versus expenditure to determine if the rate of savings is feasible? Fourth, has there been a consideration of alternative means (such as secondary financing) to purchase the house sooner? Fifth, have provisions been made to protect the plan against sickness or other adverse circumstances? The list of problems could go on forever. In short, the family could faithfully carry out their budgeted savings each and every month for four years and still not be able to achieve their goal. Why? Because they failed to take into account significant factors that affect their day to day living as well as the goals they are trying to achieve.

If the family had looked at trends in inflation, trends in the growth of real estate values, tax policies of the federal government, and their own potential for future earnings, they might well have concluded the best thing to do was buy the house immediately through the use of secondary financing. They would have been better off this way because of the tax breaks for homeownership (deduction of interest and property tax payments) and the penalties for saving (no tax deductions, taxes due on savings interest, probably resulting in a higher tax bracket). Also, they would have benefitted from the appreciation in the value of the house as opposed to having to pay more for the same house or settle for the smaller one. Finally, they would have enjoyed the use of the house immediately instead of having to wait four years. In short, their budgetary plan was too limited to enable them to reach their goals. A financial policy, being of broader scope and considering more variables, would probably have put them into their dream house sooner.

What are the lessons for local government in this story? Local governments must look beyond their immediate goals to things they want to attain in the longer run. Their budgets should not reflect only day to day concerns. They should not be limited in their consideration to a day to day balancing of receipts and expenditures. They should consider factors that will impact on the local government in the years to come. They should attempt to regularize and identify changes in their expenditure patterns and sources of revenue. Local governments should explore more than one alternate means of reaching a desired goal. In short, local governments must take a long range view of what they are trying to achieve and should make a deliberate attempt to identify those outside factors likely to influence the achievement of their goals.

The important question for the taxpayer to ask is: does local government have a financial policy? Why is this important? It is important because without a financial policy, government is living on a day to day basis that is not conducive to the achievement of any kind of long range goal, whether that goal is to increase services or to reduce taxation. The following questions are designed to help the taxpayer determine if a local government has a financial policy and the extent to which that policy considers the significant factors that affect local government operations.

1. *Are there a set of general guidelines used to determine the levels of service the local government will provide?*

Each year budget decisions are made involving the hiring of personnel and the acquisition of goods and supplies. Most of these resources go to provide services that continue year after year. In some years when tax resources are plentiful a slightly higher level of service may be provided than in the previous year. In times of fewer resources a slightly lower level of service will be funded. In this instance, the level of service is determined by the relative availability of financial resources. In good times all departments get more money, in tight times they all usually share the budget cuts. Although this appears to be a fair and reasonable approach from the point of view of elected officials, government managers, and public employee groups, it is not fair and reasonable for the taxpayers. This kind of day to day decision making serves only the priorities of the moment; it does not provide for the achievement of longer range goals and objectives. Additionally, the entire rationale is based on the assumption that whatever tax monies are available will be consumed to the last penny. Although this type of operation is unfortunately all too common in local government, there is an alternate approach that can be followed. This approach involves the establishment and use of guidelines to determine types and level of services that should be offered.

Service guidelines are important because they represent a process of deliberation and decision making aimed at identifying the optimum mix and level of service the local government should provide. Defenders of the piecemeal approach will hasten to argue that "there is no such thing as an optimum level of service and if there is local governments are not going to achieve it, so why waste time deliberating and deciding." In reality this kind of argument is nothing more than a simple-minded defense of the business as usual method of operation, i.e., keeping taxes as high as possible and spending all the funds that are available.

In formulating service guidelines, the term optimum refers to those services and to the levels of services considered to be both desirable and affordable in the minds of the citizens of the community. The ideal situation would be for citizens to take an active part in the formulation of service guidelines for each of the major functions of local government. This could be accomplished through the creation of citizen advisory committees that, working with elected officials and members of management in a given functional area such as fire protection, would formulate a statement of the level of fire service that is currently being provided along with a conclusion about the adequacy of the current service. Based on this information, a long term plan could be formulated that would include a statement of what the level of service should be, what that level of service will cost, and a set of guidelines aimed at bringing the current level of service into conformity with the desired level of service. When these guidelines have been formulated, they could be submitted to the people for a vote. If the legal structure of the local government does not permit such a direct expression of citizen desires, then at the very least these guidelines could serve as the central campaign issue in the election of local government officials. Once approved either directly or indirectly, these guidelines would serve to guide future budgetary decisions concerning what levels of service to provide.

What has been described is an ideal situation. "Ideal" is not a condition that occurs very often in local government. Therefore, citizens must be prepared to deal with less than ideal situations. The most elemental and basic question that can be asked is simply: "Are there any guidelines for services?" If this question is answered in the affirmative, then these guidelines can be reviewed and evaluated. If the answer is negative, then the citizen has a good idea of the quality of the local government and can start to do something about it. As with any relatively complex question, there are more possibilities than a straight "yes" or "no" answer. A very common answer to this question will probably be something like this: "Yes, we have guidelines. No, they are not written down, so you can't have a copy. Our guideline is to provide the best service we can with the money we have." If service guidelines do not exist in writing, if they are not readily available to the public, if they do not play a prominent part in the budgetary process, if elected officials do not appear to be familiar with them, then chances are they are not taken seriously by local government officials. Guidelines that are not taken seriously are of no value. What about the guideline of "doing the best with what we have." This is not a guideline, it is simply a confirmation of the fact that business as usual prevails, i.e., spend all the money available and give everyone their fair share.

To conclude, service guidelines are important because they communicate to the taxpayers a plan for providing a given level of service at a given cost. This plan allows taxpayers to make judgements about whether the level of service is acceptable at the level of funding stated. It also communicates that public officials are serious about their responsibilities for representing the interests of the citizens. It indicates they are making decisions about spending the taxpayers' money with some goal in mind. Lack of service guidelines reflects decision making on a day by day basis, which invariably leads to constant increases in government spending and taxation.

Service guidelines add logic and rationale to the expenditure of public funds. However, expenditures represent only one-half of the financial operations of local government. The other half is equally important to the taxpayers and in the need of logic and rationality. Therefore, the second question taxpayers should ask of their local government officials involves policies for the generation of revenues.

*2. Are there a general set of guidelines used to determine the mix of revenues that the local government uses to support its operation?*

As previously discussed, the revenues of local government come from a variety of sources including local taxes, subventions, and revenues from governmental enterprises. Additionally, local governments borrow money by selling bonds to finance long term capital improvements. Although revenue decisions are greatly restricted by state and federal law, there is still a great deal of latitude for local decision making. The question about guidelines refers to this latitude in generating revenues. The rationale for the need of revenue guidelines is essentially the same as that for service guidelines. Citizens have a right to expect their local officials to have some long term plan or goal in mind when they make decisions regarding taxes, bonds, and fees. Additionally, citizens have the right to know what these plans and goals are and what progress is being made toward their fulfillment.

If decisions are made every year in response only to current pressures without regard to long term consequences, then a number of unfavorable consequences can be expected. First, assuming that the need to spend as expressed in budget requests always exceeds available revenues, citizens can expect their local officials to do everything they can to raise revenues to meet these requests. As explained in the model presented in the initial chapter of this book, spending is a type of behavior that is rewarded in the political life of local government. Taxpayers can confidently expect politicians to do what they believe to be in their best interest. The second unfavorable consequence involves the question of who will bear the burden of financing increased spending. It is usually those groups of taxpayers that have the least amount of political clout. Because clout is often related to wealth, the poor and middle income people can expect to bear more than their fair share of the burden. Third, local governments will tend to gravitate toward those sources of revenue that are the least visible to those who pay the taxes or charges. They will try to utilize taxes and charges that are easy to pay. Lack of visibility and ease of payment are two ways to insure that taxpayers will not take an undue interest in taxes. To sum up, left to its own devices, hidden from the scrutiny of the taxpayers, local government will tend to seek painless, unobtrusive sources of revenue and proceed to spend all of the funds that become available.

The previous paragraph summarized what happens without revenue guidelines. What happens when they exist? First, they serve to communicate the revenue policies of the government to the interested taxpayer. Does the government levy charges covering the full cost of the services with which they are associated? Or are these services subsidized by taxes on the general public? Does the local government intend to continue a heavy dependence on the property tax? Does the local government know what percentage of its residents' income it takes in local taxes? Does it have an optimum percentage that it believes it should take? How much total debt should the local government incur for capital improvement?

Citizens have the right to know the answers to these questions. But even more importantly, they have the right to know whether or not local officials even consider these questions in a logical, reasonable way. A formal set of revenue guidelines should provide citizens with the opportunity to evaluate all aspects of their local government's revenue structure. Guidelines serve to uncover hidden taxes and services that appear to pay for themselves but do not. Third, guidelines provide a means to compare the actions elected officials take in regard to revenues with the principles they say they stand for.

As in the case of expenditure guidelines, citizens will find they receive answers from public officials more complex than "Yes, we have guidelines and here is a copy of them" or "No, we don't have any guidelines." The same rules of interpretation apply to revenue guidelines as apply to expenditure guidelines. For guidelines to be useful they must be explicit, easy to understand, well known to elected legislative officials, and readily available to the general public. Otherwise they will not fulfill the functions that make them valuable.

3. *Are there general guidelines available describing the personnel policies and practices the local government follows?*

The model presented in Chapter Nine mentioned that there were two major types of resources requiring the attention of management: financial and human. Just as it is important for a local government to have guidelines governing the use of its financial resources, it is no less important to have guidelines for the budgetary decisions that govern the management of human resources. There are two major reasons why human resources deserve equal attention with financial resources. First, local governments spend the majority of their funds to pay the salaries of their employees. Salaries are the single largest budgetary item. Second, it is the people in any organization who get the work done. Local government is no different. The overall quality of the labor force and the way in which it is managed have as much effect on the quality of government services as any other factor. Just as services are affected by the quality of the personnel, so are the taxes that support those services.

On the issue of personnel policies taxpayers are likely to find themselves allied with the public employees. It is to the advantage of both groups that the local government have a readily available and explicit set of principles that serve to guide every day decisions, budgetary and otherwise, concerning personnel matters. The policy guidelines should cover, at a minimum, the following points: salary policies (with special emphasis on such questions as how competive the local government wants to be in its salary structure), the nature and funding arrangements for pension plans (i.e., what percentage of the benefit premiums is the government prepared to pay for), fringe benefit packages (including sick leave and vacation pay), and the position of the local government toward the personal and professional development of its employees (specifically, the government's willingness to spend the taxpayer's money for the personal development of job-related skills). For the employee, these issues have a great deal to do with determining the quality of the working life the government offers as an employer; therefore, they have a right to know the position of the government on these issues as well as any changes that are contemplated. Similarly, the taxpayer has a right to know how these issues are decided now and how they are likely to be decided in the future.

Unfortunately, it is at this point that the taxpayer and the employee may find themselves parting company as allies. Quite rightly, the employee is interested in getting high levels of salary and benefits in exchange for honest, conscientious work. The taxpayer, on the other hand, is interested in getting the maximum amount of productivity for the minimum salary expense. This conflict is unavoidable, especially when there are public employee associations involved. They tend to complicate matters even further because their leaders must be concerned not only with the quality of the work place, but with the numbers of workers. As explained in Chapter One, employee association leaders have the same needs to expand their organizations as managers in government or business. While the presence of explicit personnel guidelines cannot alleviate conflict, they can at least help to keep the negative consequences of the conflict controlled. Alienation between government workers and taxpayers leads to poorer services, poorer working conditions, less worker satisfaction, and, ultimately, to higher taxes.

When explicit personnel policies do exist, they serve to educate both workers and taxpayers. They place pressure on politicians to be honest in their positions with both groups, rather than taking the easy way out and telling both groups what they want to hear at election time. In budget decisions they can conserve much time and energy in trying to resolve the conflicting demands of the taxpayers and the employees. Lastly, explicit personnel policies lead to better decisions about personnel matters because they provide a framework for decisions removed from the pressure of the budgetary process and questions such as "How much will our next raise be?" The process of creating or changing personnel policies can have much wider participation and more logical and useful deliberations when removed from the confines and pressures of the budgetary process. Rather than be a part of the budgetary process, these guidelines should be a major part of the environment in which budgetary decisions are made.

In evaluating answers to this question, taxpayers must follow the same approach used with the previous two questions. If no policies exist, then the obvious step is to push elected officials to start creating them. If they do exist, they should be examined by taxpayers in order to determine their compatability with the funding level the taxpayer is able and willing to support. As stated before, informal policies, policies not written down, policies not used in the budgetary process, are no policies at all and should be treated as such.

Three questions have been presented and discussed that will help taxpayers to evaluate the overall financial policies of their local government. These questions, along with those dealing with the responsibilities of the local government, set the stage for the next step in "getting to know your local government." By now, it is possible to have a good idea about the competency, political honesty, and professionalism of the local government officials encountered. However, not much has been said about how to evaluate the actual financial position of the local government in terms of the possibility of lowering taxes and/or increasing the level of services. The next three sets of questions deal specifically with this issue.

## HOW TO EVALUATE THE REVENUES AND EXPENDITURES OF LOCAL GOVERNMENT

Thus far the evaluation of local government revenues and expenditures has been discussed only in general terms. These discussions are essential if taxpayers are to make informed judgements about the financial condition of any given local government. In addition to this background information, another component is needed. That component is specific information about the financial status of local government. For the average citizen to get enough detailed financial information in an understandable format may be very difficult indeed. What is needed is a relatively simple format that can be used to summarize the financial activities of local government for a number of years. This format must be simple enough to be usable by the average taxpayer, yet accurate enough to present a true and realistic picture. This section presents forms to be used to gather financial information about local government. Their format is one that should be compatible with the operations of most general purpose local governments, i.e., cities, counties, and towns. Some adaption might be necessary for use with specialized local government units such as school districts.

When the necessary information has been gathered and entered on the forms, they should reflect a true and accurate picture of local government finance. However, users are cautioned that the information they have will in most cases consist of approximations rather than exact figures. This is because local government finances are so complex that a summary of them accurate to the last dollar would involve a level of time and effort far beyond that which most taxpayers would be willing to devote.

### Summarizing Revenues

The form for the collection of the revenue data utilizes information for three years of actual government operation plus projections for the coming year of operation. Revenues are broken down into four broad categories: taxes, miscellaneous, intergovernmental revenues, and capital revenues. Each of these categories is further broken down showing individual items. The information needed to fill in the form is the amount of revenue generated from each item for the current fiscal year and each of the two previous years. Additionally, projected revenues for the coming year are required. Also, brief notes should be made to indicate the rate of the tax and whether or not the rate has changed in the period covered by the data. Because of its importance in local government finance, a separate section is provided for the property tax. In addition to the amount of taxes collected in each of the years, the amount of the tax base (total assessed valuation) and the tax rate (mill rate) should also be entered. (Note: Chapter Four contains a description of the operation of the local property tax that some readers may wish to review before starting to collect this information.)

The categories used in the *Summary of Local Government Revenues* are designed to cover virtually every type of revenue source occurring in local government operations. Not all of these are used by every local government, and in some cases the terminology will vary. There may be some instances where a revenue source may appear not to belong in any of the categories listed. If this occurs, a judgement should be made to list the revenue wherever it seems to most logically belong. Exact categorization is not important. What is important is that these judgements be consistent in each of the four years for which data is gathered. Additionally, some taxpayers may find that the government they are examining has changed reporting or accounting systems during the four year period under examination. In these cases, every effort should be made to assure that the information in the *Summary* is presented in a consistent fashion for each of the four years. Consistency is very important because the prime purpose of the chart is to provide a review of revenues over time. This type of review allows for the identification of patterns in revenues. For instance, the earlier chapter on local government finance discussed each of the major sources of revenue and presented historical data that showed the trends in yields for each of these sources. The patterns of the local government's revenues can be compared with these historical national trends. This comparison will give the taxpayer an idea of how the local government compares with the national averages.

Using comparisions, the taxpayer will be able to determine which sources of revenue are declining in importance and which are becoming a more important part of the overall revenue picture. Also, taxpayers will be able to quickly estimate how important any given revenue source is to the overall operation of the government. This analysis could reveal that a great deal of time is being spent trying to decide on a fee structure that yields very little in revenues, when there are other issues being ignored that have a major impact on the local government. When used in this way, the *Summary* can pinpoint those key areas of revenue policy requiring the attention of taxpayers and their elected officials.

The four year trends can also reveal potential problems in local government revenues. For instance, a trend in decreasing sales tax revenues could be spotted early and consideration given to what alternate revenues could be generated, what could be done to keep revenues from declining or what services could be reduced to keep the budget in balance. Similarly, a trend of increasing property tax revenues due to rapidly rising assessments could be a signal that taxpayers should start to put pressure on local officials to reduce the property tax rates as the assessments rise. Citizens who are active or want to be active in the affairs of their local government will find that there are a vast number of ways in which the data contained in the *Summary* will be useful.

In looking at the *Summary* from a broad perspective, taxpayers should give some thought to evaluating the overall impact of the

FIGURE 11.1
**Summary of Local Government Revenues**
(thousands of dollars)

| Source of Revenue | Two Yrs. Ago | Last Year | Current Year | Next Year | Comments |
|---|---|---|---|---|---|
| 1.0  Tax Revenues | | | | | |
| 1.1   Property tax | | | | | |
|         Total assessed valuation | | | | | |
|         Mill rate | | | | | |
|         Total property tax | | | | | |
| 1.2   Non-property taxes | | | | | |
| 1.21    Individual income tax | | | | | |
| 1.22    Corporate income tax | | | | | |
| 1.23    General sales tax | | | | | |
| 1.24    Selective sales tax | | | | | |
| 1.241    Motor fuel | | | | | |
| 1.242    Alcoholic beverages | | | | | |
| 1.243    Tobacco products | | | | | |
| 1.244    Utilities | | | | | |
| 1.245    Other | | | | | |
| 1.25    Motor vehicle licenses | | | | | |
| 1.26    Operators licenses | | | | | |
| 1.27    Other | | | | | |

## Summary of Local Government Revenues (continued)

| Source of Revenue | Two Yrs. Ago | Last Year | Current Year | Next Year | Comments |
|---|---|---|---|---|---|
| 2.0  Miscellaneous Local Revenues | | | | | |
|   2.1   Interest earned on cash balances | | | | | |
|   2.2   Sales of property and other assets | | | | | |
|   2.3   Special assessments | | | | | |
|   2.4   Fees and charges | | | | | |
| 3.0  Intergovernmental Revenues | | | | | |
|   3.1   Federal government | | | | | |
|     3.11   Grants-in-aid | | | | | |
|     3.12   Revenue sharing | | | | | |
|     3.13   Shared taxes | | | | | |
|     3.14   Other payments | | | | | |
|   3.2   State government | | | | | |
|     3.21   Grants-in-aid | | | | | |
|     3.22   Revenue sharing | | | | | |
|     3.23   Shared taxes | | | | | |
|     3.24   Other payments | | | | | |
|   3.3   Other local government | | | | | |
|     3.31   Grants-in-aid | | | | | |
|     3.32   Revenue sharing | | | | | |
|     3.33   Shared taxes | | | | | |
|     3.34   Other payments | | | | | |

**Summary of Local Government Revenues** (continued)

| Source of Revenue | Two Yrs. Ago | Last Year | Current Year | Next Year | Comments |
|---|---|---|---|---|---|
| 4.0 Capital Development Funds | | | | | |
|   4.1 General obligation bonds | | | | | |
|   4.2 Revenue bonds | | | | | |
| 5.0 Revenues from Public Enterprises | | | | | |
| 6.0 Other Receipts | | | | | |

revenue system. Some questions that might be asked are: What groups in the community are bearing the heaviest load? Are they the ones who are best able to pay the taxes? Are property taxes proportionate to the level of services property owners receive? Do fees and charges contribute in a significant way to overall revenues? Are fees more trouble to collect than they are worth? Is there a trend toward increased reliance on aid from the state and federal governments? Are public enterprises contributing their fair share to support local government operations? Does the government's indebtedness appear to be growing or decreasing? The answers to these questions and others like them can be determined with a fair degree of accuracy. But this is only the first step. Taxpayers must then ask themselves how they feel about what they have learned. They must start to develop a philosophy about government revenues. They must ask themselves: What do I think about the way this revenue system operates? They must develop personal opinions about questions such as: Should property tax revenues be used to support general government operations or just for property related services? Should property tax burdens be lifted by shifting reliance to less painful taxes such as those on sales and incomes? Should fees and charges be adjusted so users pay the full cost of the services they receive? Or should services be subsidized so that all citizens have the opportunity to make use of services for only a nominal charge? In short, taxpayers should use the information they have gathered from the *Summary* to form their own point of view about local government revenues.

Once taxpayers are well informed about revenues, they will be able to make better decisions about how to get what they want from local government. They will be better able to force elected officials out of the spending syndrome and into having more concern for the conservation of tax dollars. Most of all, taxpayers will be able to make thoughtful, informed decisions about the way they want local government revenues to be structured, rather than simply striking out at local government's property tax because it is visible and painful to pay while other, more burdensome taxes escape unnoticed and unchallenged.

## Summarizing Expenditures

The form used to summarize local government expenditures follows the same general format as the *Summary of Local Government Revenues*. It summarizes expenditures made during the two past years, and for the current year, and expenditure projections

for the coming fiscal year. Additionally, it provides a space for
listing the number of people employed in each of the major oper-
ational areas of local government. The categories used are based upon
standards developed by the National Committee on Governmental
Accounting.[2] There are three types of categories commonly used
to present expenditure figures: functions, activities, and units.
Functions refer to broad purposes for which local governments
expend funds. Activities are specific operations taking place within
the broader functions. Items are expenditures made in order to carry
out the functions and activities. The listing of items represents the
major budgetary categories likely to be found in local governments
across the country. The functions listed are inclusive enough to
cover the activities of virtually any local goverment unit. When the
form is used for special purposes of local governments only a few of
the functions will apply. Activities are listed for only the first category because the extreme diversity of local governments makes
it impractical to attempt to predict what the major activities will be
for the other functions in any particular local government. The
activity names should be filled in with the titles used by the local
government. The form provides three spaces for activities under each
function. More should be added if they are necessary. The complete
list of items is to be used under each and every activity. (Note:
Chapter Nine provides information that may be helpful in gathering
the data. It is important to keep in mind that while terminology
will differ from government to government, consistency in placing
expenditures into categories is more important than any one actual
placement.)

When the *Summary of Local Government Expenditures* is
completed the taxpayer will have an overview of how the local
government spends its funds. As in the case of the summary of
revenues, it is important to look for trends in spending of particular
interest. These trends serve the purpose of providing basic information for the taxpayer and as a means of comparing the public
statements of government officials with the actual facts of government operation. As an example, elected officials like to champion
the cause of economy in government even though they must spend in
order to retain their offices. Therefore they attack spending in areas
that generate good publicity, but do not seriously disturb their
relationships with other government officials, special interest groups,
or public employee groups. A favorite area is travel. However, in
virtually all local government budgets, travel is a very small percentage of overall expenditures. Therefore, even significant reductions in travel expenditures are unlikely to have a measurable impact

on overall expenditures or on the tax burden. A taxpayer who is armed with the expenditure facts can successfully challenge officials who make these kind of misleading statements. These challenges will put pressure on officials to take a more serious view of curbing government expenditures. But if taxpayers are not informed, then they are susceptable to the kind of deception that has just been described.

Taxpayers will find the information on personnel costs to be particularly enlightening. Personnel will prove to be the largest expenditure category for virtually every local government. Also, taxpayers will undoubtedly notice that once added to the payroll, employees are there to stay. Even in units whose budgets have remained stable or decreased, it is not unusual to find that the number of employees has remained constant. The lesson of this trend should be clear. Budget proposals calling for the addition of new positions to the government payroll should be scrutinized very carefully because in all likelihood once added those employees will remain. If the service appears to be needed and taxpayers want to avoid the permanent employee trap, contracting out for the service may prove to be a viable alternative. Government managers and elected officials are much more likely to cancel a contract than they are to face up to the firing of public employees once the need for a particular service has disappeared.

The value of knowing a government's expenditure habits is limited only by the imagination and energy of the taxpayer. Virtually every public issue a local government faces is influenced in some way by how government spends and raises its funds. Naive taxpayers can easily be manipulated by those in government who have an interest in preserving the pattern of growing government expenditures. A taxpayer who is serious about wanting to curb spending and limit taxes should be knowledgeable about government finances, if for no other reason than to choose intelligently between alternatives elected officials present.

## Getting the Information

It is now appropriate to raise some points about the process of getting the information necessary to complete both summary forms. First, all of the information on both of the forms is a matter of public record; that is, the public has a legal right to such information and government has a legal obligation to provide it. Despite these legal guarantees, taxpayers may experience some difficulty in securing the information. Clerks in city hall may say it is not available or cannot be given out. Or they may lead the taxpayer to a desk, piled up with

## FIGURE 11.2
## Summary of Local Government Expenditures
(thousands of dollars)

| *Category of Expenditure* | *Two Yrs. Ago* | *Last Year* | *Current Year* | *Next Year* | *Number of Personnel* |
|---|---|---|---|---|---|
| 1.0  General Government | | | | | |
| 1.1   Legislative | | | | | |
| 1.11  Personnel | | | | | |
| 1.12  Contractual Services | | | | | |
| 1.13  Travel | | | | | |
| 1.14  Equipment | | | | | |
| 1.15  Supplies | | | | | |
| 1.16  Capital Outlays | | | | | |
| 1.17  Other | | | | | |
| 1.2   Judicial | | | | | |
| 1.21  Personnel | | | | | |
| 1.22  Contractual Services | | | | | |
| 1.23  Travel | | | | | |
| 1.24  Equipment | | | | | |
| 1.25  Supplies | | | | | |
| 1.26  Capital Outlays | | | | | |
| 1.27  Other | | | | | |
| 1.3   Executive | | | | | |
| 1.31  Personnel | | | | | |
| 1.32  Contractual Services | | | | | |
| 1.33  Travel | | | | | |
| 1.34  Equipment | | | | | |
| 1.35  Supplies | | | | | |
| 1.36  Capital Outlays | | | | | |
| 1.37  Other | | | | | |

**Summary of Local Government Expenditures** (continued)
(thousands of dollars)

| Category of Expenditure | Two Yrs. Ago | Last Year | Current Year | Next Year | Number of Personnel |
|---|---|---|---|---|---|
| 2.0 Public Safety | | | | | |
| 2.1 Police | | | | | |
| 2.11 Personnel | | | | | |
| 2.12 Contractual Services | | | | | |
| 2.13 Travel | | | | | |
| 2.14 Equipment | | | | | |
| 2.15 Supplies | | | | | |
| 2.16 Capital Outlays | | | | | |
| 2.17 Other | | | | | |
| 2.2 Fire | | | | | |
| 2.21 Personnel | | | | | |
| 2.22 Contractual Services | | | | | |
| 2.23 Travel | | | | | |
| 2.24 Equipment | | | | | |
| 2.25 Supplies | | | | | |
| 2.26 Capital Outlays | | | | | |
| 2.27 Other | | | | | |
| 2.3 | | | | | |
| 2.31 Personnel | | | | | |
| 2.32 Contractual Services | | | | | |
| 2.33 Travel | | | | | |
| 2.34 Equipment | | | | | |
| 2.35 Supplies | | | | | |
| 2.36 Capital Outlays | | | | | |
| 2.37 Other | | | | | |

**Summary of Local Government Expenditures** (continued)
(thousands of dollars)

| Category of Expenditure | Two Yrs. Ago | Last Year | Current Year | Next Year | Number of Personnel |
|---|---|---|---|---|---|
| 3.0 Highways and Streets | | | | | |
| 3.1 | | | | | |
| 3.11 Personnel | | | | | |
| 3.12 Contractual Services | | | | | |
| 3.13 Travel | | | | | |
| 3.14 Equipment | | | | | |
| 3.15 Supplies | | | | | |
| 3.16 Capital Outlays | | | | | |
| 3.17 Other | | | | | |
| 3.2 | | | | | |
| 3.21 Personnel | | | | | |
| 3.22 Contractual Services | | | | | |
| 3.23 Travel | | | | | |
| 3.24 Equipment | | | | | |
| 3.25 Supplies | | | | | |
| 3.26 Capital Outlays | | | | | |
| 3.27 Other | | | | | |
| 3.3 | | | | | |
| 3.31 Personnel | | | | | |
| 3.32 Contractual Services | | | | | |
| 3.33 Travel | | | | | |
| 3.34 Equipment | | | | | |
| 3.35 Supplies | | | | | |
| 3.36 Capital Outlays | | | | | |
| 3.37 Other | | | | | |

**Summary of Local Government Expenditures** (continued)
(thousands of dollars)

| Category of Expenditure | Two Yrs. Ago | Last Year | Current Year | Next Year | Number of Personnel |
|---|---|---|---|---|---|
| 4.0 Planning and Zoning | | | | | |
| 4.1 | | | | | |
| 4.11 Personnel | | | | | |
| 4.12 Contractual Services | | | | | |
| 4.13 Travel | | | | | |
| 4.14 Equipment | | | | | |
| 4.15 Supplies | | | | | |
| 4.16 Capital Outlays | | | | | |
| 4.17 Other | | | | | |
| 4.2 | | | | | |
| 4.21 Personnel | | | | | |
| 4.22 Contractual Services | | | | | |
| 4.23 Travel | | | | | |
| 4.24 Equipment | | | | | |
| 4.25 Supplies | | | | | |
| 4.26 Capital Outlays | | | | | |
| 4.27 Other | | | | | |
| 4.3 | | | | | |
| 4.31 Personnel | | | | | |
| 4.32 Contractual Services | | | | | |
| 4.33 Travel | | | | | |
| 4.34 Equipment | | | | | |
| 4.35 Supplies | | | | | |
| 4.36 Capital Outlays | | | | | |
| 4.37 Other | | | | | |

## Summary of Local Government Expenditures (continued)
### (thousands of dollars)

| Category of Expenditure | Two Yrs. Ago | Last Year | Current Year | Next Year | Number of Personnel |
|---|---|---|---|---|---|
| 5.0 Sanitation | | | | | |
| 5.1 | | | | | |
| 5.11 Personnel | | | | | |
| 5.12 Contractual Services | | | | | |
| 5.13 Travel | | | | | |
| 5.14 Equipment | | | | | |
| 5.15 Supplies | | | | | |
| 5.16 Capital Outlays | | | | | |
| 5.17 Other | | | | | |
| 5.2 | | | | | |
| 5.21 Personnel | | | | | |
| 5.22 Contractual Services | | | | | |
| 5.23 Travel | | | | | |
| 5.24 Equipment | | | | | |
| 5.25 Supplies | | | | | |
| 5.26 Capital Outlays | | | | | |
| 5.27 Other | | | | | |
| 5.3 | | | | | |
| 5.31 Personnel | | | | | |
| 5.32 Contractual Services | | | | | |
| 5.33 Travel | | | | | |
| 5.34 Equipment | | | | | |
| 5.35 Supplies | | | | | |
| 5.36 Capital Outlays | | | | | |
| 5.37 Other | | | | | |

**Summary of Local Government Expenditures (continued)**
(thousands of dollars)

| Category of Expenditure | Two Yrs. Ago | Last Year | Current Year | Next Year | Number of Personnel |
|---|---|---|---|---|---|
| 6.0 Health | | | | | |
| 6.1 | | | | | |
| 6.11 Personnel | | | | | |
| 6.12 Contractual Services | | | | | |
| 6.13 Travel | | | | | |
| 6.14 Equipment | | | | | |
| 6.15 Supplies | | | | | |
| 6.16 Capital Outlays | | | | | |
| 6.17 Other | | | | | |
| 6.2 | | | | | |
| 6.21 Personnel | | | | | |
| 6.22 Contractual Services | | | | | |
| 6.23 Travel | | | | | |
| 6.24 Equipment | | | | | |
| 6.25 Supplies | | | | | |
| 6.26 Capital Outlays | | | | | |
| 6.27 Other | | | | | |
| 6.3 | | | | | |
| 6.31 Personnel | | | | | |
| 6.32 Contractual Services | | | | | |
| 6.33 Travel | | | | | |
| 6.34 Equipment | | | | | |
| 6.35 Supplies | | | | | |
| 6.36 Capital Outlays | | | | | |
| 6.37 Other | | | | | |

**Summary of Local Government Expenditures** (continued)
(thousands of dollars)

| Category of Expenditure | Two Yrs. Ago | Last Year | Current Year | Next Year | Number of Personnel |
|---|---|---|---|---|---|
| 7.0 Welfare | | | | | |
| 7.1 | | | | | |
| 7.11 Personnel | | | | | |
| 7.12 Contractual Services | | | | | |
| 7.13 Travel | | | | | |
| 7.14 Equipment | | | | | |
| 7.15 Supplies | | | | | |
| 7.16 Capital Outlays | | | | | |
| 7.17 Other | | | | | |
| 7.2 | | | | | |
| 7.21 Personnel | | | | | |
| 7.22 Contractual Services | | | | | |
| 7.23 Travel | | | | | |
| 7.24 Equipment | | | | | |
| 7.25 Supplies | | | | | |
| 7.26 Capital Outlays | | | | | |
| 7.27 Other | | | | | |
| 7.3 | | | | | |
| 7.31 Personnel | | | | | |
| 7.32 Contractual Services | | | | | |
| 7.33 Travel | | | | | |
| 7.34 Equipment | | | | | |
| 7.35 Supplies | | | | | |
| 7.36 Capital Outlays | | | | | |
| 7.37 Other | | | | | |

## Summary of Local Government Expenditures (continued)
### (thousands of dollars)

| Category of Expenditure | Two Yrs. Ago | Last Year | Current Year | Next Year | Number of Personnel |
|---|---|---|---|---|---|
| 8.0 Culture and Recreation | | | | | |
| 8.1 | | | | | |
| 8.11 Personnel | | | | | |
| 8.12 Contractual Services | | | | | |
| 8.13 Travel | | | | | |
| 8.14 Equipment | | | | | |
| 8.15 Supplies | | | | | |
| 8.16 Capital Outlays | | | | | |
| 8.17 Other | | | | | |
| 8.2 | | | | | |
| 8.21 Personnel | | | | | |
| 8.22 Contractual Services | | | | | |
| 8.23 Travel | | | | | |
| 8.24 Equipment | | | | | |
| 8.25 Supplies | | | | | |
| 8.26 Capital Outlays | | | | | |
| 8.27 Other | | | | | |
| 8.3 | | | | | |
| 8.31 Personnel | | | | | |
| 8.32 Contractual Services | | | | | |
| 8.33 Travel | | | | | |
| 8.34 Equipment | | | | | |
| 8.35 Supplies | | | | | |
| 8.36 Capital Outlays | | | | | |
| 8.37 Other | | | | | |

**Summary of Local Government Expenditures** (continued)
(thousands of dollars)

| Category of Expenditure | Two Yrs. Ago | Last Year | Current Year | Next Year | Number of Personnel |
|---|---|---|---|---|---|
| 9.0 Education | | | | | |
| 9.1 | | | | | |
|   9.11 Personnel | | | | | |
|   9.12 Contractual Services | | | | | |
|   9.13 Travel | | | | | |
|   9.14 Equipment | | | | | |
|   9.15 Supplies | | | | | |
|   9.16 Capital Outlays | | | | | |
|   9.17 Other | | | | | |
| 9.2 | | | | | |
|   9.21 Personnel | | | | | |
|   9.22 Contractual Services | | | | | |
|   9.23 Travel | | | | | |
|   9.24 Equipment | | | | | |
|   9.25 Supplies | | | | | |
|   9.26 Capital Outlays | | | | | |
|   9.27 Other | | | | | |
| 9.3 | | | | | |
|   9.31 Personnel | | | | | |
|   9.32 Contractual Services | | | | | |
|   9.33 Travel | | | | | |
|   9.34 Equipment | | | | | |
|   9.35 Supplies | | | | | |
|   9.36 Capital Outlays | | | | | |
|   9.37 Other | | | | | |

## Summary of Local Government Expenditures (continued)
### (thousands of dollars)

| Category of Expenditure | Two Yrs. Ago | Last Year | Current Year | Next Year | Number of Personnel |
|---|---|---|---|---|---|
| 10.0 Debt Service | | | | | |
| 10.1 | | | | | |
| 10.11 Personnel | | | | | |
| 10.12 Contractual Services | | | | | |
| 10.13 Travel | | | | | |
| 10.14 Equipment | | | | | |
| 10.15 Supplies | | | | | |
| 10.16 Capital Outlays | | | | | |
| 10.17 Other | | | | | |
| 10.2 | | | | | |
| 10.21 Personnel | | | | | |
| 10.22 Contractual Services | | | | | |
| 10.23 Travel | | | | | |
| 10.24 Equipment | | | | | |
| 10.25 Supplies | | | | | |
| 10.26 Capital Outlays | | | | | |
| 10.27 Other | | | | | |
| 10.3 | | | | | |
| 10.31 Personnel | | | | | |
| 10.32 Contractual Services | | | | | |
| 10.33 Travel | | | | | |
| 10.34 Equipment | | | | | |
| 10.35 Supplies | | | | | |
| 10.36 Capital Outlays | | | | | |
| 10.37 Other | | | | | |

## Summary of Local Government Expenditures (continued)
### (thousands of dollars)

| Category of Expenditure | Two Yrs. Ago | Last Year | Current Year | Next Year | Number of Personnel |
|---|---|---|---|---|---|
| 11.0 Intergovernmental Expenditure | | | | | |
| 11.1 | | | | | |
| 11.11 Personnel | | | | | |
| 11.12 Contractual Services | | | | | |
| 11.13 Travel | | | | | |
| 11.14 Equipment | | | | | |
| 11.15 Supplies | | | | | |
| 11.16 Capital Outlays | | | | | |
| 11.17 Other | | | | | |
| 11.2 | | | | | |
| 11.21 Personnel | | | | | |
| 11.22 Contractual Services | | | | | |
| 11.23 Travel | | | | | |
| 11.24 Equipment | | | | | |
| 11.25 Supplies | | | | | |
| 11.26 Capital Outlays | | | | | |
| 11.27 Other | | | | | |
| 11.3 | | | | | |
| 11.31 Personnel | | | | | |
| 11.32 Contractual Services | | | | | |
| 11.33 Travel | | | | | |
| 11.34 Equipment | | | | | |
| 11.35 Supplies | | | | | |
| 11.36 Capital Outlays | | | | | |
| 11.37 Other | | | | | |

copies of budgets for the last several years, and say "help yourself." There is a better way to gather the information.

1. Using the form as a guideline and drawing on knowledge of the local government involved, put together a list of requests that when filled will yield the required information. For instance, "Please provide the budget figures for the fire department for the last three years along with the projected budget for the coming years. Also, I would like to know the number of employees for each of these years."

2. When the list is completed, send it with a cover letter to the chief administrative officer or the elected official who functions as the chief executive of the local government.

3. Allow a reasonable time for a response. It could take two or three days for a single employee to gather the required information if the local government does not have an adequate record-keeping system.

4. If a response is not received within a reasonable time, send a follow-up letter pointing out that by law this information must be made available. Send copies of this letter and the original letter to the elected official who represents the ward or district you live in.

5. This should get some action. If it doesn't, contacting the local press might help.

If the information proves difficult or impossible to secure, this is a clear demonstration of a lack of concern for taxpayer interests. In such a case the best course to follow is to form a local taxpayer group to bring pressure to get the information and to work on replacing those public officials who were non-cooperative. Another tactic that can be used is to have an item placed on the agenda of the legislative body to inquire why this information is not readily available to citizens. Most local governments have regular meetings of the council or board that permit citizens to raise questions and issues. However, to get on the agenda for a particular meeting usually requires a request be made one to two weeks in advance. This kind of public action will almost always serve to involve the local press and in most instances will result in government officials agreeing to provide the necessary information.

## CONCLUSION

This chapter has been devoted to explaining means taxpayers can use to learn more about the operation of their local government. The more a taxpayer knows about the finances of local government, the more able the taxpayer will be to bring about changes in spending habits and tax rates. This knowledge is not without a price. It will require the taxpayer to learn a good deal about local government, to probably spend some time in government offices or at meetings with elected officials, and to spend some time reflecting on the way in which the government operates.

Without some knowledge taxpayers cannot expect to make meaningful changes in their government or their taxes. Local officials have not demonstrated the ability to curb spending and taxation. On the contrary, they have every reason to try to maintain business as usual despite the spread of the taxpayer revolt. They will try to mollify taxpayers with rhetoric, insignificant cuts in spending, and one-time tax refunds. The taxpayer who accepts these actions as real solutions to the problem of rising taxes and government spending is going to be sadly disappointed. Knowledge can serve to insulate the taxpayer from the dangers of these false promises. Knowledge allows the taxpayer to understand the changes that are the most likely to bring about the results desired.

## NOTES

1. The author is indebted to Lennox L. Moak and Albert M. Hillhouse for their fine work in this area. Their book, *Concepts and Practices in Local Government Finance* (Chicago: Municipal Finance Officers Association, 1975), provides many of the ideas for this chapter. These have been transformed somewhat to take into account the difference in view point between government managers and taxpayers.

2. National Committee on Governmental Accounting, *Governmental Accounting, Auditing and Financial Reporting*, p. 27.

# PART IV Alternatives to Higher Taxes

# 12 BETTER MANAGEMENT OF LOCAL GOVERNMENT

The taxpayer revolt has focused a spotlight of interest on the operations of local government. One of the key points is the relationship between levels of service and levels of taxation. Leaders of the tax revolt movement have consistently maintained that it is possible to make significant cuts in taxes without suffering significant erosion in levels of service. They say this can be accomplished by the elimination of waste and overlapping services. Local government officials present the counter argument that tax cuts of necessity mean service cuts. The experiences of the tax revolt in the late 1970s have not resolved this dispute because where significant tax cuts were achieved, state governments filled the budget gap with bailout funds. As a result, even those local governments most affected by the taxpayer revolt were never really forced to reduce their levels of spending significantly.

This chapter will attempt to provide some answers to the debate over the question of whether or not better management of local government operations can result in significant tax savings. Three specific approaches to the betterment of management operations will be presented. Implementing any of them in a manner calculated to bring about significant savings requires a high level of technical expertise and competence from local government managers and their staffs. In order to attract and retain people with the necessary expertise, local governments must pay salaries at least equivalent to those paid in private industry. Taxpayers who feel that the better management of local government is one way to reduce taxes and maintain services must be prepared to pay the salaries required to attract people who have the competence and training to do the job. Poorly paid and, hence, poorly motivated employees cannot be expected to improve the quality of local government operations. Substandard salaries for local government personnel will result in substandard performance costing taxpayers more money for fewer and poorer services.

In addition to qualified professional managers and employees, the improvement of local government requires that elected officials have an understanding, however rudimentary, of modern management techniques. They must know enough to be able to communicate intelligently with their managerial staff. At the minimum, they should understand some of the basic differences between the operations of public organizations and private, profit-oriented organizations. Of course, they must also be committed to the idea that local government should operate with the goal to provide the maximum amount of service for the minimum cost. It is the job of the elected officials to provide leadership and set the tone that will steer local government employees and managers in the right direction. If elected officials don't care about bettering the quality of the operations of local government, then the managers and staff certainly can not be expected to do their utmost to make improvements and conserve taxpayers' dollars.

Citizens have a role to play in the betterment of local government operations. They must be realistic in terms of salaries and benefits paid to both their elected and appointed officials. The old axiom of "you get what you pay for" applies very well to local government personnel. Citizens should also be prepared to accept that the improvement of local government operations may result in the loss of some services they value. Improving operations may involve the elimination of services benefitting only a small percentage of the people in the community. Citizens must understand these reductions are for the benefit of the entire community and, thus, should accept the reductions as part of the improvement of local government operations. Finally, just as elected officials must have some knowledge about the management and operations of local government, citizens also must have some understanding of how their government works and what they can legitimately expect from it. Without this understanding they will not be able to identify those improvements that should be supported or those proposals that work against the improvement of local government operations. The intent of this chapter is the same as the previous chapters, to assist in this educational process.

## HOW TO INCREASE THE EFFICIENCY AND EFFECTIVENESS OF LOCAL GOVERNMENT

Increasing efficiency and effectiveness is the most popular remedy for high taxes. It is popular because it represents the best of both worlds for the taxpayer: lower taxes and the same or perhaps even a higher level of service. The sad fact is that it is highly unlikely that local governments have either the capacity or the potential for improving their efficiency and effectiveness to a degree that will result in significant savings to the taxpayers without corresponding significant reductions in service. Most local governments just do not have enough "fat" in their operations to make much of a difference to the taxpayer. This is not to say that some improvement is impossible or that the effort should not be made. The point is that taxpayers should not have unrealistic expectations about the savings possible from this kind of effort. In addition to the relatively low potential for savings, the capacity to achieve the savings available is almost completely dependent on the amount of expertise available in the local government's work force. In addition to expertise, the work force must have a commitment to improve operations and must be well motivated, well led, and reasonably paid. A local government fortunate enough to possess such a work force has the opportunity to achieve some significant savings if the proper leadership is exerted by elected officials and is supported by taxpayers and citizens' groups. However, a local government lacking competent and expert management, whose work force is poorly motivated and poorly paid, has little chance of achieving significant advances in efficiency and effectiveness. In extreme instances improvements in management, staff, and working conditions will have to preceed any serious attempt to upgrade efficiency and effectiveness.

Regardless of a local government's potential for achieving real savings through improved efficiency and effectiveness, the political realities of the taxpayer revolt require that strong efforts be made in this direction. If for no other reason than to satisfy taxpayer expectations, elected officials should do all they can to improve local government operations. No matter what the condition of the local government and its workforce, there are a number of steps that can be taken to increase efficiency and effectiveness.

## Use Cost/Benefit Analysis

There are numerous management techniques that offer the potential for increasing the efficiency and effectiveness of operations in any type of organization. Many of these are unsuitable for small and medium size local governments because they require large investments of time and money or they require a level of expertise far beyond that which is available. Cost/benefit analysis is a technique that can be used on a grand scale, employing high priced consultants and requiring hundreds of hours of additional staff time. However, it can also be used in a much simplified format by any competent government manager or elected official.

Cost/benefit analysis is a technique for making decisions. At its core is the simple notion of identifying the positive results (benefits) and the negative results (costs) likely to occur as a result of any particular action. It offers a decision rule that states the benefits from any action should outweigh the costs by an appreciable margin. There are three simple steps to cost/benefit analysis. They are: costs must be identified and evaluated, benefits must be identified and evaluated, and costs and benefits must be compared with one another to determine if the action under consideration should be taken. If the benefits are greater than the costs, then action should be taken.

The technique is flexible because the calculation of costs and benefits may be done in any number of ways ranging from the most sophisticated to a simple, common sense probing of the likely consequences of any action. The value of the technique in improving operations lies primarily in the conscious search to identify costs and benefits. The type of calculation used to evaluate them is secondary to the process. Cost/benefit analysis can be introduced into an organization in a piecemeal fashion with minimal time devoted to the training and orientation of staff. Because the start-up costs are very low, the risk involved in trying the technique is almost nonexistent.

An additional benefit of this technique is that it can be easily understood and used by citizens interested in observing and participating in local government operations. When cost/benefit analysis is used as a part of the budgetary process, it has the added benefit of presenting the decision processes in a manner that taxpayers can understand and evaluate. If there is less mystery in the financial operations of local government, there is a better opportunity for cooperative action between citizens and public officials. Cooperation will give citizens a good return on their investment in government.

Cost/benefit analysis can make a positive contribution to the efficiency and effectiveness of local government by illuminating the negative and positive consequences likely to result from any decision. This kind of systematic evaluation of consequences can help local government officials avoid situations where an apparent short term gain is counteracted by a long term cost undiscovered before the decision was made. By emphasizing the values of efficiency, effectiveness, and economy in analyzing costs and benefits, public officials will be able to make improvements in these areas to the extent their expertise and knowledge allows. The technique is as useful to a small rural local government as it is to a large urban government possessing a high level of technical expertise.

## Contract for Services

Many times local governments fail to seriously consider the alternative of contracting for services. The seemingly high initial cost makes hiring the necessary employees, buying the equipment, and providing the service directly appear to be the best and cheapest alternative. However, this kind of short term cost analysis can be very deceiving. One of the organizational characteristics of any local government organization is a tendency to retain employees and positions once they are created. This is because public officials, whether elected or appointed, have a built in bias against terminating public employees (after all, they are voters too!). Elimination of the service or even substantial reductions are next to impossible even if it is clear the service is no longer needed. In addition to this bias against reduction and elimination, the nature of the budgetary process almost guarantees gradual increases in the amount of money spent to provide the service. While not technically uncontrollable, most government activities show a slow but steady rate of growth over the years that is virtually impossible for elected officials to stop. Also, civil service rules and collective bargaining agreements can hamstring public management in its efforts to improve the efficiency and effectiveness of service delivery.

For many local governments, contracting out for services may be a means of solving the problems mentioned in the previous paragraph. Contracts are normally written for a short period of time, one or two years. Public regulations almost always require contracts to be put up for bid so the local government has some assurance it is getting a fair and competitive price for the services it receives. Contracts that are properly written have service specifications assuring the quality and quantity of the service provided. If these are not met, it is relatively easy for public officials to enforce the provisions of the contract. Contracting for services has another advantage for the local government because the local government doesn't have to terminate employees in order to eliminate the service. It is much easier for elected officials to terminate a service by merely failing to renew a contract than it is for them to vote the layoff of 20 or 30 employees.

In terms of efficiency and effectiveness, the advantages usually far outweigh the disadvantage of the higher initial cost of contracting for services. The initial cost is usually higher because of the profit margin the contractor must have to stay in business. Both taxpayers and elected officials must look beyond this initial disadvantage to the longer range benefits. An additional benefit of contracting is its contribution to the business base of the community, which in turn serves as part of the tax base for the local government. Local governments usually derive tax revenues from the business they give to local contractors, thereby lessening the initial cost disadvantage.

Contracting out is a particularly attractive alternative in instances where the local government is considering a new service or a significant expansion of an existing service. Replacing an existing service with a contractual arrangement will usually require a significant number of public employees to be laid off. The political consequences of such an action are usually more serious than elected officials are willing to bear unless they are under severe taxpayer pressure. When used properly contracting out for local government services can be a significant means of increasing efficiency and effectiveness.

## Evaluate Programs and Services

It is common practice in almost all local governments to evaluate the performance of employees on a periodic basis. Elected officials receive a form of evaluation when they campaign for reelection. Local governments provide for the evaluation of people working for them, but they usually do not have a means for the systematic evaluation of the programs and services they offer. In theory programs should be evaluated as a part of the budgetary process. This usually does not occur because at budget time elected officials and government managers are concerned with the number of dollars being spent by government, not with determining which programs are working well and which are having problems or have become obsolete.

A system of periodic evaluation of the performance of local government programs and services is needed. To avoid the complicating factors of personnel decisions and budget decisions, this evaluation should be a separate process carried out at a different time of the year. Although they should be separated from personnel and budget activities evaluations will yield information and recommendations that will undoubtedly affect future personnel and budgetary decisions. The emphasis of these evaluations should be two fold: 1) Does the need for the service still exist? If it no longer does, is the service meeting new, vital needs that have developed since the service was first initiated? 2) If there is an identifiable and legitimate need for the service, is the service doing a good job of meeting the need? Negative answers to either of these questions should be the signal for strong action by the local government officials. The evaluations can be adjusted in complexity and sophistication to meet the level of expertise available to the local government. As in the case of cost/benefit analysis, the basic procedure is more important than the complexity with which it is carried out. For service evaluation to make a maximum impact on the overall operations of government it must be regularized so that all services and programs are evaluated on a periodic basis. The schedule of evaluation should be enacted as an ordinance by the legislative body. This assures that evaluations will be carried out and demonstrates the support of elected officials for these actions.

One means of accomplishing these periodic evaluations are the "sunset" laws that have been adopted by some state and local governments. They strengthen the evaluation process by requiring programs to go out of existence unless there is legislative action to continue them. This legislative action is usually based upon the results of a vigorous evaluation process. These sunset laws can be an extremely useful means of improving the operations of local government by identifying unnecessary and obsolete programs.

As in the case of contracting out for services, sunset laws and periodic evaluations are easier to institute with new programs because there are fewer entrenched political interests to support and defend them. Citizen and taxpayer groups should insist that these evaluations include a process for seeking inputs from people who receive the services as well as from the general public. Evaluations conducted entirely within the bureaucratic structure of government are likely to be narrow in focus and without regard for the attitudes and values of the general public. In addition to citizen input, it is important for evaluations to be seriously considered by decision makers during the budgetary process. Formal processes such as those used in sunset laws should exist to assure that critical evaluations of programs do not end up gathering dust in some manager's office. Program and service evaluations will only enhance the efficiency and effectiveness of local government to the extent they are used by elected officials in making spending and taxing decisions.

## Train the Workforce

In times of taxpayer unrest over high taxes employee training programs tend to be high on the list of items scheduled for elimination by elected officials. The protests of managers are easily brushed aside with the argument that training does not contribute directly to the services local governments provide. The funds saved may be an insignificant part of overall expenditures, but they represent tangible evidence that the officials can cut spending without reducing services. The reasons given below demonstrate that these are false economies.

As an initial point, the training funds expended by any local government usually do not amount to more than a very small percentage of the overall budget. Therefore, the likelihood of these savings affecting tax rates even in the long run is very remote. Second, almost every government employee requires some degree of training and skill development to do a competent job. Employee costs are the single largest expenditure local governments make. A poorly trained work force represents an enormous cost to taxpayers in terms of decreased efficiency and effectiveness. Machines are regularly scheduled for maintenance and periodic overhaul. Human skills require the same kind of periodic attention. Additionally, properly designed training programs demonstrate to employees that management is interested in the quality of work they do and is willing to devote time and money to improve their work. A work force well motivated and well trained is an invaluable asset to a local government interested in achieving a high level of efficiency and effectiveness.

As strange as it may sound to some people, taxpayers concerned about high taxes and low levels of service should encourage proper training of government employees and support reasonable salary levels and good treatment in general for government employees. The number of people on the payroll is the most significant factor influencing personnel costs. Money spent for training employees is a small part of personnel costs and can pay big dividends in terms of increased efficiency and effectiveness. Taxpayers should beware the false savings offered by politicians as a result of gutting employee training and development programs.

## Take Advantage of "Free" Services

In the previous paragraphs, the importance of technical competence and expertise has been mentioned several times in connection with improving efficiency and effectiveness. Technical competence and expertise are usually determined by the size of the administrative staff the local government can afford and the salaries it can pay. However, there are actions that small and relatively poor governments can take to increase their management capacity without spending a great deal of money.

Most state governments have a department of local government affairs offering "free" services to local government. These may range from an investment plan for excess funds that pools local government monies in order to earn a higher interest rate to "circuit rider" programs where professionally trained public managers serve as advisors to a number of local governments on a shared-time basis. When used wisely and in conjunction with local needs these services can be of real help in improving the operations of local government with no loss in local autonomy and control. In addition to state governments, there are a wide variety of organizations offering training and technical services to small governments at little or no cost. Examples are the Municipal Finance Officers Association, the National Municipal League, and the International City Management Association. Local universities may have institutes and departments that provide useful services with little or no charge. These "free" services must be used wisely so that they contribute to local goals and provide a reasonable return on the time invested in them.

Taxpayers usually view money spent on organization dues or for travel to conferences with great suspicion. In some cases this suspicion is justified, in other cases real benefits are being lost by the reluctance to spend a small amount of money in an unpopular way. The point is that improving local government operations requires technical skills and competence. These can be cheaply and easily attained by the means described. The funds involved should be considered an investment that can yield big returns in terms of increased efficiency and effectiveness. However, taxpayers and local officials are justified in demanding that money spent for these purposes be accounted for in terms of the benefits likely to result. In short, cost/benefit analysis can and should be applied to the question of whether or not to take advantage of some of the "free" services that have been mentioned. Also, it should be kept in mind that the time of employees involved in these activities is usually a far more significant expenditure of funds than any money spent for travel and similar expenses.

The five means of improving the operations of local governments discussed here are relatively unique because they do not usually get taxpayer support. Yet it should be clear at this point that each of these techniques and ideas when used properly can result in real savings for government and taxpayers. Taxpayers should do two things: initiate and support the use of these techniques in their local government and require evidence that they are being used properly and productively.

## PAYMENT-FOR-SERVICES PROGRAMS

In the years prior to the taxpayer revolt most local governments derived some of their revenues from arrangements in which they charged citizens a fee for a service or the use of a public facility. In many cases these fees did not cover the actual costs associated with the activity and were used to regulate and limit the use of the service or facility. Fees were not a significant part of local government revenues and they certainly were not viewed as a means to improve the management of local government. The taxpayer revolt is bringing about a drastic change in the role these revenues can play in local government finance.

Fees-for-services as a revenue source have been discussed in the previous chapters describing the progress of the taxpayer revolt. Now they are examined as a means for increasing the operating efficiency and effectiveness of local government. Payment-for-services programs are based on the fundamental proposition that, in some instances, the users of a public service should pay the full cost of providing that service. When appropriate services have been identified for the program they must be isolated from other revenue operations. The device used to do this is called a revolving fund.

Revolving funds are an accounting device that provides for the earning and expenditure of funds in a manner similar to a small business. However, revolving funds are not intended to make a profit. Their goal is to provide the appropriate level of service for the least possible cost. They are expected to "break even," to neither generate a profit (excess revenues) nor to run at a deficit. They should collect just enough revenues to pay all of the costs associated with the service plus reimburse the local government for overhead and support services.

In addition to being accounting devices, revolving funds should represent an organizational unit separate from the general administrative structure and subject only to the authority of the elected officials. The managers of these units must have the authority to set the rates charged for the service. They must also have complete freedom in spending funds to provide the service. This means they must not be forced to use the city service garage to service their vehicles, be required to purchase their supplies through the usual government supplier, or be forced to use any of the other city staff services. These managers are being asked to function as though they were in a market-oriented environment. They must be given adequate authority to carry out this responsibility.

Revolving funds and their related administrative structures contribute to operating efficiency and effectiveness by placing the manager in the position to control both revenues and expenditures. This control allows managers to determine the best means of operating because they are able to experiment with various alternative courses of action and thus determine which is best suited for their operation. They can see the effects of whatever changes they make clearly and directly. The situation is not unlike private industry where a merchant may experiment with various combinations of business hours until the best one is discovered. By gaining operating experience, the revolving fund manager is able to develop a means of operation that provides the required services for the least possible cost to the users and at no cost to local government.

As in the case with any management device, there are some potential problem areas that require attention. The first is the determination of which services should be placed on a self-paying basis. Some services are by their nature so vital and so expensive that they require subsidy from general tax revenues. Health, fire, and police services are examples of these. Other services are less vital and their actual cost is such that most people can afford to pay for them. These can be placed on a self-supporting basis. Examples of these are building and zoning services, recreational services, and utilities. The decision of which services to place on the self-payment program must be made individually in accordance with the particular needs and circumstances of each local government and the surrounding community.

The second area of concern grows out of one of the primary characteristics of the revolving fund system, autonomy. Managers must not be allowed to be so independent that they are not responsive to the direction of local officials. Because elected officials represent the people in administrative matters, for them to lose control of an operation means that the citizens have also lost control over it. Elected officials must be able to control these operations because they are ultimately responsible to the people for them. Revolving fund managers must have operating control, but they must be responsive to the direction of elected officials.

Revolving funds are the best means of structuring payment-for-services programs in most circumstances. There are other ways, however. One of the most common is the use of earmarked revenues to provide specific services. This device is more common than revolving funds, but many times does not contain the managerial structures necessary to improve government operations. Most earmarked funds go into the general revenues of the local government, and then a similiar amount is spent on the activity the funds are designated to support. Usually there is no direct linkage between the provision of the service in terms of quality or quantity and the amount of revenue produced. Management cannot control both revenues and expenditures. However, with an organizational structure that parallels the one described for revolving funds, earmarked revenues can be significant contributors to the increased efficiency and effectiveness of government.

In terms of potential problems, they suffer most from a lack of control. Earmarked revenues are generally taxes (such as an excise tax on gasoline sales earmarked for road maintenance) whose revenues are not easily controllable by elected officials. Therefore, there is a danger that more funds may be generated than are actually needed to provide the sercice. In this instance efficiency and effectiveness can not be served. Overall, in order for earmarked revenue operations to make a positive contribution to better local government, they must be closely controlled, have a unified management structure, and be well suited to the particular circumstances in which they are used.

To sum up, payment-for-services programs can make a positive contribution to the betterment of local government operations. They can help curb unnecessary government spending and insure that only those revenues actually needed are collected. As with other means of improving management, they require a reasonable level of expertise and technical competence. They also require that elected officials and citizens have a basic understanding of what they are designed to do as well as their principle advantages and disadvantages.

## HOW TO REDUCE AND ELIMINATE GOVERNMENT SERVICES

The reduction and elimination of local government services was one of the anticipated results of the taxpayer revolt against the property tax. However, because large state revenue surpluses were used to sustain local government spending, no significant reductions took place in many instances. Despite the rhetoric of the anti-tax campaign, neither proponents of the tax revolt nor opposing local government officials seemed very eager to begin a wholesale reduction in the scope of local government activities. Elected officials found such reductions to be politically difficult and taxpayers did not want to give up services unless they had to. State bailouts helped both groups to avoid the unpleasant business in most instances. This is ironic because reducing and eliminating government services is the surest and most direct way of curbing local government spending and of reducing tax burdens. If and when state bailout funds dry up, taxpayers and local officials will come face to face with the necessity for drastic action.

Taxpayers who are serious about reducing their tax burden will have to consider this alternative because it offers the best and most effective means of cutting down the size of local government operations. In reducing or eliminating services, the goal should be to maximize the amount of funds saved while minimizing the reductions and eliminations of service. In order to achieve this goal, there are five points that must be considered. These are discussed below.

## Consider What Services Can Legally Be Reduced or Eliminated

Many areas of local government operations are controlled by the laws of the state and federal governments as well as by the state constitution and perhaps even by the charter of the local government itself. The first step in a program of elimination and reduction is to identify all of those areas within the discretion of local government. Each of these must be examined to determine if there are state or federal matching funds attached to the services under study. If there are, then the savings to the taxpayers may not be as great as they first appear. This may affect the decision of which services to cut. Additionally, local governments must be wary of cutting services in areas that might effect their eligibility to receive state and federal grants-in-aid. For example, some community development grants require an independent local planning commission. If such a commission were eliminated as an economy measure, the local government would no longer be eligible for the federal grant program. This could result in local taxpayers having to pay for programs that might otherwise be funded by the federal or state governments. This kind of savings would be a false economy indeed.

Once areas of potential reduction are identified, the nasty business of deciding whose priorities will be served and whose will suffer can begin. Taxpayers must have a role to play in this decision process if it is to result in significant savings. The anti-cut bias of local officials requires taxpayers to be active enough to break officials out of their usual behavior and to convince them that the majority of the people want reductions and are willing to fight for them at the next election. Taxpayers must also be prepared to sacrifice some of the services they personally enjoy. To expect other people to suffer the entire service loss is totally unrealistic and will present a serious obstruction to attaining any real saving.

## Consider the Different Types of Reduction Decisions

In considering what program and service cuts to make taxpayers and elected officials will find it useful to consider the various types of decisions available. At least three types of reduction decisions should be considered. The first is to lower the quality of a particular service. An example might be to limit garbage pickups to curbside and to only pick up trash in plastic bags of a certain dimension. This kind of service is of lower quality than one where anything will be picked up that is placed outside of a garage door. Presumably it will also lower the cost. The second type of decision would be to lower the frequency of service. Again, using trash pickup as an example, pickups might be changed from once a week to once a month, resulting in a cost savings. Obviously, both frequency and quality of service could be lowered as a part of the same decision, i.e., once a month pickup at curbside of plastic bags only. The third type of decision would be to totally eliminate a service. If trash pickup was eliminated, presumably people would haul their own trash to the dump or private contractors would fill the void.

If a service is being paid for out of general revenues, it could be switched over to a payment for service basis, e.g., local government charges for the pickup of trash. The key point in this decision from the point of view of the taxpayer is whether the government charge for pickup is less than a private contractor would charge for a comparable level of service. If operations were of equal efficiency and effectiveness, government should be less expensive because it does not make a profit. By removing a service from general revenue funding, a reduction in taxes is achieved. However, if people must pay a service charge instead, are they any better off? If the fees exceed the amount saved in taxes, then the answer is no.

In cutting a program or service all of the different types of reduction decisions should be considered in order to find the one that maximizes the tax savings and minimizes the loss of service. It is extremely important that savings be expressed in the form of taxes, rather than merely expenditures. Tax savings are the only ones that really affect the economic well-being of the citizen. Savings in a particular area of expenditure can easily be "lost" when the budget is considered as a whole.

## Link Reductions in Services to Reductions in Taxes

In selecting areas for reduction and elimination there is another criterion to be considered. This criterion is based upon the assumption that there should be a linkage between taxes paid and the services received. Services chosen for elimination or reduction should be those closely related to the taxes reduced. For instance, reductions in the property tax should be made by reducing property related services such as road clearing, landscaping, and fire protection. The basic idea is that the public is entitled to only those services for which it is willing to pay.

This criterion would not apply in a situation where reductions are made in program areas not specifically linked to a particular tax. General service reductions should be linked with a reduction in the taxes that have the broadest base, so that all members of the community may benefit equally from the savings achieved. As a general rule, the savings resulting from program reductions should be passed on to those citizens who must suffer the reduced services. This direct relationship between reductions in taxes and reductions in services is a test that local government officials can apply to taxpayers to measure the depth of their sentiment and commitment. Taxpayers who are unwilling to put up with reduced services in return for lower taxes are being unrealistic about what it is possible to achieve in the way of government reform. Aside from improving the quality of local government operations and increased reliance on the state and federal governments, reduced taxes must usually result in reduced services.

### Involve Citizens in Reduction and Elimination Decisions

In reducing or eliminating services, citizen participation is one of the most important considerations. Taxpayers provided the impetus for cutting government operations through their demands for a lightening of the tax burden. Therefore, they should be expected to participate in making the difficult decisions concerning the reductions in programs. To leave these unpleasant chores to the elected officials is bad practice for two reasons. First, elected officials are quite likely to hesitate at every step of the way to avoid making cuts in government operations. Additionally, the cuts that they do manage to make are likely to be those that are the least painful to the majority of taxpayers. They will also be the cuts that involve the least political unrest. The result of these cuts will probably be some small savings now and higher expenses later on in the future. (Public officials are unlikely to cut personnel costs, instead they make the easy reductions such as deferring maintenance and needed capital expenditures.)

The second reason for not leaving reduction decisions exclusively to the elected officials is that they are unlikely to be in touch with the service priorities of the citizens. That the drastic measure of cutting government operations was necessary in the first place demonstrates how out of touch incumbent officials are with the sentiments of the citizens. Citizens must be willing to take an active part in the decisions to reduce and eliminate government services.

There are at least two means of participation. One means is through a series of community meetings in which alternatives are discussed complete with information about the loss in services and the resulting savings in taxes. A series of meetings held through out the community can give officals a fairly good sense of what kind of reductions people prefer. The second means of citizen input is through the ballot box. Advisory or binding referenda can be used as a means for citizens to directly state their preferences for cuts in programs. The advantage to this method is that it includes all citizens who are interested enough to cast a ballot. The disadvantage is that the alternatives must be presented in writing at a very simple level. This may result in insufficient information being available for citizens to make intelligent decisions. The use of either of the two methods will depend on the nature of the reductions being considered and the particular circumstances of the situation.

## Look for Special Constraints on Service Reductions

One of the first steps in evaluating areas for possible reductions should be to look for special considerations that may hamper cutting efforts. These should be identified early so that time and effort is not devoted to implementing a reduction alternative only to have it stymied at the last minute by some unforeseen consideration. Examples of these kinds of factors are labor agreements, insurance requirements, and adverse economic impacts on the local community.

## Concluding Comments About Reductions

Reducing the scope of government operations is a very difficult business for government officials and employees. This difficulty is compounded when the change is made necessary by a violent action of the taxpayers. In these situations a crisis mentality prevails and the chances of accomplishing intelligent reductions in services that achieve the highest possible tax savings are often remote. One factor that can help is the active involvement and participation of citizens in the reduction process. Citizens must be realistic in their expectations of what can be achieved and they must be willing to give up some of the government services from which they personally benefit. If citizens make every attempt at intelligent participation and if elected officials cooperate with this effort, then there is every reason to believe that significant tax savings can be achieved through an intelligent reduction in local government services.

## CONCLUSION

The intent of this chapter has been to illustrate some of the means available to improve the quality of local government operations. Improved operations are an alternative to high tax rates. The ultimate definition of the quality of local government operations has to be made by the citizens. For this reason, even the elimination and reduction of services can constitute an improvement in government operations. Any type of improvement will require the active, informed participation of the citizenry, the whole-hearted cooperation and leadership of elected officials, and a level of technical skill and expertise that is consistent with the complexity of the improvements being attempted.

There is one other possibility for the improvement of the operations of local government that has not been discussed so far. This possibility is for innovation to provide a higher level of service for a lower cost to the taxpayer. The following chapter provides a description of an innovation that could be of real use in providing high quality local government services at a reduced cost.

# 13 A NEW ALTERNATIVE TO PAYING TAXES: VOLUNTEER PERSONAL SERVICE

Up to this point, the discussion has focused on reducing government spending and ways in which local government can raise new revenues in order to reduce the burden of the property tax. In addition to these traditional means of attacking the tax problem, imagination and creativity is needed in developing new ways to reduce the tax burden. In this chapter a new approach to the payment of taxes is described. It draws upon the idea of volunteer service, which has a long and honored tradition in this country. Volunteer Personal Service (VPS) is a sensible way for people to pay their fair share of taxes with as little hardship as possible.

Like any new idea that seems to threaten the status quo, the concept of Volunteer Personal Service will be greeted by politicians and government officials with claims of: "It won't work," "It costs more than it's worth," "It can't be done," "It's not in the public interest." The astute taxpayer will translate these arguments and get their real meaning: "It won't work *because I didn't think of it,*" "It costs more than it's worth *because it will cause me political problems,*" "It can't be done *because I don't see any real benefit in it for me,*" "It's not in the public interest *because it's not in my interest.*" These arguments should not be accepted. Any reform worth having is going to take a fight to achieve. As will be demonstrated, Volunteer Personal Service is an idea whose time has come.

## HOW VOLUNTEER PERSONAL SERVICE CAN WORK

Volunteer Personal Service is based upon the simple notion that people should be allowed to substitute their labor for the monetary payment of their taxes. Volunteer work is accepted as a means of paying taxes!

| original tax bill | LESS | the value of VPS | EQUALS | adjusted tax bill |
|---|---|---|---|---|

Although VPS could and should work with any level of government, this description is of how it can work with local government because it is at this level that the chances of implementation are the greatest.

There are two types of local government taxes that are well suited for adaption to the VPS program: property taxes (both real and personal) and user fees such as charges for water, sewers, recreational facilities and the like. Property tax bills normally come out once or twice a year. It would be a relatively simple matter for these bills to be adjusted with the dollar value of the credits earned by an individual under the VPS program. User fees billed on a regular basis, such as sewer and water charges, could be adjusted every month in a similar fashion. Government-owned recreational facilities could be authorized to honor "credit cards" that represent the dollar value of services volunteered to the local government. These losses of revenue would be offset by an equal saving brought about by reduced personnel costs resulting from the VPS program. A typical implementation of VPS program might occur in the following way.

1. *In keeping with the basic notion* of substituting volunteers for salaried employees, government officials would identify jobs that could be performed by volunteers with a minimum of on-the-job training. Because most governments have job classification systems that specify required skills for each job, it should be relatively easy to determine what type of job for which a particular volunteer is qualified. The jobs selected for the VPS program should possess the following characteristics. They should be jobs that can be learned by someone with the basic skills within a short period of time. Typical jobs that might be made available to volunteers are keypunch operator, receptionist, switch board operator, library assistant, or recreation program assistant. The basic idea is that the jobs do not require a thorough knowledge of the on-going operations of the government agency. Rather the jobs must be those that are primarily concerned with the completion of specific tasks or assignments relatively independent of other operations. This independence from other operations allows the flexibility necessary to accomodate

the scheduling of a number of different volunteers throughout the day. Previous experience with volunteers has shown that this flexibility is necessary in order to make effective use of volunteer talents and skills.

Another criterion for position selection for the VPS program is the availability of qualified personnel for the supervision and training of volunteers. Handling volunteers effectively requires a certain kind of skill and attitude that not all people possess. Supervisors and trainers must be selected for more than their knowledge of the jobs to be performed. They must be sensitive to the needs and concerns of volunteers as well as the needs of management to have the work done in a timely and efficient manner. The selection of supervisors and trainers is the key factor in the success of the VPS program from the point of view of the volunteer as well as the government agency.

Success in the VPS program is defined for the volunteer as being able to pay taxes with labor rather than with dollars. This means there should be as many job slots available as there are volunteers to fill them. From the point of view of government the substitution of labor for dollars should not result in the loss of operating effectiveness or in any added costs. A negative effect on either performance or cost would work against the overall goals of the VPS program.

In terms of cost, the idea is that the loss of tax revenue will be offset on a dollar for dollar basis by the salary savings achieved through the use of volunteers. The cost of training and supervision would be borne by the volunteers through a start up charge that must be "earned" by each participant before each begins to earn credits against taxes.

2. *The second step in creating the* VPS system involves development of the accounting and records system that will convert the dollar value of the volunteer's work to a credit against an individual tax bill. The system would work in the following way. As soon as a citizen registers for the VPS program, an account is set up that shows the amount of property tax or other tax owed. It would also indicate whether or not the citizen desires to have a "credit" card for use in paying fees imposed by government owned recreational facilities.

As credits are earned through volunteer service, the dollar value of these is added to the citizen's account. The amount added would be determined by the hourly pay rate for work the volunteer is performing. These hourly rates would be derived from the official salary scale for each position filled by the volunteer. Before credit is earned against the tax bill, the volunteer must first work off the initial training and registration fee. The registration fee is assessed only once when a person enters the VPS program. The training fee is applied whenever a volunteer qualifies for a new position. It should be emphasized that these "assessments" are not paid in cash by the volunteer, but rather they must be worked off the volunteer's account. The volunteer receives a statement on a regular basis reflecting the amount of credit earned.

It would be possible for people to work off all of their property taxes and utility charges and to earn an unlimited amount of credit toward the use of government facilities for which a fee is usually charged. Practically speaking, it may be wise to limit the amount of usage fee credit that may be earned by any one individual within a given period of time. These credits would not be transferable to any person nor could they be carried over from year to year.

3. *The final phase of VPS* implementation is to match volunteers with specific jobs and to establish a system for matching the job needs of the government with the availability of volunteers on a daily basis. Associated with each position would be a list of volunteers who had qualified to work in that position. This list would also contain information on the time availability of each volunteer. A coordinator of volunteers (this position might even be staffed by volunteers) would be responsible for securing the volunteers for the positions in need of staffing. This coordination function is crucial to the success of the VPS program. There must be sufficient volunteer time available to take care of the work needs of government. Also, there must be a sufficient amount of work available to provide a meaningful level of tax relief for those people who want to work in the VPS program.

## HOW VOLUNTEER PERSONAL SERVICE BENEFITS THE TAXPAYER

The most obvious benefit of the VPS program is to the taxpayer who elects to volunteer time and labor in lieu of paying taxes in the conventional manner. This trade off of labor for dollars might have the most appeal to those taxpayers who do not hold down full-time jobs. This category includes retired persons and people whose family responsibilities prevent them from taking a full-time job. For these people, the VPS program provides a means of paying their fair share of taxes while at the same time conserving hard earned dollars—thus improving the quality of their lives as well as contributing to the overall economic health of the community. Taken in aggregrate across the entire country, these saved dollars could represent a considerable amount of new economic input, which might have a real beneficial effect on the local, state, and national economies. Taxes paid to government with labor rather than with dollars represent a positive contribution to the economy rather than an addition to generally non-economically-productive spending of government.

In addition to economic benefits, some participants in the program may be able to develop new job skills they can use if they decide to enter the work force at a later date. The overall extent of this job training could be significant enough to replace a substantial portion of federal funds currently being spent for job training programs. Although this might seem to be a somewhat intangible benefit of VPS, it falls in line with the notion that every decrease in government spending adds to the economic well-being of the country through decreased taxes and increased spendable income.

Still another benefit accruing to taxpayers who involve themselves in the VPS program is that they will gain a better understanding of the day to day workings of their local government. This knowledge will enable them to be more effective in bringing pressure to bear on politicians to reduce taxes. As we have seen in previous chapters, generalities are usually ineffective in pressing for tax relief and reduction of public expenditures. Firsthand knowledge can go a long way toward convincing a reluctant public official. The volunteer may be in the envied position of knowing more about a particular program or activity than a member of the town council. In government affairs knowledge is an indispensable partner to success. In addition, if elected officials know they are dealing with informed citizens, there is a greater likelihood of cooperation and constructive effort. Politicians find it very difficult to respond to specific questions or suggestions with only vague generalities. VPS should serve as a means to encourage citizens to become more aware of how their government operates. This increased awareness will equip citizens to have a more direct and significant impact on their government. An informed citizenry is the vital component in reducing taxes and unnecessary government spending.

## HOW VOLUNTEER PERSONAL SERVICE BENEFITS THE GOVERNMENT

All too often, plans that promise relief for the taxpayer seem to promise nothing but trouble and hard times for government and government officials. At least this is the story generally heard in response to tax relief proposals that have any significant impact on the amount of tax dollars collected and spent. The VPS program when proposed will undoubtedly be regarded by government officials as one of the worst (and craziest) ideas ever put forth by citizens as a means to cut down the amount of taxes they must pay. Fortunately, while VPS may indeed cause some hard times for government officials who resist it, it will in fact make a positive contribution to the efficiency and effectiveness of the government agencies that adopt it.

This increase in efficiency and effectiveness will be brought about by two direct effects of the VPS program. First, the people working under VPS will be volunteers. This means they will be bringing a different attitude to their "job" than the civil servant who probably feels under paid and overworked. For the volunteer the "job" is a source of new ideas and experiences—a break from the routine of housework, child rearing, or retirement. There is ample evidence to show that the attitude and motivation of a worker is perhaps the prime factor in determining what kind of work the person turns out. Someone who is interested in the job is less likely to make mistakes and is less likely to try to avoid or pass off problems than someone who is tired of the same old routine. All of us at one time or another have encouraged those government employees who thought that we were working for them instead of the other way around, who thought that it was too much trouble to explain some government regulation or provide the answers that we needed. It is hard to imagine a volunteer having this kind of attitude toward the public. After all, the volunteer is the public! We can confidently expect the volunteer employee to have an attitude superior to that of many of the government employees that we encounter.

In addition to better motivation, the volunteer worker can be expected to bring a new viewpoint to the job—a viewpoint that has not been stifled by years of employment at the same tiresome task. If utilized in the proper manner, this fresh perspective can be of real value to the management of the government agency in improving the quality of service without increasing the cost of that service. In most cases, the volunteer worker will perform better than the average employee because of the volunteer's superior motivation and fresh approach to the job.

In addition to the higher quality of work, there is another substantial benefit that will accrue to the government agency sponsoring a Volunteer Personal Service program, a benefit that can be calculated quickly and directly in terms of dollars saved. For most local government agencies, fringe benefits for full-time employees run at least 20 percent or more of the employee's base pay. VPS workers will not require fringe benefits. This means that, even though the salaries associated with VPS positions are not saved (because of the tax credits earned by the volunteers filling that position), an amount equal to 20 percent of the tax credits earned will be saved. If a given VPS program generates $100,000 in tax credits in any one year, the local government can expect a direct reduction of $20,000 in its expenditures for employee fringe benefits. In larger government agencies this can amount to very significant savings indeed. An additional direct monetary saving will be generated from savings on cost-of-living and merit increases that do not have to be given to the volunteer worker. To be sure, some adjustment will have to be made in "pay" rates for the VPS worker, but these adjustments need not be as high or as frequent as would be necessary for a full-time employee. Overall, a properly run VPS program should generate significant dollar savings for the government at the same time that it contributes to the increased efficiency and effectiveness of the government's programs.

There is still another direct benefit that will accrue to the government that sponsors a VPS program. Many times politicians will make the comment that they cannot seem to get the government employees to be responsive to the needs and desires of the people. This lack of responsiveness may sometimes be due to the loss of perspective that occurs among many government workers. They tend to see themselves as government employees and not as taxpayer-citizens. Among some government employees "taxpayer" is a dirty word for a group of people that seem to have nothing better to do than to try to deny "well-deserved and long-overdue" raises to government employees. This type of attitude is particularly unwelcome in an employee whose job it is to serve the needs of the public. Exposure to the VPS volunteer should serve to soften, if not change, the attitude of the government worker toward the citizen. This change in attitude will be manifested in terms of improved service to citizens. Similarly, volunteers can be expected to spread the word that the public employee is a human being who really is concerned about doing the job in the best way possible.

Citizen participation in government affairs has long been viewed as a desirable goal by those who wish to retain or achieve political office. All too often citizen participation has been limited to a few neighborhood meetings for most people, or membership on relatively powerless boards and commissions for a few people. In either case there is little or no contact between the average citizen and the typical government employee. It is precisely this sort of contact that is the most valuable in improving citizen-government relations. Add to this the direct economic benefit that will result for both the government and the private citizen and it becomes very hard to imagine why an idea such as VPS would not enjoy wide and trouble-free adoption. But, as might be suspected, the road to implementing Volunteer Personal Service programs will not be smooth and easy. On the contrary, it will meet with fierce resistance from many of the power groups concerned with the affairs of local government.

In order to be an effective advocate of VPS, taxpayers must be prepared to answer these attacks when they come. The following paragraphs will preview some of the arguments likely to be made by those opposing VPS and will present some effective answers to these arguments. Prior knowledge of the arguments likely to be encountered should make taxpayers more effective advocates for VPS and thus hasten the day when the average citizen will have the choice of paying a fair share of taxes with either labor or dollars.

## HOW TO FIGHT FOR THE VOLUNTEER PERSONAL SERVICE PROGRAM, OR WHAT TO SAY WHEN THEY TELL YOU IT CAN'T BE DONE

Probably the first objection to be raised against VPS will be that it costs too much. But, in fact, it represents a substantial dollar savings when the elimination of fringe benefit costs and expensive cost-of-living and merit increases is taken into consideration. Despite the fact the charge of "it costs too much" is not true, it is still made and pursued vigorously. First, "it costs too much" is a great argument to make when a politician needs time to find out more about a proposal. Even if it can be proved that a new idea will not "cost too much," no one will fault a politician for being overprotective of the taxpayer's purse. In addition, "further study" can be made to show that the cost for the new program is not high at all or is at least reasonable. Therefore, the politician can easily change positions if this seems to be the expedient thing to do. The second factor that makes the "cost too much" argument very popular is directly related to the overall reason for this book. Taxpayers are tired of having to pay an increasingly larger percentage of their income to support government operations when it appears that government is failing in its major duties of protecting and enhancing the economic well-being of the citizenry. Most politicians are astute enough to realize this feeling and use it to their own purposes. Ten years ago the most common argument used against a new program was that it wasn't in the public interest or was unthinkingly conservative. But times change, and today's all-purpose argument against change and innovation is "it costs too much." The fact that VPS will actually cost less is not going to stop the "it costs too much" argument.

The second and most serious argument against the VPS program is going to be that it will cause some public employees to lose their jobs. This argument will receive support from a powerful coalition of public employee unions and government officials. Unions and government officials on the same side of the fence? That's right. There are certain areas of common interest between union and management in the public sector and this is one of those areas. This common interest involves the leadership of both organizations. Both union leaders and government officials have a vested interest in maintaining or increasing the total number of government employees.

Government officials have a well-known inclination to try to maximize the number of employees under their control. For the government manager a larger work force is one of the requirements for promotion and for moving on to bigger and better things. For the elected official public employees mean jobs. The facts about patronage systems are well known and do not need an extensive explanation here. Suffice it to say that when a politician's fortune is dependent on the number of jobs to be given out, there is a strong need to maintain, if not increase, the number of public service jobs. Even in government agencies that enjoy the use of a civil service system instead of a patronage system, there is a built-in incentive for the elected official to maintain and increase the number of full-time public service jobs. More employees usually mean more programs in operation. Programs are one of the few tangible ways that politicians have of showing the good job they have done for their constituents. Increased programs and services translate into political promises that have been kept. They are accomplishments that can be pointed to with pride during reelection campaigns. Unfortunately, the uninformed taxpayer-citizen often accepts these programs as real accomplishments rather than seeing them for what they are—a device to ensure reelection.

It's obvious why government officials want more employees, but why do labor leaders want to see the employment roster grow? Such growth usually means an increase in the union membership, which in turn brings more power and influence for the labor leaders. In addition to this obvious reason, there are more subtle reasons why union leaders yearn for a larger number of public employees. These reasons lie within the nature of the management process itself. Managing a labor organization is not unlike managing any other type of general complex organization. Managers judge others and themselves by the same criteria: how large a membership has been built. It is the same reasoning as the public manager counting how many employees have been added to the "empire" over the years. Also, a larger union membership leads the way for more staff, again increasing prestige. A large membership means more pay and more status in the world of national and international unionism. In short, the union manager has just as much stake in empire building as the government manager. In fact, there have been a number of cases where unions have resisted a cut in the number of employees even though no one would be fired or laid off. The reason is that union leaders are not immune from the empire building syndrome.

Understanding these arguments does not mean accepting them. The plain fact is that to cut taxes jobs must be cut. Too much of the government budget goes into the payroll for it to be any other way. The Volunteer Personal Service program will cut jobs, not services. Even though it maintains or improves services, it will be fought as vigorously as any "meat-axe" approach to cutting government jobs and spending.

The only answer to the negative arguments is a straight foward one. VPS will maintain services while reducing costs and the numbers of full-time employees. This is exactly what every concerned taxpayer should be fighting to achieve.

# 14 WHAT SHOULD TAXPAYERS EXPECT FROM LOCAL GOVERNMENT?

Taxpayers are generally quite vague about what they expect from their local government. If it were not for runaway inflation and the high degree of visibility attached to local government and its property tax, it is unlikely that taxpayers would think much about local government at all. However, as the examination of the tax revolt has demonstrated, taxpayers are thinking about local government in serious terms. They are quite clear about what they do not want from local government: higher spending and higher taxes. But what about the positive side of the issue? What should taxpayers expect from their local government?

## RESPONSIVENESS

Local government in the United States is a form of representative democracy. In essence, the people select representatives to hold public office with the understanding that these individuals will represent the interests of those who elected them. Elected officials should have the desire as well as the ability to carry out the public's will. Therefore, the responsiveness of government is something that people have a right to expect. The only limitation on this responsivenesss is government's obligation to protect the rights of minority groups from perverse actions as required by the state and national constitutions.

This right of responsiveness should be the fundamental expectation all citizens have of their government. When citizens perceive their government is not being responsive to their desires on a particular issue, they must take some action. Ideally, the government structure provides for some type of direct input from the people such as an initiative or referendum and the right to hold elections for the purpose of recalling public officials in the middle of their terms. The initiative, referendum, and recall are all means citizens can use to enforce their right of responsiveness from the government. If these means are not part of the local government structure, citizens must rely on placing pressure on elected officials and on supporting candidates who give promise of being responsive in public office. Additionally, citizens who do not have the right of initiative, referendum, or recall should work to institute these processes in their local government structures. As a beginning, elected officials should be asked to go on record in favor of these devices for public input. All citizens should place responsiveness high on their list of expectations from local government.

When government is responsive or when citizens make a direct input to government operation, as with a referendum election, this creates a corresponding responsibility for citizens to be informed about issues and to look at the issues from the viewpoint of the public good rather than from a perspective of pure self-interest. Additionally, citizens must be realistic in their expectations of responsiveness. Elected officials are the ones who bear the full force of the demand for responsiveness. Citizens must realize that elected officials do not have complete power to control the actions of local government. They share that power with government managers, with public employee groups, and with special interest groups. In judging the performance of any one elected official, citizens should evaluate what that person has tried to do, as well as what has actually been accomplished. It takes more than the efforts of a single elected official to make an entire government responsive to the desires of its citizens.

## COMMUNICATION

The idea of responsiveness requires citizens to be able to communicate freely and directly with public officials, both elective and appointive. Communication is a process requiring the active participation of both parties. Citizens must be willing to take the time and energy to communicate their desires and concerns to local government. Citizens also have a right to expect local government officials not only to converse willingly with citizens, but to go out of their way to seek opportunities to learn what the people want. All government officials have an obligation to take affirmative actions to involve citizens in the decision-making processes of government, especially when the matter under consideration will have a direct impact on the lives and prosperity of some or all of the citizenry.

Citizens should expect to be consulted when improvements in roads and other public facilities are planned for their area. This consultation should not be a superficial, "What do you think of what we want to do?" approach. It should be more basic and should start by asking citizens what *they* would like to see done in their neighborhoods. If citizens do indicate they would like a certain improvement or service, they have the right to be fully informed of what these improvements will cost before they are started. The public official who gets citizens to express interest in a project, gets the project started, and then uses it as an excuse to raise taxes or collect more revenues is not being honest with the people. The informed citizen should not be content to express a desire for improved services without finding out what these services will cost and where the money will come from. Public officials have an understandable tendency to present only the benefits of an improvement to the citizens they talk to. Citizens have the right to hear both sides of the issue without having to force the information out of an official.

## ACCESSIBILITY

Accessibility to the people is one of the characteristics of local government that sets it apart from the state and federal governments. It is, in fact, one of the great assets local government possesses. Citizens have a right to expect local government to be receptive to their ideas and concerns. However, citizens must be realistic in their expectations and they must also guard the ability of the local government to respond to these expectations. Previous chapters have pointed out the clear trend toward increased reliance on state and federal funds by local government. It was also made clear that the usual consequence of accepting outside money is a loss of local autonomy and freedom of action. Sometimes when this issue is raised citizens may feel it is of no great importance to them, that it only involves the prerogatives of a power hungry politician down in city hall. Nothing could be further from the truth. If citizens are unhappy with the level of responsiveness in city hall, they should do something about it: replace those officials with others who will be more responsive. If citizens allow their personal dislike for incumbents to lead them to complacently accept a loss in the autonomy of their government, they, not the politician, are the real losers. Politicians can be replaced, but once lost to the state or federal government, autonomy is almost impossible to regain.

Regaining autonomy is difficult in the best of circumstances. It will usually involve the loss of substantial amounts of funds that provide needed employment in the community and needed services to the citizens. Few of the people involved will want to give up these tangible benefits for the seemingly obscure purpose of having a responsive and accessible government.

In addition to the "strings" attached to state and federal dollars, there are a large number of other restrictions local governments must operate under and that cannot be changed by local action. Citizens must be cautious not to place unrealistic expectations on their local government. Local governments are at the bottom of the governmental structure and have the least power and autonomy. They are also the most accessible and visible. Because they are visible and accessible is no reason to make them the scapegoats for the transgressions of the higher level governments.

The taxpayer revolt in California provides a perfect example of what can go wrong when one level of government is made to pay for the sins of another. Taxpayers were infuriated by high property taxes and a huge state tax surplus. They voted to slash property taxes by more than half. They allowed state government to bail out local governments with surplus funds and, by doing so, to place many severe restrictions on the operations of local government. As long as local governments continue to accept these funds, they will continue to give up their autonomy. If precedent is a prediction for the future, the funds will be accepted for as long as the state can afford to give them. Without the ability to control its own operation, local government cannot be expected to be responsive to the desires of its citizens. California taxpayers have destroyed part of the ability of their local governments to be responsive to their desires. This ability can only be restored by ceasing to rely on state funds. How many local communities will make this sacrifice? Only a very few have refused state aid thus far. The result? The accessibility and responsiveness of local governments all across the state of California have been seriously weakened.

From California's experience it is reasonable for citizens to conclude that accessibility is an expectation of local government that cannot be abused. Because local government is accessibile to citizen input, it is vulnerable to citizen action in a way that the state and federal governments are not. Citizens must exercise this prerogative with care and restraint. A perceived lack of responsiveness on the part of local government may not be the fault of the elected officials. It may be due to factors beyond their control. Citizens must try to differentiate between instances when local government *will* not respond to their desires and when it *can* not respond to them. If citizens expect local government to be responsive, accessible, and open to communication, they have a corresponding obligation to maintain the ability of the local government to carry out these obligations. Measures taken to correct the failures of local government should not destroy the ability of the local government to respond as it is expected to.

## HONESTY

Honesty is a quality that has always been high on the list of expectations that citizens have of their local officials. Elected officials are not expected to profit from their government service. They are expected to be honest with citizens when explaining action or the lack of action by local government. For citizens who are concerned about curbing government spending and taxation, honesty about the costs and funding of desired services is particularly important. It is also one of the areas where even the most conscientious officials sometimes fall down. Most public officials are well enough informed about the way people behave to realize that people prefer to hear good news rather than bad. So if people say, "We want this or that service," the elected official does everything possible to bring it about because the people want it. The official does not mention that this added service along with one or two others is going to add to the tax burden next year. Is this dishonest behavior on the part of the official? Most people would probably say no, it's not dishonest in the way that the term is commonly used. It doesn't involve graft, cheating, or other illegal activities. Yet in a very important way, it is dishonest.

Whenever citizens take an active part in the affairs of government they have a right to be made aware of all of the facts regarding a particular issue. They must be made fully aware of the costs of what they want, not just be assured that it can be done. Elected officials must take the risk of sharing the bad news with the citizens along with the good. Citizens must realize that in government, like everywhere else, every benefit is likely to have a cost. The officials that dampen ideas for services with the sad news about costs must not be punished for their honesty; they should be respected for having the courage to tell citizens some of the facts they might not like to hear.

Unless citizens have a true picture of the costs associated with the services they want, they cannot make an informed decision about the issue. Depriving them of information is the same as depriving them of the right to full and complete participation in the process of governance.

There is another dimension to the expectation of honesty. It is that elected officials must work in the public interest rather than in their own self-interest. In cases where self-interest is expressed in terms of financial rewards, it is relatively easy to judge the quality of the elected official's action. The vast majority of elected officials would not even think of attempting to profit economically from their association with government. Yet there is a form of self-interest they work for that must be made compatible with the public interest. Being an elected official in local government can be a rather thankless task, particularly in smaller governments where officials are part time and receive insignificant salaries. Why do these officials choose to serve? Perhaps the most common reason is they want to contribute to their community and to society as a whole. They want to perform a service for their fellow citizens. These are good and noble reasons that other citizens should applaud. However, they are not the only reasons that people serve in elective offices.

The very nature of human beings requires that feelings of self-worth and importance play a prominent role in the actions of every individual. Every healthy individual needs to feel that who they are and what they do is important, to others and to themselves. For people in elective office these needs are satisfied to some extent by things that they do and attempt to do while in office. For this reason most elected officials either intentionally or unintentionally will seek out situations and opportunities that can contribute to their self-esteem. This fulfillment of self-interest is as important and legitimate for public officials as it is for people in other situations. Therefore, citizens should expect their elected officials to try to fulfill this type of self-interest along with the public interest. When dealing with public officials citizens should realize that these self-interest needs must be served and should not go out of their way to deprive elected officials of this needed gratification. In fact, by helping elected officials find a way to reconcile their self-interest with the public interest, the chances for cooperation and success are greatly enhanced.

Activist citizens may find this merging of interests is a key factor in bringing about some of the changes they would like to see in government. The expectation of honesty from local government and local government officials carries with it the requirement of candid understanding on the part of the citizen. As citizens become more involved in the activities of their government, they should not be surprised to see the same type of need for self-esteem start to develop in themselves. When this happens, this interest will have to be served just as surely as the economic self-interest of citizens is served by reducing taxes and curbing government spending.

## SATISFACTION

This point may seem to be self-evident, but it does require some explanation. In recent years a great deal of attention has been focused on the extent of citizen dissatisfaction with government. The blame for this dissatisfaction has been placed upon politicians, circumstances, and the people themselves. Very little is ever said about citizens being satisfied with their government, perhaps because dissatisfaction is more worthy of note. For instance, "A Taxpayer's Guide to Satisfaction" would hardly be a provocative title for a book such as this. Despite the fact that satisfaction with government is rarely mentioned in a positive sense, it is one of the legitimate expectations a citizen can and should have of local government. Because government in this country exists for the purpose of serving the people's interest and because government taxes the economic resources of its citizens in order to achieve this goal, the people have the right to expect government will perform its functions at a satisfactory level.

Satisfaction may be achieved in a number of different ways. Citizens who are ignorant of anything government does and who are not suffering economic hardship may simply assume that government is doing a good job and therefore feel satisfied with it. Citizens who are ignorant about government, but suffering from economic troubles, may blame the government for them. They are dissatisfied with government, perhaps for good reason, perhaps not. When and if their economic troubles are solved, they will again lapse into a state of satisfaction with government. The satisfaction of these people is not important to this discussion because it is neither caused nor denied by the actions of government, especially local government. The satisfaction of those citizens who are knowledgeable about how their government operates and who are concerned about the quality of services they receive for their tax dollars is the important topic.

Citizens should be satisfied that they have had an opportunity to make their views known to government officials. They should be satisfied that these views have received a fair and impartial evaluation. If their views are those of the majority of the citizenry, then they should have the satisfaction of knowing that their position will become a reality. These are the basic satisfactions all citizens have the right to expect from their local governments. Citizens do not have the right to expect government to satisfy every desire for increased services or decreased taxes that they have. Citizens should not expect that local government has the ability to cure their economic ills. They cannot demand economic satisfaction from local government. Local government, like every other level of government, must serve the needs of the majority of the people in a way that is consistent with the constitutional guidelines under which it operates. This means it is inevitable that a certain portion of the citizenry is going to be dissatisfied with the services it receives and the amount of taxes it pays. This is acceptable and inevitable in a democratic society.

What is not inevitable or acceptable is citizen dissatisfaction with the process by which inputs are made to the operation of government. The people have a right to be heard, to have their views evaluated, and to have those views acted upon if they represent the views of the majority of the people. This right to satisfaction with government is the essence of a free and democratic society.

## ORGANIZATIONAL CONSIDERATIONS

Thus far the expectations discussed have focused on the relationship of citizens with local government. There is another class of expectations worthy of note. These expectations have to do with the manner in which local government operates. In many ways local government organization is like any other type of organization in our society. It is subject to the same stresses and pressures as private organizations. It must comply with the same work rules and government regulations. Because of this similarity, citizens tend to have the same kind of expectations of local government organizations that they have of business organizations with which they are familiar. While these expectations may be reasonable to some extent, there are certain differences that must be taken into consideration when formulating expectations about government operations.

The most significant difference is in the source of revenues these organizations have. Private business derives its revenues from sales and investments. It uses these for the costs of doing business, for further investment, and for the payment of profits to the owners of the business. Local government, on the other hand, derives most of its revenues from taxes. The amount of revenue needed is to a large extent determined by budget requirements. In local government expenditures dictate what revenues will be. In business usually the opposite is true; revenues determine what expenditures can be made. The significance of this difference is that local government does not have the same built-in control on spending as business does. Therefore, local governments generally have followed the regrettable practice of spending all of the revenues available to them. This lack of a built-in spending limitation has created an attitude on the part of government officials that implies one of their prime tasks is to keep revenue yields as high as possible. The reasoning behind this attitude is that government should provide the maximum amount of service possible.

Because of this natural tendency toward spending on the part of local government, citizens should have the expectation that some control be exercised by elected officials. The principles upon which this control is based are those of efficiency, effectiveness, and economy examined in detail in Chapter Ten. Citizens should expect local government to have some limitation on spending based upon these three notions (with economy being predominant). Citizens must give an indication to their local government officials of how strict they want the government to be about conserving their tax dollars. They must also realize that economy in government will inevitably result in a reduction in the quality of the services that government offers. Efficiency and effectiveness also limit the services government can offer because these qualities can only be achieved through regularization and routinization of services. The citizen who wants an old sofa picked up by the city trash department must realize that this type of personalized service is usually not consistent with an efficient and effective operation. When citizens firmly present their expectations for efficiency, effectiveness, and economy, they can help to provide a spending control on government not ordinarily present.

One of the most important organizational characteristics citizens should demand from local government is a clear relationship between the provision of a specific service and the visibility of the cost of the service. The relationship between cost and service must be clear to citizens and elected officials alike, so that they are able to make informed judgments about the services they want and for which they are willing to pay. This relationship can be established and made visible by breaking down the cost information on local government into the smallest units possible and by using either a performance or program type of budgeting system. Another way to maintain the cost/service relationship is through the use of earmarked revenues and fees-for-services arrangements. Both of these arrangements provide citizens with a clear view of what a particular service is costing them. Without this kind of information citizens and elected officials cannot make informed judgments about the services they want to keep, reduce, or enhance. If citizens find they cannot easily determine the cost of a particular service or activity, they can assume that this activity probably is in need of their scrutiny. They should demand that local government operate in a fashion that permits easy review and comparison of services and costs.

## CONCLUSION

Responsiveness, communication, and accessibility are all necessary characteristics of a government that is truly representative of the wishes of the public it exists to serve. Honesty is a characteristic that citizens must demand from both their elected and appointed officials. In considering the organizational characteristics of local government, citizens should demand that some spending restraints be built into the operations of local government to serve the same purpose as the earnings restraint on the spending in business organizations. Citizens should also demand that local government function in a manner that permits an easy association of costs with the services. Cost/service information is a necessity if citizens are to make informed judgments about the level of government services they desire and are willing to support.

All of these expectations are summarized in the idea of satisfaction with government operations. It is not necessary or even possible for all citizens to be satisfied with the services they receive and the level of taxes they pay, but they must be satisfied with their ability to affect changes in local government goals, services, and policies. Unless citizens feel comfortable in their ability to do this as a group, the concept of a representative, democratic form of government will not function as it was intended.

When citizens feel their legitimate expectations are not being met by government and its elected officials, they have the obligation to do something about the situation. They can take direct action if the appropriate means exist. Referenda and initiatives are excellent means of direct citizen action. Also, recall elections are a good way of convincing uncooperative elected officials that they are failing in their responsibilities to the people who elected them. When these direct means do not exist, citizens must use the indirect means of political pressure: forming groups to work for specific reforms and working for or against particular candidates in local elections.

These are extreme measures. Often a candid discussion with local officials will convince them that there is a problem in need of attention. The majority of elected officials are trying to provide a genuine service to the people they represent. Often all that is needed is for them to know the concerns people have and to know that these concerns are shared by a large number of people.

Citizens with clear expectations about the nature of their relationship with local government have the capability of making a positive contribution to the quality of that government and have a good chance to bring about specific changes, whether increased services or decreased taxes. On the other hand, citizens who care only about the amount of taxes paid, who want to eliminate or reduce all services except those that are personally received, are working against the interests of good local government and the general public and are not likely to be successful in making the changes they desire.

# INDEX

Admissions and amusements tax, 58-59
Alabama: property tax limitation measure, 95
Alcohol and tobacco tax: federal, 25-26; local, 58-59; state, 36-38, 44-45
American Tax Reduction Act of 1979, 131-132
American Tax Reduction Movement (ATRM), 131-133
Arizona: Economic Estimates Commission, 108-109; expenditure limitation measure, 108-111; legislature, 108-111; Tax Commission, 111
Atiyeh, Victor, 92

Balanced budget, 105, 155
Bonds, 101
Brown, Jerry, 69, 73, 76-77, 81, 97
Budget balancing tax, 52
Budgetary process, local: economy, 165-166; effectiveness, 164-165; efficiency, 164; legal and ethical requirements, 166-167; methods of, 169-173; types of, 167-169

California: cities, 83; counties, 74, 83; courts, 83; Department of Finance, 82-84; initiative process, 70-71; legislature, 74, 78; property assessment, 71-72, 74; rent control, 84; state income tax, 72; Supreme Court, 76 (see also Proposition 13; Spirit of 13; Commission on Government Reform)
Capital funds, 153-154
Carter, Jimmy, 24

Circuit rider program, 226
Cities or towns, 144; commission form, 145-146; council-manager form, 146-148; mayor-council form, 146; services, 159-161
Colorado: Department of Local Affairs, 118; expenditure limitation measures, 116-118; legislature, 116-117; sunset law, 117
Commission on Government Reform, 81-82, 85, 97
Constitutional amendment, 126, 128
Consumer Price Index, 104
Consumer protection, 97
Contracting for services, 223-224
Cost benefit analysis, 221-222, 227

Earmarked revenues, 102, 229
Education, 97, 98
Electoral process (see Promise Model)
Employees, public: associations, 9-11, 13, 73, 79, 83; personnel policies, 193-195; retirement systems, 101; training programs, 225-226
Employment tax, federal, 20-23
Estate tax, 27-29
Excise tax: federal, 25-27; state, 34-38, 43-45
Expenditures, 101-103; increase of, 12-14, 15; limitation of, 103-108; maintaining program, 11-12, 15; reduction of, 8-11, 15, 230-235

Federal Constitutional Convention, 127-128

Fees and charges, local, 47, 49, 63-65, 79-80, 98, 152-153, 227-230

Gann, Paul, 73, 77, 84, 121
Gift tax, 27-29
Gross receipts taxes, 57-58

Hatch, Francis, 95-96
Hawaii: Council on Revenues, 116; expenditure limitation measure, 115-116; legislature, 115-116; tax credit, 115
Health and welfare, 83, 85, 97
Hotel and motel tax, 58-59

Idaho: counties, 88-89; legislature, 88-89; property tax limitation measure, 87-90; State Tax Commission, 89; tax burdens, 87-88
Illinois, 120-121, 137; advisory referenda, 120; constitution, 142; legislature, 120
Income tax, federal: corporate, 23-25; personal, 16-20, 23-25
Income tax, local: corporate, 60-63, 64-65; personal, 60-63, 64-65
Income tax, state: corporate, 38-42, 43-46; personal, 38-42, 43-45
Inflation, 18, 19, 29, 39, 71-72, 103-104, 110-112, 117, 119, 129-133
Insurance trust payments, 48-49
Intergovernmental revenue, 32-33, 47-49, 106, 152, 154-155
Internal Revenue Service, 17, 40

Jarvis, Howard, 73, 77, 85, 127, 131-133

King, Edward J., 95-96

Libraries, 82-83, 85, 97-98
License fees, state, 42-45
Line item budgeting, 170-171
Liquor stores revenue, 48-49
List, Robert, 90
Local government: better management of, 219-235; charters, 141; counties, 143-144, 161; financial policies, 182-189; functions and services, 149-162; general, 143-144; personnel policies, 193-195; revenue guidelines, 191-193; service guidelines, 189-191; state constitution, provision for, 141-142; state statutes on, 142; taxpayers' expectations of 246-256; taxpayers participation in,

167-215, 233-234 (*see also* Cities or towns; Process Model of local government; Budgetary process)
Los Angeles County, 73

Massachusetts, property tax limitation measure, 95-96
Michigan: education, 93; property tax limitation measures, 93-94
Missouri, property tax limitation measure, 96
Montgomery County, Maryland, property tax limitation measure, 95
Motor fuel tax: federal, 25-26; local, 58-59; state, 36-38

National Tax Limitation Committee (NTLC), 127-131
National Tax Reduction Plan, 127
National Taxpayers Union (NTU), 127, 131
Nevada: expenditure limitations, 90-91; gambling and tourism, 90; legislature, 90-91; property tax, 90; property tax limitation measure, 90; sales tax on food, 90; school districts, 91
New Jersey: expenditure limitation measure, 111-115; legislature, 111-113
North Dakota, 136

Old Age, Survivors, and Disability Insurance trust fund (OASDI), 21-23
Oregon: legislature, 92-93; low income home owners, 92; property tax limitation measures, 91-93; senior citizens, 92

Parks and recreation, 83, 85, 97
Performance budgeting, 170-171
Police and fire, 83, 85, 97
Post, A. Alan, 81
Post Commission (*see* Commission on government Reform)
Presidential powers, 125-126
Process Model of local government: allocation of financial resources, 155-156; audit and expenditure review, 157-158; identification and pricing of productive outputs, 151-152; management of fiscal and human resources, 156-157; raising revenue, 152-155
Program budgeting, 171-172

## ABOUT THE AUTHOR

ROBERT J. DWORAK is Professor of Public Administration at the University of New Haven. Previously, he taught at universities in Illinois and California.

Dr. Dworak has served as a consultant to state and local government and has published widely in the field of public administration. He received his graduate education at the School of Public Administration, University of Southern California.

Program evaluation, 143-144
Promise Model: being in office, 8; getting elected, 6-8; getting re-elected, 14-15
Property tax, 96-99; assessment of, 50-52, 54; exemptions, 51, 53-54; local 49-55, 64-65; state, 33-34, 43-44
Proposition 13, 69-86, 96-97, 123-124, 125, 131, 135, 159, 179-180
Public enterprises, 153

Revenues, public: federal government, 16-30; local, 47-65; state, 31-46
Revolving funds, 228-230

Sales tax: local, 55-59, 64-65; state, 34-36, 43-45
Serrano vs Priest, 78
Social Security (*see* Old Age, Survivors, and Disability Insurance trust fund (OASDI) )
South Dakota, 136
Spirit of 13, 84, 121-122, 124
Straub, Robert, 92
Subventions (*see* Intergovernmental revenue)

Sumptuary taxes, 26, 34-38, 44-45
Sunset laws, 225 (*see also* Colorado)

Tax anticipation notes, 154
Tax Reform Act of 1976, 39-40
Taxes: expenditure, 23; increase of, 5-15; indirect, 3; percapita burden of, 3-4, 31-32
Taxpayer activism, 133-138
Taxpayer revolt, 69, 87, 96-100, 125, 136-137, 219, 227-228, 249
Tennessee: constitutional convention, 119; expenditure limitation measure, 119
Texas, expenditure limitation measure, 118-119
Thompson, James R., 120

Unemployment Insurance trust fund, 22-23
Utility revenue, 48-49, 58-59, 80

Volunteer personal service, 236-245

Windfall profits tax, 24
Wisconsin, 136

Younger, Evelle J., 69

Zero base budgeting, 172-173